An *artist's view of the City of Washington in 1833. The Navy Yard is at the right on the far side of the Potomac. On the hilltop just above it is the Capitol. The White House stands on the elevation to the left of center, and the Long Bridge spans the river at the extreme left.*

THE I. N. PHELPS STOKES COLLECTION,
NEW YORK PUBLIC LIBRARY

THE PRESIDENT WHO WOULDN'T RETIRE

By the same author

FORGE OF LIBERTY
PAINTED LADY
Eliza Jumel: Her Life and Times

The President Who Wouldn't Retire

LEONARD FALKNER

COWARD-McCANN, Inc.

NEW YORK

To Lisa, Christina and Jimmy

Illustrations follow p. 160

INTRODUCTION

JOHN QUINCY ADAMS, sixth President of the United States, achieved more after he left the White House than most men accomplish in a lifetime. Retired to genteel obscurity by the advent of Jacksonian Democracy, he—the frosty New England aristocrat, the Puritan intellectual—emerged again to forge a new career for himself that took him to far greater eminence than the Presidency had been able to provide.

This is the story of that second career, of the former President who became the stormy petrel of the House of Representatives and the pioneer advocate of civil rights for the Negro race in America. No other President, before or after, has a comparable distinction. Most of them have withdrawn to private life, to live out their years cloaked in the ermine of elder statesmen: George Washington at Mount Vernon, John Adams at Quincy, Thomas Jefferson at Monticello, Andrew Jackson at the Hermitage, James Madison, James Monroe, and in our time Dwight Eisenhower on his farm in Gettysburg and Harry Truman at the old homestead in Independence, Missouri. While a few tried unsuccessfully to regain the Presidency a second time—Van Buren, Theodore Roosevelt, Grover Cleveland—only Cleveland succeeded. William Howard Taft became Chief Justice of the Supreme Court.

7

The notable exception was Herbert Hoover, who performed prodigious service in the subsequent Truman Administration as coordinator of food supplies for thirty-eight countries depleted by the Second World War and later as chairman of the Commission on Organization of the Executive Branch of the Government.

But none of them had the temerity to allow the electorate to return them to the heat and fury of legislative politics. Seeing what Adams was able to accomplish, it is regrettable that the example he set has not been followed since. Truman in the House or Senate and Eisenhower across the aisle from him to challenge, defend, to raise their voices in experienced counsel, in the give-and-take of debate, could be a noble and profitable experience for the country.

As a member of Congress, Adams succeeded where he most probably would have failed, had he tried, as President. The President is constitutionally detached from the other branches of the government. He can direct and advise; he can cajole, propose, veto; he can attempt to dictate. But he cannot enter into legislative activity, and his responsibilities are too many and too great for him to give strenuous and effective attention to a deserving minority—as Congressman Adams championed the civil rights of the Negro.

No other President, aside from his father, has left such a voluminous record as did John Quincy Adams of his day-by-day experiences, his thoughts and trials and achievements. The voluminous diary he kept in his palsied longhand, his letters, his detailed reports to his constituents, even his account books, are all preserved in the Adams Trust at the Massachusetts Historical Society. I am deeply indebted for the privilege of researching them. Adams' son, Charles Francis, published a condensation of the diary in twelve thick volumes in 1874-77. But Charles Francis considered much of the material inconsequential or too personal to include, and it is those parts that, to me, reveal the true character of his contentious and extraordinarily principled father.

Of equal help were the *Register of Debates in Congress* and the *Congressional Globe,* predecessors of today's *Congressional*

Record, and the letters and diaries of Adams' contemporaries and the newspapers of the day. The dialogues and monologues, the conversations, are all authentic. The only liberty I have taken is to turn them into direct discourse.

I am indebted to George Wilson Pierson for permission to quote from his book, *Tocqueville and Beaumont in America,* and to Dwight L. Dumond for excerpts from the letters of Theodore D. Weld to his wife, Angelina Grimké Weld. Of further help were the typescripts, newspaper clippings and other documents relating to the *Amistad* captives deposited in the New Haven Colony Historical Society by William A. Owens, author of *Slave Mutiny: the Revolt on the Schooner* Amistad. For a scholarly study of Adams' statesmanship the definitive source is the two volumes by Samuel Flagg Bemis, *John Quincy Adams and the Foundations of American Foreign Policy* and *John Quincy Adams and the Union.* My particular thanks for the use of their facilities go to the Sterling Memorial Library at Yale University, the Butler Library at Columbia, and the Massachusetts and New York Historical Societies.

A historian friend said when he heard I was working on John Quincy Adams' career in the House of Representatives, "He wasn't a great President, but he was one hell of a great Congressman!"

Leonard Falkner

Candlewood Isle, Conn.
1967

➤➤➤ I ⧫⧫⧫

FEW men could have been more deserving of a tranquil retirement than the elderly John Quincy Adams, pruning his apple and peach trees behind the old Adams mansion in Quincy that September day of 1830. Two months past his sixty-third birthday, he knew his public career was over. "After fourteen years of incessant and unremitted employment," he wrote in his diary, "I have passed to a life of total leisure, and from living in a constant crowd to a life of almost total solitude."

Four of those fourteen years, 1824-28, had been spent in the White House as sixth President of the United States, the eight previous years as President Monroe's Secretary of State and co-author of the Monroe Doctrine. Prior to that he had headed the peace commission which signed the Treaty of Ghent ending the War of 1812, and had gone on from there as President Madison's minister to unfriendly England.

The second President Adams had actually spent most of his life in the nation's service, and held more public offices of distinction than any American statesman has held before or since. He was only twenty-six when President Washington appointed him minister to The Hague, an important listening post for neutral America as the French Revolution spilled Europe into years of war. President John Adams, assured by Washington that young Adams was "the most valuable character we have abroad," then named his son minister to Berlin. At the end of his term in the White House, Adams recalled John Quincy to prevent his hostile successor, Thomas Jefferson, from doing so.

Back in Boston, at thirty-five, with a wife and young son, John Quincy returned briefly and halfheartedly to the law practice he had started before entering the foreign service. By 1802 he had been elected to the Massachusetts Senate. The next year, the state legislature sent him to Washington as U.S. Senator. Six years later, when James Madison succeeded Jefferson as President, he appointed Adams minister to Russia, where, in the palace gardens of St. Petersburg, he took long walks with the moody Tzar Alexander I and watched from a royal box the debacle of Napoleon's march on Moscow. The War of 1812 and his subsequent appointment to the peace commission began those "fourteen years of incessant and unremitted employment."

It was a brilliant career in any statesman's book, but John Quincy, in retirement, remembered only the frustrations of his four-year Presidency and the crushing rejection of his bid for a second term by the nation his father had helped create and to whose service he had devoted all his energies and talents. "The sun of my political life," he brooded, "sets in the deepest gloom."

Adams was a scholar, a bookworm. He read the Latin of Cicero and Tacitus as effortlessly as he did his favorite poets, Shakespeare and Milton. He spoke French like a native, and was fluent in German, Dutch and Italian. He was a rigid Puritan, and had read the Bible through so many times, as well as commentaries and foreign texts, that he knew it by heart. A good statesman but a poor politician, he scorned party loyalty. He possessed his famous father's pugnacity and a broad streak of his conceit. What tenderness he had inherited from his brilliant and warm-hearted mother, the incomparable Abigail, he kept well hidden, except in the soul-revealing pages of his diary.

His manner was cold, contentious, headstrong. As a result, his circle of friends was small, the roster of his enemies large and studded with the politically powerful. Andrew Jackson, his successor as President, was in Adams' estimation "a barbarian who could scarcely spell his name." He thought the Virginia statesman, John Randolph of Roanoke, "the image and superscription of a great man stamped upon base metal." Senator Thomas Hart Benton, "Old Bullion" of Missouri, was "a liar of magnitude." And so on through Daniel Webster, Henry Clay, Martin Van Buren, John Calhoun, William Crawford, all of whom had "used their faculties in base and dirty tricks to thwart my program in life."

Adams' contemporaries found it hard to like him. His bristling temper, his quickness to sense malice in whoever opposed him, make it understandable. Yet, as we see his personality emerge through the years still ahead of him, he takes on new dimension and stature. For far from being through with public service at sixty-three, he was on the threshold of his second, indeed his most brilliant, career; the career in which the very qualities that had kept him from becoming a popular figure were to make him great.

But no such challenging prospect was in sight for the former President as he settled into disconsolate retirement in that Indian summer of 1830. He had been a minority President. Andrew Jackson, the hero of New Orleans, had polled 99 electoral votes, Adams 84 and Henry Clay 37. Since no candidate had obtained a majority, the election went to the House of Representatives. There Adams won, with the support of Clay, who reasoned that, of the two—Adams and Jackson—Adams was the lesser evil. When Adams subsequently appointed Clay his Secretary of State, the Jackson forces immediately cried "Deal!" But no deal was ever proved. Actually, it was typical of Adams' political ineptitude—or inflexible statesmanship, if you will— that he appointed Clay, fully realizing the implication involved. He simply informed his critics that Clay was the best man for the job.

It did not quiet them. Nor did the radical opposition, which controlled the next Congress, accept his ambitious program of internal improvements: construction of federal highways and canals to open the country's primitive interior, adoption of a national bankruptcy law, and the establishment of an astronomical observatory, a national university, and a naval academy.

They were four years of frustration and martyrdom. In 1828, Jackson, with his log-cabin and frontier-fighter background, captured the imagination of the newly enfranchised farmers, piling up 178 electoral votes to only 83, mostly in staid New England, for Adams.

It had been a dirty contest. Neither candidate campaigned—it was not yet the custom actively to seek public office—but the newspapers, which then had the power to break a public figure, attacked Adams relentlessly. Adams had bought, and paid for himself, for a total of $84.50, a billiard table and chess set while in the White House. To the opposition press this was "gambling paraphernalia," and they implied it had been bought with public funds. They pictured Adams as a monarchist and a European aristocrat, a demagogue scorning the rights of free men. They accused his administration of corruption and hinted at dire scandals involving misappropriation of funds, none of which was true. They even went so far as to charge that, while minister to Russia, Adams had pimped for the Tzar, providing Alexander with an innocent Boston girl from his household.

Decorum prevented President Adams from answering this canard, but he turned the facts over to his friend, Congressman Edward Everett of Massachusetts, who presented them to the House of Representatives. A nursemaid in the Adams household, Martha Godfrey, had written a gossipy letter to a friend back home, retelling stories she had heard about Alexander's amatory escapades. It was intercepted by the Russian post office. The Emperor and his Empress were amused by the girl's credulity and invited the Adamses to bring her, together with her charge, young Charles Francis Adams, for an informal visit to see what the royal family was really like. That, in sum, was the extent of Adams' procuring.

The newspapers supporting Adams were not idle. They called Jackson a bloody duelist and murderer, a compulsive gambler, a bigamist. The bigamy charge particularly infuriated Jackson. He and his beloved Rachel had been married in the belief that her first husband had already divorced her. When they learned their mistake, the divorce was obtained, and they were married a second time. He was deeply devoted to her, and anyone who spoke disrespectfully about Rachel became Jackson's enemy for life.

While Adams could dish out vitriolic invective, he could not take it with equanimity. "I go into retirement," he wrote, "with a combination of parties and of public men against my character and reputation such as I believe never before was exhibited against any man since this Union existed."

But worse was to come. Adams' wife, Louisa, daughter of a former American consul in London, was not well when they left the White House in March of 1829. The Massachusetts winters were too harsh for the delicate, London-born daughter of a Maryland family who, her grandson, Henry, claimed, possessed the fragile beauty of a Romney portrait. Until the weather softened, they moved to Meridian Hill, then to the outskirts of the capital, sharing the big Porter mansion there with their second son, John, and his young wife and daughter. Their eldest son, George Washington, and youngest, Charles Francis, were living in Boston, where the precocious young Charles Francis had just finished reading law in the office of Daniel Webster and had been admitted to the Massachusetts bar. George, twenty-eight, was also a member of the bar, but he was a desultory attorney, a poet of sorts, neurotic, erratic. His warmhearted mother worried about his health and deep depressions, while his father, in long, preaching letters, pleaded with him to stop his dissipations.

In April they sent for him to help bring his mother home to Quincy. Unknown to the family, George's mind was snapping. He began to have vivid hallucinations—that strangers were following him, breaking into his rooms at night, that birds were speaking to him. He took the stage to Providence and there boarded a steamboat for New York. During the night, he leaped overboard. His parents got the news of his suicide two days later from the Baltimore *American*. Despite Adams' chilly exterior, he was a loving parent. The tragedy was doubly hard on him because he had to mask his own grief to keep his wife from a breakdown.

As if this were not trouble enough, a political antagonist, meanwhile, had embroiled him in a dispute that turned the leading families of Boston against him. William B. Giles, governor of Virginia, dug into the past to reveal that Adams, while serving in the Senate as a nominal Federalist in 1808, had told President Jefferson that a group of Massachusetts Federalists, known as the Essex Junto, were apparently in collusion with British agents to break away from the United States and establish a Northern Confederacy if Jefferson's Embargo Act were not lifted. The nation was on the verge of war with Britain, following the high-handed attack on the U.S. frigate *Chesapeake* and the impressment of four of her crew who were forced to join Britain's war with Napoleon. The Embargo Act, strong-armed through Congress by Jefferson to support American neutrality, was violently opposed in New England because it choked off her shipping and commerce.

Adams' conference with Jefferson had been confidential. Although he had been sent to the Senate by the Massachusetts Federalists, who feared and hated Jefferson and his Republicans, politics for Adams always stopped at the water's edge. He was, and always would be, a Man of the Whole Nation. With his help, the embargo was rescinded and a milder Non-Intercourse Act substituted. The Northern Confederacy never got beyond the talking stage.

Governor Giles' revelation, however, stirred up a teapot tempest in Boston. Thirteen of her leading citizens, whose relatives were possibly involved, asked Adams to name the conspirators. A more dexterous politician might have ducked out of the kitchen and let the teapot cool for lack of fuel. But Adams could never be silent when he knew he was right. He published a statement saying that he had "unequivocal evidence . . . that their [the New England conspirators] object was, and had been for several years, a dissolution of the Union, and the establishment of a separate confederation." The Boston that Adams had hoped to live with in friendly retirement cut him cold. His mood, in virtual isolation in the run-down old mansion he had inherited from his father, was as black as the ink that recorded it in his diary:

16

No one knows and few conceive the agony of mind that I have suffered from the time that I was made by circumstances, and not by my own volition, a candidate for the Presidency till I was dismissed from that station by the failure of my re-election. They were feelings to be suppressed; and they were suppressed. No human being has ever heard me complain. Domestic calamity, far heavier than political disappointment or disaster can possibly be, overtook me immediately after my fall from power, and the moment of my distress was seized by an old antagonist [Giles] to indulge a hatred overflowing with the concentrated rancor of forty years, and who could not resist the pleasure of giving me what he thought [was] the finishing blow at the moment when he saw me down. . . . In the French opera of *Richard Coeur-de-Lion,* the minstrel, Blondel, sings under the walls of his prison a song beginning: *"O, Richard! O, mon Roi!/ L'univers t'abandonne"* [the entire world is abandoning thee]. When I first heard this song, forty-five years ago, at one of the first representations of that delightful play [at the court of Versailles], it made an indelible impression upon my memory, without imagining that I should ever feel its full force so much closer to home. . . . Scarce a day [has] passed that did not bring it to my thoughts. . . . I should consider my public life closed, and take as little part in public concerns as possible.

So we find him in reluctant solitude in his garden in rural Quincy that Saturday, September 4, 1830. He is a small man, five feet seven, with a slight paunch, a round face, wrinkled as a dried persimmon, shiny bald head, with a crown and sideburns of white hair. His lips are thin and habitually compressed, his eyes red and watery; they bother him constantly, but he will go without spectacles all his life. The knee breeches he wore in young manhood have been out of fashion for thirty-odd years. He is dressed in old trousers and a faded vest, a cravat loosely tucked in his shirt collar. He has a nagging cough and complains of twinges of lumbago and rheumatism. He is certain he is not much longer for this world. His daily swim in Quincy Bay tires him of late, forcing him to remember that when he was President he used to disrobe under an old sycamore behind the

17

White House and swim a mile effortlessly in the Potomac. Now he does a half mile, down and back between Daniel Greenleaf's upper and lower wharves, in the raw except for a white nightcap to protect his head from the sun. Does it in sixteen minutes. And this at sixty-three!

He awakes and is up early, usually at around four o'clock, and says his prayer, kneeling beside his bed, loud enough for anyone in the house to hear. In his study, lighting his shaded whale-oil lamp with his old tinderbox (and, on cold mornings, the fire), he rereads three chapters from the New Testament, reads some passages of Cicero and writes until nine, mostly in his diary, that massive compendium of his thoughts, observations and activities that he has been compiling since he was ten years old and living in Paris with his father, on the elder Adams' historic mission for the Continental Congress in 1778. He writes with a quill, plucked from a goose, its point carefully heated and sharpened into a pen with his penknife. Steel pens have been on the market for two years, but it will be a long while before John Quincy will change to one.

The day being clear, he leaves his work table a few minutes before six (solar time) to go to the window and check his chronometer against the sunrise over the distant village church. At nine he goes down to breakfast in the dining room with its old Queen Anne furniture from his father's time, the Sèvres service bought in Paris the year he saw Napoleon return from Elba, the heavy coin-silver teapot and sugar bowl and cream jug. The portraits of George and Martha Washington, which John Adams had painted when he left the White House, look down from the west wall. The middle-aged servant, in a simple housedress (Adams will have no truck with uniforms), serves "the President," as he is known in the household, and "the Madame," Louisa, his wife.

Little talk passes between the two. John Quincy is wrapped in his own brooding. Louisa, fragile and singularly peaceful—a vision of silver-gray to her grandson, Henry—has learned long ago that small talk and tender compatibility are not Adams characteristics. "As it regards women," she wrote to her son, Charles Francis, upon his engagement to Abigail Brooks, "the

18

Adams family are one and all peculiarly harsh and severe in their characters. There seems to exist no sympathy, no tenderness for the weakness of the [female] sex."

Back in the study, the big east room across the hall from his and Louisa's bedrooms, he tries to get down to the task to which he expects to dedicate the rest of his life: compiling the papers of John Adams, his father. He has barely begun, and will never get far into it; years later his son Charles will finish the task.

The work table is littered with papers. So is the mantel shelf, and scattered among them are the dried cores of apples and pears eaten and tossed aside days ago. The walls are covered ceiling-high with books. John Quincy's library, some 8,600 volumes bound in embossed leather, is the finest privately owned in the country. Its overflow fills his bedroom walls. In the closet is a shelf of tumblers inverted over caterpillars he expects to see turn into butterflies; they never do. On other shelves are some of his wife's best Waterford glass dishes—until she finds and rescues them—containing peach and plum pits and acorns he is observing. The acorns, he has noted, take two months to sprout. He is deeply interested in horticulture.

In the afternoon he goes for a long walk down to the village center and back across his uncultivated fields, three and a half miles to the hour, carefully clocked. Then into his nursery, where he is raising a row of seedling white oaks for future generations of Adamses to stroll under. Dinner is between five and six. Afterward, more reading—Cicero's *Eighth Philippic* —over a glass, "sometimes two and occasionally three," of Bual Madeira. The post rider drops off the Boston newspapers.

That Saturday's issue of the Boston *Courier* was filled with the usual listings of ship arrivals and departures, advertisements for "A Bakehouse to Let," "A Certain Cure for Dispepsia," "A Shipment Recently Received from Liverpool of Dyed Shirtings," "M. Pelletier's French School at 4 Haymarket Place." On an inside page John Quincy read, with cynical surprise, an article that was drastically to change his life and embroil him in his second career. It read:

19

ELECTION: The election of Governor, Senator and Representative to the State Legislature and of Representatives to the next Congress, will take place in Maine on Monday. A similar election will be held in Vermont on Tuesday. From indications in the papers we apprehend that there will be a warm contest in both states, between the friends of the present National Administration and the opposition.

The election of Representatives to Congress in our own state will return in about two months. No movement to affect any changes in our present delegation has yet been made to our knowledge, except one or two communications in the Boston *Gazette* which, if we understand them right, are intended to operate against the re-election of Mr. Gorham in this district, an effect which we trust and hope will be entirely unavailing.

We would not wish to be considered meddlesome, but we take the liberty of suggesting to the National Republicans of Norfolk, that they would do well to elect Mr. Adams, the ex-President, as their next Representative. There are many considerations which might make such an election desireable to them as a party, and unless we mistake entirely Mr. Adams's disposition, there are as many which might render an election agreeable to him.

Adams was an old hand at suspecting an oblique attack upon himself. He could think of no good reason for the *Courier* to want to promote him back into public service. Its editor, Joseph Tucker Buckingham, was one of his many political enemies in Boston. Besides, his Quincy home was in the Plymouth, not the Norfolk, congressional district. He dismissed the article as "in no spirit friendly to me."

Nine miles away, in Boston, his youngest son, Charles Francis, read it and called the article "a nomination with a sneer." At twenty-three, Charles was one of the brightest young men in Boston. A natural scholar, he was deeply versed like his father and grandfather in the classics, and destined to succeed them as the third Adams of distinction. Besides acting as his father's financial manager, he had a growing law practice. Only a year before, he had married into a prominent family. His bride was Abigail Brooks, daughter of Peter Chardon Brooks, well-to-do insurance man of Boston and Medford. Charles' father-in-law had built the young couple a house on Hancock Avenue, in the patrician Beacon Hill district.

With discernment unusual for his age, Charles read the motive behind the *Courier* nomination. The editor, Buckingham, was helping to promote Henry Clay of Kentucky as the next candidate of the conservative National Republican party to oppose the radical Jackson for the Presidency. Regarding Adams as a possible rival, Buckingham intended to get him out of the way.

Three days later, a letter to the editor appeared in the *Courier,* from a resident of Duxbury, in the Plymouth congressional district that included Adams' homestead. The Duxbury subscriber wrote:

I was highly gratified by the suggestion in your paper of Saturday in favor of electing Mr. Adams to Congress. It is many years since the Plymouth District has been represented by any man of eminent standing, and the electors have now an opportunity of doing honor to themselves and of testifying their respect for this much-abused fellow-citizen. . . . Could it be ascertained that he would accept if chosen, I believe he would receive the support of every National Republican in the District, with the exception of those who wish to be candidates themselves. To Mr. Adams himself, I should suppose it would be desireable to be thus placed in a situation where he could have so good an opportunity of publicly defending the measures of his administration when attacked; and to the state of Massachusetts it is surely an object to strengthen her delegation in Congress. With such men as Webster, Everett, Davis, etc., it is already a strong one, but with the addition of Mr. Adams's preeminent talents, it would be decidedly a more powerful representation than that of any other state. A place in Congress is of course no object of ambition, on account of the honor thereof, to Mr. Adams, but it surely can in no way be derogatory to his dignity to represent in part his native State in the great Councils of the Nation. . . . There surely can be no impropriety in a past President's accepting such a distinguished trust as that which the electors of Plymouth District can now place in the hands of Mr. Adams.

Young Charles Francis, busy with his own career and social life, was annoyed at the assumption that his father, after being President of the United States, would accept a seat in the lower house of Congress. There was as yet little charity in Charles' makeup, but he felt sorry for his father for being subjected to this newest indignity. Charles considered him well out of public service, with its harassments and unwelcome publicity. That Adams might accept the nomination apparently did not occur to him. "He is beyond ambition," said Charles.

Ten days later, on September 17, John Quincy Adams made one of his infrequent trips into Boston. It was the city's second centennial of its settlement, and the committee in charge had invited him to take part in the ceremonies, although three members of the committee, including the mayor, Harrison Gray Otis, had feuded with him over the Essex Junto. Joining the assembled dignitaries in the Senate chamber of the State House, he was pleased to discover that a prominent place had been assigned him in the forthcoming procession. He then marched, with his own escort of two marshals, down Tremont, Court and State streets to the head of Long Wharf and back to the old South Meeting House, where his friend of many years, Josiah Quincy, president of Harvard, delivered the oration. Afterward, there were fireworks on the Common and then a party at the home of Lieutenant Governor Winthrop.

The Winthrop gathering had political overtones. There were a few old-line members of the declining Federal party, a scattering of Jacksonian radicals, who were taking the name Democrats, but the majority of those attending were National Republicans, violently opposed to everything Jackson's Administration did and stood for. It was the first time since his retirement that Adams had encountered many of the guests. He was pleased by the comparative warmth of his reception. Even Mayor Otis and William Sullivan, chief marshal of the celebration and another of the Essex Junto protestants, shook his hand. His old friend, Edward Everett, National Republican Representative in Congress from the Middlesex district, was there. So were two other National Republican Congressmen, the Reverend Joseph Richardson from Adams' home district of Plymouth, and John Davis of Norfolk.

Between glasses of punch strongly laced with Madeira, Davis and Richardson drew Adams aside. "We wish an opportunity to converse with you," said Davis in the stiff, Latinate upper-class manner of the day. His was the district that the *Courier* editor had suggested might nominate Adams. "May we call on you tomorrow?"

Adams, who seldom wasted words, said merely that he would be at home to them in Quincy. Later that evening, he had a talk with Everett.

"What do you say to going to Congress?" Everett asked.

"I have nothing to say to it," Adams replied.

"Mr. Richardson, of your district, is declining reelection for the Twenty-second Congress, which convenes, as you know, in December a year hence."

Adams was noncommittal. He acknowledged that he had read the items in the *Courier,* but added, "As the editor of the paper has been uniformly hostile to me, I supposed the nomination was made in the same spirit, and did not imagine it was seriously thought of by anyone."

Everett let it go at that. You did not argue casually with John Quincy.

Adams was spading in his garden the next afternoon when he was informed that John Davis was at the door. To the Congressman, familiar with the austere brick homes of Beacon Hill, the old white frame mansion, with its picket fence, its worn brick walks, ivy and shaggy boxwoods, had an old-fashioned, country air. From the entrance hall, a narrow open stairway led up to the bedrooms and the President's study. The parlor, to the left, had been paneled in richly grained Santo Domingo mahogany by the original Tory owner when he built the house in 1731, but John Quincy had had it covered with white paint

23

to brighten the room in the gloomy New England winters. The furniture was Queen Anne, gracious and comfortable but out of date.

Adams and Davis were stiffly exchanging greetings when Rev. Joseph Richardson arrived. Davis opened the conversation.

"I have seen in the newspapers," he said to Richardson, "that you have declined a reelection to the next Congress."

"It is a determination long since taken," Richardson answered. "I think it due to the people of my congregation. They have been exceedingly reluctant at my going even to the present Congress." He turned to Adams. "I have come purposely to inquire if you would serve, if elected, as member for our district. If you would agree to serve, I believe the election could be carried by a large majority." Receiving no reply and seeing no alteration in Adams' stern expression, he went on: "I think that service in the House of Representatives of a former President of the United States, instead of degrading the individual, would elevate the Representatives' character."

"I have in that respect no scruple whatever," Adams told him. "No person could be degraded by serving the people as a Representative in Congress. Nor, in my opinion, would a former President of the United States be degraded by serving as a selectman of his town, if elected by the people. But age and infirmity have their privileges and their disqualifications. I have not the slightest desire to be elected to Congress, and I cannot consent to be a candidate for election. The state of my health, the degree of opposition to the choice, the character of the candidate in opposition, might each or all contribute to my determination."

Richardson quickly understood the essence of what Adams was saying: that he would not *seek* public office. If the people overwhelmingly wanted him, he might agree to serve. Adams might appear unduly coy, but his experience as a minority President was still painfully fresh in his memory, and he never wanted anything like it again.

Richardson stood up.

"This is sufficient," he said. "I shall go to work."

A few days later, one of his neighbors, Deacon Spear, tried, with no more success, to pin Adams down.

"Well, do you consider yourself an inhabitant of Quincy?" the deacon finally asked.

"Certainly," Adams replied. "If not an inhabitant of Quincy, I am an inhabitant nowhere."

"That is all I wish to know," said the deacon.

A Mr. Bailey accosted Adams next.

"I have been asked by several persons whether you would accept the office of Representative if elected," he said. "Might I answer that question if it is again put to me, and it certainly will be?"

"I cannot answer it myself," Adams told him, and added with carefully chosen words: "To say that I would accept would be so near to asking for a vote, that I do not feel disposed to go so far."

Bailey pointed out that, if Adams should decline the nomination, it was doubtful that the National Republicans could agree upon a candidate who would poll enough votes to retain the district's seat in the House. The Massachusetts constitution required that, to be elected, a candidate had to have a majority of the votes cast. Two of the state's districts were already without a Representative because they had failed to elect a majority candidate. But Adams had gone as far as he would go.

So September came to an end, and Adams gave up his daily half-mile swim in the frosty bay, and suddenly felt better. He noted that his shellbark hickory tree had "fall'n into the sere, the yellow leaf," the red oaks' leaves were turning crimson, the chestnuts' pale yellow, while the English oaks and the peach and plum and apple trees were still green. The Hingham *Gazette*, the home-town paper of the retiring Representative, the Reverend Mr. Richardson, came out strongly for Adams. And he observed that, as he passed them on his daily walks through the village, his neighbors seemed to regard him with a new interest.

Adams wrote that his family opposed his return to politics. If Louisa objected, it was only for the sake of his own peace of mind. She was a Southerner at heart, and Washington, drab though the capital city still was, had a far stronger attraction for her than harsh New England. Louisa had never entirely become an Adams. She was too warmhearted, impulsive, romantic. Besides, she knew from long experience that, in matters political, her husband, with his inflexible dedication to "the nation," would go his own impulsive way.

There was no doubt about how their son Charles Francis felt about it. Back with his young wife from the Brooks' summer home in Medford, he had moved comfortably into the orderly routine of life on Beacon Hill. He installed a supply of firewood for the winter, and was pleased to find it cheaper than a year ago. He cashed the dividends on a couple of the Adams family bank stocks, attended a directors' meeting and "began the winter campaign with Cicero, which I propose to read through. I propose to make myself as much as possible master of the Latin language. It is one thing to read Latin, another to understand its force."

The Hingham *Gazette*'s campaign for Adams, prominently reported in the Boston newspapers, interrupted Charles' devotion to Cicero. He had the carriage brought around and, with a young acquaintance who wanted to meet the elder Adams, drove out to Quincy. It was a disappointing journey. He found his mother in bed with a sore throat, and hungry for sympathy. His father stubbornly avoided discussion of his candidacy. In time Charles would come to have a deep admiration for his father's extraordinary character, but youthful self-assurance dampened his opinion of him now. "My father is a singular man," he observed. "He wants the profound wisdom which gives knowledge its highest luster. He is not proof against the temporary seductions of popular distinction, which is the most solid evidence of greatness."

The next weekend he was back in Quincy, accompanied by his wife. This time he managed, after copying a letter for his father, to have a candid talk with the old man. Neither recorded the conversation, but it is evident that Adams was not at all impressed by his son's argument that it was below his, and his family's, dignity for him to go back into politics as a Congressman. He wrapped himself "in the cloak of patriotic in-clination," said the son. But Charles saw through that. "My eye is a little too deep to be blinded," he added. The old war horse was smelling the smoke of battle and chewing the bit. "His is not the highest kind of greatness," Charles wrote in his diary. "I regret the decision on his account. I regret it upon my own. To neither of us can it be beneficial to be always struggling be-fore the public without rest or intermission."

After the Sunday morning service in the village Unitarian church, the two went for a drive, and Charles took up the ar-gument again. Ignoring his son altogether, Adams blithely wan-dered off to pick up acorns for his back-yard nursery. The next morning, as the young couple were getting ready to return to Boston, Charles noticed a coldness on his father's part that was to last for some time. "My father did not seem in very good humor," he said, "probably for the course which I felt it my duty to take about the election. But I feel he ought not to take any course without having the whole ground laid out before him. The precedent is important to the whole nation."

It was a precedent. Washington, John Adams, Jefferson, Madi-son and Monroe had all retired from the White House to live out their lives as dignified elder statesmen, receiving distin-guished visitors, resuming their correspondence with old friends, occasionally delivering an oracular opinion on some noncontroversial subject. Unfortunately for John Quincy Ad-ams, he was not in a comfortable position to don the mantle of elder statesman. He had some 900 acres, part of it scattered in Quincy, the rest in Weston. He was land poor and had invested heavily in a bankrupt grist and flour mill being operated un-successfully by his other son, John, in Washington. Whether he could afford to or not, he was inclined to donate to causes he considered good. Young Charles was bringing some order into his chaotic financial affairs, but it would be years before they were back on a sound footing. Meanwhile, it is possible that the pay of a Representative had some influence on Adams: $8 a day while Congress was in session, $8 for each twenty miles traveled between the capital and home—a total of close to $1,700 a year.

Back in Boston, Charles continued to worry. "My mind always assumes a load of care when I think of my parents," he said. "Their situation is a painful one, and it is always a hard thing for a child to feel a doubt about the sound judgment of either. But I see no way to avoid it, for I always find them in some species of embarrassment and I do not often agree with their plans."

Charles Francis, who would go on to become the Free-Soil party's candidate for Vice President and Lincoln's capable minister to England during the Civil War, possessed, according to his brilliant son, Henry, "the only perfectly balanced mind that ever existed in the name." Unlike his former-President father, his judgments were painstakingly and judiciously arrived at. His attire was neat, his father's careless; his study and writing table were tidy to a fault. No ink stains on his fingers— the elder Adams' were perpetually smeared. No peaches on the mantel being over-ripened for seedlings or dried apple cores lurking under the papers. He dreaded his father's visits. By the time John Quincy left, it was "as if a whirlwind had invaded the study."

Meanwhile, the delegates from thirteen towns of the attenuated Plymouth congressional district met in the village of Halifax on October 12. A clique of Jackson men, insisting they were National Republicans, invaded the meeting to contest Adams' nomination. The Adams delegates withdrew and held their own meeting, nominating Adams by acclaim while the Jacksonians nominated a man named Arad Thompson.

The election was held on November 1. Adams kept himself aloof, recording in his diary for that day that he had read the last available fragment of Cicero's poetry and had finally completed "the perusal of everything written by him now known to be extant." It had occupied two hours of each day for ten months. In many ways, he sensed a parallel between his own life and that of the Roman politician, noting gloomily, "I am now precisely at the age when the life of Cicero was so tragically closed."

On November 6, the newspapers reported the returns in the Plymouth district. John Quincy Adams had received 1,817 votes, Arad Thompson 373, and a Federalist, William Baylies, 279.

"I am a member of the Twenty-second Congress," Adams wrote exultantly in his diary that night. He spent the next day "reflecting upon this new incident which has drifted me back amidst the breakers of the political ocean."

Of one thing he was certain: "This call upon me by the people of the district in which I reside, to represent them in Congress, has been spontaneous. I have received nearly three votes in four throughout the district. My election as President of the United States was not half as gratifying to my inmost soul. No election or appointment conferred upon me ever gave me so much pleasure."

➤➤➤ II ◄◄◄

TO understand John Quincy Adams it is essential to look upon him as an eighteenth-century man, although most of his mature life was spent in the nineteenth. The Boston Massacre, the Stamp Act, the Tea Tax, the Blockade of Boston were all vivid memories. As a child he had stood beside his father's firebrand cousin, Sam Adams, and seen the Redcoats drill in Boston's King Street. With his mother, Abigail, he had climbed Penn's Hill, near their farmhouse, to watch the Battle of Bunker Hill across the bay. He had heard his father describe his debates in the Continental Congress and his work on the Declaration of Independence with Thomas Jefferson and Benjamin Franklin. George Washington had been his youthful patron, sending him on his first diplomatic mission, to The Hague. He had known the Founding Fathers intimately. He never did warm up to the British.

The nation was as close to his heart as his family. Perhaps closer. When President Madison nominated him the country's first minister plenipotentiary to Russia, in 1809, Louisa protested in tears at leaving America for bleak and frozen St. Petersburg. England and Napoleonic France were at war, and the American merchant sailing ship assigned to take them would have to run the blockade of both belligerent nations. Adams decided to leave the two older boys with their grandparents in Quincy. Louisa had hysterics, and her father-in-law locked his door to stop her from appealing to him. But they went, taking only two-year-old Charles Francis with them on the seventy-five-day crossing. It was six years before they saw their other sons again.

Adams watched the birth of the party system: the original monolithic Federalist party of his father and Washington; the Republican party of Thomas Jefferson, since split into the National Republicans and the Jacksonian Democrats; and now the Antimasons. He was never beholden to any of them. He was, and always would be, a Man of the Whole Nation—an inflexible, if too often irascible, "guardian of her Laws and Liberties," as his mother had counseled him in a long-ago letter.

With Charles' help, he now went back to editing *The Works of John Adams*. But his interest in the warmed-over controversies of a dead generation lagged. His father's feud with Jefferson and quarrels with Hamilton and Timothy Pickering and his frosty disagreements with Washington seemed remote indeed now that he was a member-elect of Congress. He found his attention focused more often on issues of current concern: the agitation suddenly intensifying in the North for abolition of slavery; the nullification threat of South Carolina over the protective tariff, which it charged was enriching commercial New England and impoverishing the agrarian slave states; President Jackson's spoils system and "dangerous demagoguery"; the Antimasonic movement.

Although it would be a year before he took his seat in Congress, Adams was impatient to get back to Washington. Louisa, with her Southern temperament, did not have to be urged. On December 3, Adams and Charles saw her off in the family coach with their coachman and her house servant, Mrs. Pitts, to drive by easy stages to Hartford. Adams, who had some business to wind up and, besides, preferred the faster if more grueling journey by stagecoach, left four days later to overtake her. The 500-mile trip to Washington, which a modern jet could make in an hour, took Louisa fourteen days. Considering the hardships that Adams recounted so matter-of-factly in the crabbed script of his diary, and the fact that it was a journey they would make back and forth between the capital and Quincy annually for years to come (although toward the end the coming of the railroad eased it considerably), it is a remarkable feat. How many men of Adams' scholarly nature and elderly years, how many women of Louisa's frail health, could endure such a trip today?

The big Concord coach, with its leather straps for springs and iron-shod wheels, came by for Adams at his son's house at nine o'clock the morning of December 7. There were seven passengers, all bundled to the ears, in the unheated, straw-floored coach, including a Reverend Mr. Searles and his sister with her two daughters, four and two years old, and a shy and completely silent young man in foreign-cut clothes. Snow lay heavy on the road. The day started clear and cold, but by noon it clouded up, and the wind deepened the drifts across the turnpike. At Newton, three hours on their way, they stalled in the snow. A coach on runners came in from the west, and Adams and his fellow passengers were transferred to it. At Needham, where they took fresh horses, they were told that one coach from Hartford, which should have arrived the day before, had not been heard from, and that another, after trying to get through the drifts behind six oxen, had turned back. They pushed on and reached the village of Sutton at nine that night and had "a very comfortable supper." Back in the coach, they traveled till four-thirty in the morning, stalling frequently in the drifts. Adams and the minister were repeatedly enlisted to put their "shoulders to the wheel." Once they took apart a rail fence so that the coach could detour through a stubbled cornfield. Another time they helped the driver pull down a stone wall. Wherever the road was blocked, they jounced over rocks and across ditches.

A few hours' rest in a village inn, and they were on their way again, reaching Hartford the afternoon of December 9, "all safe and unhurt." Louisa and the servants were waiting for him. They loaded the carriage aboard the steamboat *Victory* and sailed down the Connecticut River, the wind cold and blustery, the hillsides deep in snow. Louisa, who dreaded steamboat travel, had hoped to go on to New Haven by land, but the road was impassible.

At Saybrook, where the *Victory* rode into Long Island Sound at sunrise, heavy swells and gale winds buffeted the little steamboat. Many passengers, including Louisa, became violently ill. Adams stayed on his feet, frustrated because, now that for the first time in days he was moderately comfortable, there was nothing to do.

At ten that night they landed in New York and put up at the City Hotel on downtown Broadway, Louisa wretchedly sick. The next day Adams visited the aged and impoverished former President, Monroe, slowly dying at the home of his son-in-law, Samuel Gouverneur. Monroe was trying to recall a Cabinet meeting during his Presidency, in 1818, when Jackson, then a major general, had nearly precipitated war with England and Spain by pursuing the Seminole Indians into Spanish Florida without official sanction and summarily executing two British subjects who tried to stop him. President Jackson had recently heard that John Calhoun, then Secretary of War and now Vice President and his heir apparent, had wanted him court-martialed. Anyone who had ever opposed Jackson was never forgiven. Calhoun's old enemy, William H. Crawford, of Georgia, Secretary of the Treasury at that time, had instigated the charge and was asking Monroe to support him, while Calhoun was asking support for his defense that the entire Cabinet, and not he alone, had opposed Jackson's action. Monroe's memory was vague. Adams' was not. He had been Secretary of State at the time and had been the *only* Cabinet member who had defended Jackson. But he had no desire either to ingratiate himself with the President or to get involved in the feud between Calhoun and Crawford. "I would be walking between burning plowshares," he said.

The next day he saw Louisa and the family coach aboard a steamboat to sail down the coast and up the Raritan River to New Brunswick, New Jersey. From there they would go overland to Trenton. He followed her a day later by boat and stagecoach. From Trenton they steamed down the Delaware to Philadelphia. Today it is hard to visualize a former President of the United States traveling unnoticed in public carriers. But the elderly gentleman with the dour manner could easily get lost in a crowd. His steamboat and stagecoach companions seldom recognized him, and Adams never enlightened them. Now and then he met one who interested him, but most of them he found "dull beyond ordinary."

When he and Louisa walked into the Manor House in Philadelphia, the clerk casually informed the former President that there were no rooms available. So they put up at the United States Hotel. In Philadelphia, his old friend, Nicholas Biddle, head of the Bank of the United States, which Jackson was threatening to abolish, entertained the Adamses at dinner. Biddle heartily supported Adams' acceptance of a seat in the lower house of Congress. The House, he said, needed men of Adams' stature. The others at the table, all prominent Philadelphia politicians, were divided. Judge Joseph Hopkinson thought it was beneath the dignity of a former President. So did several others. Adams listened with equanimity. On national issues he could be savagely contentious, but where his own impulses were involved he was always polite.

The road from Philadelphia to Baltimore was tolerable, but from there to Washington it meandered bewilderingly through the pine forests, drivers picking their way from one clearing to another, detouring fallen trees, bogging down in swamps, getting lost. Louisa had gone on ahead again, but somewhere in the winter dusk Adams' stagecoach passed the carriage, and he reached their son John's house on Washington's Sixteenth Street an hour ahead of her. It was the night of December 17. Louisa had started out on the morning of the third! Adams remarked, "Even with all the modern facilities for traveling, the trip is arduous at this season." He was remembering that in his father's time the entire journey had been by land.

A week later he and Louisa were still not recovered. He had "a hoarse sore throat every night," and his chronic cough was worse. Young Dr. Hunt prescribed "trash which will tease me and leave me just where I am. Rye mush and milk for breakfast, a plaster on my breast, Seidlitz powders, and no supper." He added, scornfully, "I do not sup!" But by New Year's when, according to the custom of the day, the gentry held open house for their friends, the Adamses ladled out punch to 300 guests.

Adams slipped back easily into his old routine in the capital. Up before dawn, with one of his dozen-odd canes for companion, he walked the two blocks to the White House and up the great mile-long emptiness of Pennsylvania Avenue to the Capitol and back. Washington was still a raw town of 20,000. The wide avenues laid out by Andrew Ellicott beside the Potomac were so strewn with potholes and open gullies at the street crossings that the carriages of statesmen and foreign dignitaries frequently broke down or overturned, spilling their occupants. Wide clearings littered with tree stumps and reclaimed by alder brush and snake-infested swamps separated the starkly new stone government buildings, the clusters of brick homes, the taverns and the boarding houses. Few Congressmen, judges or visiting politicians brought their families. Instead, they crowded into the boarding houses. Chief Justice John Marshall of the Supreme Court and his six associate justices boarded together in one house. The Jacksonians favored Gadsby's Indian Queen Tavern at Pennsylvania Avenue and Sixth Street. The National Republicans had their own haunts. So did the Antimasons. Statesmen from the Northern states mingled with the slaves of the Southerners to shop for roasts, turkeys, oysters, cheese and pickled apricots at the sprawling open stalls of the Central Market on Pennsylvania Avenue. President Jackson rode on horseback through the streets and country lanes, accompanied only by "Little Van," his Secretary of State and new favorite. Foreign diplomats cursed the mud that splattered their boots and complained of the poor draft of American fireplaces. Urns of Old Scotch snuff adorned the House and Senate lobbies, and every office had its spittoons for the chewers of Wedding Cake plug and Brown's Very Best.

An Indian in the dress of a tribal chief stopped Adams on one of his morning walks and, in sign language, proffered his respect. Adams thought he was one of the Cherokees he had tried to help during his Presidency. Unlike Jackson, the man of the people, Adams the aristocrat had always shown a warm sym-

35

pathy for the plight of the Indians being driven from their eastern lands. Another morning a man shyly asked to shake his hand because he had been "my President." Adams began to feel he was part of things again, enjoying "a degree of tranquillity such as I never before experienced, interrupted only by . . . the consciousness that it must be speedily changed for a return to all the cares, mortifications and perplexities of ungracious public life."

William Wirt, the Maryland lawyer and writer who had been his Attorney General, came by to discuss the failing health of seventy-five-year-old Chief Justice Marshall. Adams shared his worry that, if Marshall should retire, Jackson would appoint in his place "some shallow-pated wildcat like Philip Barbour [House member from Virginia], fit for nothing but to tear the Union to rags and tatters."

Vice President Calhoun, who had also been Adams' Vice President, called and tried to renew their old friendship. Adams was frosty. "Mr. Calhoun's friendships and enmities," he wrote in his diary, "are regulated exclusively by his interests." Calhoun was still trying to recover Jackson's friendship and needed all the help he could get. He got none from Adams.

The visitor to the house on Sixteenth Street who profoundly affected Adams' future career as "Old Man Eloquent" was Benjamin Lundy, the Quaker abolitionist and editor of the Washington weekly, *The Genius of Universal Emancipation.* Abolition of slavery had suddenly become a great moral crusade among the middle classes of the North. Partly it was inspired by Great Britain's action to end slavery in her West Indies, accomplished in 1833, and by the prohibition of slavery in some of the South American states breaking away from Spain. But there was an emotional, a religious fervor behind the new cause, linked intimately to the evangelical awakening of the day. In the Burned-Over district of western New York—burned over with religious zeal—the evangelist, Charles Finney, and the persuasive propagandist, Theodore Weld, were denouncing slavery as a moral offense against God, and winning support in rural congregations throughout the East. In Boston, William Lloyd Garrison was publishing his fiery *Liberator.*

The Quakers had long been dedicated to wiping out "the sin of slavery." A practical place to start, in Lundy's opinion, was the District of Columbia, which, like the territories, was under the jurisdiction of Congress. But they were having a hard time finding members of Congress who would present their petitions.

Adams had always abhorred slavery. As "one of the smallest poets of my country," he had, while in the White House, written a sonnet ending:

> That nature's God commands the slave to rise,
> And on the oppressor's head to break his chain.
> Roll, years of promise, rapidly roll round,
> Till not a slave shall on this earth be found.

Still he would have no part of the abolitionist movement, and he made that clear to Lundy. Any action now to abolish slavery in the South would rend the nation. Until the North became strong enough to work its will upon the South, the only hope was for abolition to come from within—within the South itself. How, he did not know. The South's "peculiar institution," he was convinced, was economically as well as morally unsound. And the countryside bore the mark of this instability. While in the North the farms were well kept, the houses and barns in repair, the village greens with their white meeting houses tidy as a swept floor, in the South, the plantations were unkempt, careless-looking, and run-down. Slave labor could not compete with free workers. The South had to depend on Northern shippers to carry most of its cotton and tobacco to market because of the risk in letting its working class, the slaves, man ships sailing outside its jurisdiction.

Adams had once hoped, along with Washington and Jefferson, that the emancipation begun in the North years before (Massachusetts had outlawed slavery in 1783) would eventually spread throughout the South. But Eli Whitney's invention of the cotton gin had so increased the demand for raw cotton and the consequent need for cheap and plentiful help to grow and harvest it that the South had become unyieldingly and defiantly opposed to change.

Petitions to Congress were another thing. The First Amendment to the Constitution, as sacred to Adams as the Bible, proclaimed that Congress could not abridge the freedom of the people to petition the government for a redress of grievances. That was the law of the land, and Adams would uphold it with all his fierce combativeness for years to come, against abuse, ridicule and threats of assassination.

On April 21 the public stage was at the door again, and Adams followed Louisa and the family coach on the long journey by land and water back to Quincy for the summer. In his baggage was a fat portfolio of poems written during the winter mornings: Psalms of David translated from the Latin and a long narrative poem on the Irish rebellion, *Dermot MacMorrough*. They would come out in limited editions and be forgotten. The beautiful Twenty-third Psalm which begins "The Lord is my shepherd" was set by Adams:

> My shepherd is the Lord on high;
> His hand supplies me still;
> In pastures green He makes me lie,
> Beside the rippling rill;
> He cheers my soul, relieves my woes,
> His glory to display;
> The paths of righteousness He shows
> And leads me in His way.

He still had seven months until he would take his seat in Congress, and he was restless. "My occupation of idleness encroaches upon the slumbers of the night," he complained. The role of elder statesman had completely lost its savor. Charles Francis tried to direct his attention back to the monumental work of editing the John Adams papers, only to discover that his father had "the most unaccountable indifference on the subject. He moves neither hand or foot in an undertaking that might be a very honorable one."

To Charles' displeasure, Adams was showing a lively interest in the country's first third-party movement, the Antimasons.

The movement had begun in western New York's evangelical Burned-Over district, which was leading the crusade to abolish slavery in the South. William Morgan, a former Mason of Batavia, New York, had written a book revealing the secret oath and ritual of the Royal Arch Order. In an unsuccessful attempt to prevent its publication, members of the order had kidnapped Morgan and, it was charged, had drowned him in the Niagara River. None of them was convicted: critics, led by two young New York politicians. Thurlow Weed, a friend of Adams, and William H. Seward, then a state Senator, charged that the officials who reluctantly brought the ringleaders to trial were themselves Masons.

The churchgoing farmers and villagers were aroused that a darkly secret organization apparently existed among the influential and well-to-do, binding its members in a blood oath so powerful that violators of its code would suffer a savagely painful death. The party sponsored by Weed and Seward declared it would support no Mason for public office. Adams fervently agreed: the young republic should not tolerate a secret organization that might have a prior claim on its members' loyalty. Both President Jackson and his Secretary of State, Edward Livingston, were Masons, and, Adams discovered, proud of it. So were many of the leading citizens of Boston and members of the slaveholding gentry of the Southern towns. Henry Clay of Kentucky, the National Republicans' candidate to oppose Jackson in the coming election, was temporizing, hoping to get both the Masonic and Antimasonic vote. Unless Clay made a clean break with the order, Adams proclaimed, the Antimasons must choose a candidate of their own.

Charles Francis, considering Antimasonry a working people's movement, appealed to his father to keep his opinions to himself. "He has partaken of late rather largely of this heated feeling," Charles wrote in his diary, "and I tried as mildly as possible to put a rein over indiscretion, which I must confess he will commit at times. . . . It is the character of my father vehemently to attack. He does it through all his writings more or less, and attacks in every community creates [sic] defenses. Controversy rises, from which issues anger, and ill blood. All this,"

39

he added sorrowfully, "is not to my taste. I must be set down as preferring insignificant and inglorious ease."

The Antimasonic party dwindled away after a few years— and so did Adams' interest in it—and its adherents were absorbed into the future Whig party. But that summer of 1831 it brought William Seward to Quincy in the hope of making Adams the third party's candidate for President. Seward, who would go on to become governor of New York, United States Senator and Lincoln's Secretary of State, was surprised at the plainness, even shabbiness, of the former President's house. The "old-fashioned knocker" brought a woman servant, who ushered him into the little parlor. "The house," Seward wrote in his autobiography, "is very plain and old-fashioned; no Turkey [Oriental] carpets, no pier tables, no 'pillar and claw' piano. Very plain ingrain carpeting covers the floor." The chairs were old-fashioned; they were Queen Anne, almost priceless today. The piano was straight-lined, probably Sheraton. A portrait of John Adams hung over the mantel, one of Jefferson on another wall.

Adams came down the stairs from his study. Seward saw "a short, rather corpulent man, of sixty and upward. . . . He was bald, his countenance was staid, sober almost to gloom or sorrow, and hardly gave indication of his superiority over other men. His eyes were weak and inflamed. He was dressed in an old olive frock coat, a cravat carelessly tied, and old-fashioned, light-colored vest and pantaloons. It was obvious that he was a student, just called from the labors of his closet. Without courtly air or attitude, he paused at the door of the parlor. I walked quite up to him, while he maintained his immobile attitude, and presented my letter of introduction from Tracy [Albert H. Tracy, a member of the House of Representatives from upstate New York]. He asked me to sit, read the letter, said he was happy to see me, sat down in the next chair."

Seward explained that he and Tracy had come to Boston to sound out the Massachusetts Antimasons on a Presidential candidate. Tracy had expected to accompany him to Quincy, but had been detained. Adams said, "Yes. Mr. Tracy was in the vicinity of the outrage in your state [William Morgan's abduction], and his attention was therefore early drawn to the subject."

Seward went on: "He . . . said he had not wished to do anything which would injure Mr. Clay's prospects of obtaining the Presidency and had therefore been restrained. He had long felt an anxious desire to discharge the duty which evolved upon him in relation to Freemasonry but, situated as he was, had hoped that other and younger men enough would engage in the cause to dispense with his exertions. But he was satisfied this was a crisis which required every man to do his duty, and he should not shirk from it. . . . He said he would not desire to be President of the United States again, though he should have the assurance of a unanimous vote. He had had the office; he knew its duties, privations, enjoyments, perplexities, and vexations. But if the Antimasons thought his nomination would be better than any other, he would not decline."

Seward would in time become an ardent Adams admirer, and his biography, written years later, is a paean of adulation. The conclusion of his account of that first meeting is revealing: "Our interview lasted three hours. He was all the time plain, honest and free in his discourse; but with hardly a ray of animation or feeling in the whole of it, . . . hardly possessing traits of character to inspire a stranger with affection. Occasionally a flash of ingenuous ardor was seen, but it was transitory, and all was cool, regular and deliberate. As I left the house I thought I could plainly answer how it happened that he, the best President since Washington, entered and left office with so few devoted personal friends."

The Antimasonic Convention, held in Baltimore in October, the nation's first political convention, divided on Adams, compromising instead on his old friend, William Wirt of Maryland. But by then Adams was on his way back to Washington to begin his first session in the House of Representatives. A month before his departure he attended a dinner in Boston given by his friend, Alexander Everett, Edward's brother and editor of the *North American Review*, for two young French intellectuals, Alexis de Tocqueville and Gustav de Beaumont. The two were officially on a government mission to study the

American prison systems, but they were more interested in how the democratic process was working. The result of their tour was de Tocqueville's *Democracy in America*, which made him famous.

Adams was the most distinguished American statesman de Tocqueville had met so far. The young Frenchman was seated next to him at the table and was delighted to discover that the former President spoke his language "with facility and elegance." He promptly made the most of it. They discussed "the character of Americans in general," and a remark by Adams enabled de Tocqueville to steer him onto the controversial subject of slavery. Adams' position on the South's "peculiar institution" would antagonize abolitionists as well as Southerners in the years ahead. De Tocqueville drew from him a frank explanation of his views.

"There are two facts," Adams said, "which have a great influence on our character: in the North, the religious and political doctrines of the first founders of New England; in the South, slavery."

Did he believe slavery a great evil in the United States?

"Unquestionably," Adams answered. "It's in slavery that are to be found all the embarrassments of the present and the fears of the future."

"Are the inhabitants of the South aware of this state of things?"

"Yes, at the bottom of their hearts. But it's a truth, concern over which they are not aware that they show. Slavery has modified the whole state of society in the South. There the whites form a class which has all the ideas, all the passions, all the prejudices of an aristocracy, but don't deceive yourself: nowhere is equality among the whites greater than in the South. Here [in New England] we have a great equality before the law, but it ceases absolutely in the habits of life. There are upper classes and working classes. Every white man in the South is a being equally privileged, whose destiny is to make the Negroes work without working himself. We cannot conceive how far the idea that work is dishonorable has entered the spirit of the Americans of the South. No enterprise in which Negroes cannot serve as the inferior agents can succeed in that part of the Union. All those who do a large trade at Charleston [South Carolina] and in the cities have come from New England. I remember that a Representative from the South being at my table in Washington could not keep from expressing his astonishment at seeing white domestics occupied in serving us. He said to Mrs. Adams, 'I find it a degradation of the human race to use whites for domestics. When one of them comes to change my plate, I am always tempted to offer him my place at table.' From this laziness in which the Southern whites live, great differences in character result. They devote themselves to bodily exercise, to hunting, to racing; they are vigorously constituted, brave, full of honor; what is called the point of honor is more delicate there than anywhere else; duels are frequent."

"Do you think that it is really impossible to get on without the blacks in the South?"

"I am convinced of the contrary," Adams replied. "The Europeans work in Greece and in Sicily. Why should they not in Virginia and the Carolinas? It is no hotter there."

"Is the number of slaves increasing?"

"It is diminishing in all the states [where] . . . they cultivate wheat and tobacco, cultures for which the Negroes are rather a charge than useful. Therefore, one exports them thence to the provinces where cotton and sugar are cultivated. In those of the western states where they have been introduced, they remain in very small number."

"I then spoke to him of nearer dangers to the Union," de Tocqueville said, "and of the causes which might bring about its dissolution." De Tocqueville was particularly interested in nullification, the militant challenge of South Carolina to President Jackson over the protective tariff. But Adams apparently considered the current states rights crisis too explosive to discuss with a foreigner.

"He did not answer," said de Tocqueville, "but it was easy to see that on this point he had no more confidence than I in the future."

On October 27 Adams came into Boston again to take the

43

stage for Washington, and to get $300 from Charles to pay his expenses. Charles, who had "noticed a growing disposition to extravagance" in his father, tried to impress on him that, as his financial manager, he was having a hard time keeping the estate solvent. But Adams briskly told him to do the best he could. Money never seriously concerned him, causing Charles to complain, "He must add one more to the long list of men who, having good advice, neglect it." He saw his father off and, the next day, drove out to Quincy to see that the outside entrance to the cellar and the windows were calked with seaweed for the winter. He weeded the strawberry bed, which needed it badly since Adams had lately lost interest in his plants and seedlings. "My father in all practical matters wants the power of executing anything like a connected system," Charles grumbled. "The consequence is that his farm, his house, his garden are all exhibiting the progress of decay."

John Quincy now had a more immediate interest. At eleven-thirty on the morning of December 5, 1831, he walked into the south wing of the old Capitol and took his seat, number 203, in the first semicircle before the elevated Speaker's chair in the House of Representatives.

⇥⇥⇥ III ⇤⇤⇤

THE twenty-second Congress was "the most fiery and eventful," said Thomas Hart Benton of Missouri, that he had witnessed until then; and Adams had a dynamic share in making it so. Congress was in its Golden Age of dialectical giants. In the Senate sat Daniel Webster of Massachusetts, with his magnetic eyes, his craggy countenance and overhanging brows; nobody, it was said, could be as great as Webster looked—not even Webster. In the same chamber were Henry Clay of Kentucky and "Old Bullion" Benton, with John Calhoun of South Carolina in the president's chair. With Adams in the House were Edward Everett, the Boston orator who would share the platform with Lincoln at Gettysburg, and a future President, James Polk of Tennessee. Two more future Presidents, Franklin Pierce of New Hampshire and Millard Fillmore of New York, would soon join them.

From down Pennsylvania Avenue the man in the White House cast his lean shadow over both their houses.

The two major—and historic—issues confronting the lawmakers, and the nation, were the tariff crisis and President Jackson's feud with the Bank of the United States. To Adams the tariff problem was basically linked to slavery. The plantation South depended on its crops, its cotton, sugar, rice, tobacco—produced by slave labor—for its prosperity. Where mass craftsmanship or clerical ability was required, the primitive Negroes were practically useless. So the South was dependent on the North for its manufactured goods, its farm tools and utensils, its cloth, glassware, refined staples and luxuries. The industrial North needed protective import duties for its young factories and textile mills to operate against foreign competition. In overpopulated England, and throughout Europe generally, labor was plentiful and therefore cheap. The free workers of the Northern states had to be better paid to keep them from adventuring westward to stake out a farm of their own in the vast public domain.

To the planters, the protective duties they had to pay for their necessities were impoverishing the South and enriching the North. South Carolina was leading the opposition to the tariff by threatening to invoke states' rights: refusing to let federal officials collect the import duties within its borders.

States' rights, harking back to the early days of independence, when each former colony was still a government unto itself, was also a vital element in the bank dispute. The powerful Bank of the United States, with its twenty-five branch offices, virtually controlled the country's commerce. While subsidized by the government, for which it served as a depository, it was independently owned, its stock distributed among Northern merchants, tidewater planters and foreign investors. Philadelphia, its headquarters, was the financial capital of the country.

To commercial New England and the Southern gentry, the bank, with its control over credit, was a necessary brake on speculation. In the frontier communities and the new Western states the bank was considered a monstrous monolith, straddling the path of expansion. A frontier farmer who wanted a loan to extend his land or to buy seed or a new team and wagon might not have security to offer, but the neighboring state bank would accept his signature on trust; the Bank of the United States would not. At the same time, the Jackson men charged, the bank did not hesitate to grant easy credit to its wealthy and influential clients.

So matters stood as the House of Representatives convened in the old south wing of the Capitol, now the Hall of Statuary, a semicircular chamber enclosed in massive pillars and pilasters of Potomac marble. The day was cold and gusty, and most of the Representatives hovered around the fireplaces in the lobby until called to order, and then they kept their hats on. The hardships of travel and the leisurely pace of the era usually made attendance small at the early sessions. But this particular Monday, 202 members, nearly the entire House, responded to the first roll call. The news that the former President was joining them had stimulated considerable interest.

His old colleague, Henry Clay, met Adams a few evenings later and asked, "How does it feel to be a boy again?" Adams said that so far he "found the labor light enough, but the House has not yet got down to business." When it did, Clay told him, he could expect it to become "extremely laborious." "I well know that," Adams said testily. "But labor I shall not refuse so long as my hands, my eyes and my brain do not desert me."

Clay's prediction soon materialized. In selecting the standing committees for the session, Speaker Andrew Stevenson of Virginia, a Jackson man, realized he had "an elephant on his hands." Adams' prestige required that he be given the chairmanship of an important committee. Anything less would be an affront. The logical place for the former President, because of his eight years as Secretary of State and his long service abroad, was the chairmanship of the Committee on Foreign Affairs. But the head of that committee, Stevenson felt, should be friendly to the Administration, and Adams and Jackson were not on speaking terms. Consequently, Stevenson made him chairman of the Committee on Manufacturers where, he hoped, Adams could do the least mischief. To make sure, he weighted the committee heavily with Administration men.

Adams was distraught. He knew almost nothing about manufacturing and had only a general understanding of tariff schedules, which would be the committee's main concern. He was a statesman, a scholar—a poet. His sole venture into business, the flour mill operated by his son John in which he had invested his savings, was a losing enterprise. The 1828 "Tariff of Abominations," as the slave states called it, which had brought South Carolina to the brink of rebellion, had to be revised. He asked

Edward Everett, who was on the Committee on Foreign Affairs, to change places with him. Everett was agreeable. Adams appealed to Stevenson to make the switch, pointing out that the position Stevenson had assigned him was "not suited to my acquirements and capacities." He wrote in his diary that he had, uncharacteristically, "petitioned almost on my knees to the speaker." But Stevenson said the committees, once established, could not be altered without a vote of the entire House. Adams did not want to submit to that so early in his career. So, "camel that I am," he took on the load, and got busy inquiring into the cost of slave cloth and blankets from New England and abroad, and the duties on plows and spikes and bolts, cotton bagging and ticking, ingrain and Brussels carpeting, coffee and tea and tableware.

Adams and Jackson were actually not far apart in their tariff concepts. Jackson wanted a moderate tariff that would be equitable for both the North and South; Adams could not quarrel with him on that. Jackson planned to use the tariff to pay off the national debt by the next year, the first and only time in the nation's history; Adams admitted it was a noble purpose. But as individuals they were as dissimilar as linen and homespun. Jackson was a slaveholder and one of the roughhewn first-generation aristocrats of the new South beyond the coastal plain. His keen native intelligence wore a thin veneer of education. Though his syntax was faulty, his mentality was not. His hostility to Adams went back to the election of 1824 and his belief that Adams had then cheated him out of the Presidency by making a deal with Clay. Political gossipmongers had persuaded him that Adams was responsible for the slander against his dead wife, Rachel. Adams, on the other hand, blamed Jackson for the false and outrageous charges of political corruption and maladministration spread against his Presidency.

As a Man of the Whole Nation, however, Adams was deeply concerned over South Carolina's rebellion against the protective tariff. He considered nullification of federal authority nothing less than treason. If it succeeded, it could spread to other Southern states, endangering the life of the Union. "My forebodings are dark," he wrote in his diary. He had hoped the

48

United States would endure for ages, but now brooded, "I disbelieve its duration for twenty years, and doubt its continuance for five."

He called together the Committee on Manufacturers. The room assigned to it was unheated, so he moved into the Foreign Affairs Committee room, which had a fire going. An Administration member suggested, and Adams agreed, that it would be helpful to confer with the Secretary of the Treasury, Louis McLane, to learn the executive department's thinking, since no tariff bill could get through Congress without Administration support. Adams himself met with McLane.

A few evenings later, Edward Everett called the leaders of the National Republican party in Congress to his boarding house to talk over their tariff program. Henry Clay, as titular head of the party, promptly took over. He was not worried about South Carolina's threats, he announced. He wanted revenue to carry out his "American system" of internal improvements. "To preserve, maintain and strengthen the American system," he said, "I would defy the South, the President and the devil!"

Adams pointed out that the situation was critical, and that they should go along with the Administration as far as possible to put through a tariff schedule acceptable to both the agricultural South and the manufacturing interests of the North. Clay disagreed. He was going to campaign for national highways and canals to develop the interior, for more manufacturing for the home market, and that meant adhering to strong protective duties. To Adams, Clay's manner was peremptory, dogmatic. Clay had just come from a dinner party. Representative John W. Taylor of New York noted that he was "a little flustered, and talked more freely than he would reflect with pleasure." He had had a bit too much to drink. When Adams said his committee had agreed to work with the Secretary of the Treasury, Clay answered sharply, "They have given a very foolish and improvident pledge."

From that point on, relations between Adams and Clay were decidedly cool. But Clay was not Adams' only adversary. By now he was in disagreement with both the six Administration members of his committee and Lewis Condict of New Jersey, the

only other National Republican on it. Condict wanted total repeal of duties on noncompetitive articles, and the Administration members, while wanting to reduce the rates, desired a
duty for revenue on all articles. Adams said, "I never was so
much harassed in my life!" His wife, however, did not take his
harassment seriously. Writing to Charles Francis' wife in Boston,
she said, "He is now very busy with his congressional duties,
which appear to please him extremely, and I think it is a life
which will yield him both occupation and amusement."

A week after taking his seat, Adams made his first speech
in the House. It was on the subject that "the gentleman from
Massachusetts" would belabor time and time again, until it
brought all the venom and fury of the Southern members and
their Northern supporters down upon him, calling him "the
madman of Massachusetts," "a mischievous, bad old man,"
"scoundrel," and "old harlequin." But that would take time.
As former President, he had the full attention of the House and
the gallery.

It had been so long since Adams had made a public address
that he found himself "not a little agitated by the sound of my
own voice." He had never been an extemporaneous speaker; he
had none of the resonant delivery and graceful poise of Webster
and Everett and the other orators of the day. His voice was high,
and cracked when it tried to soar. He spoke in spurts, stooping
over his desk, grimacing.

He had fifteen petitions to present, he announced, all of
the same tenor. He sent one up to the clerk to be read. It declared that "the undersigned inhabitants of Pennsylvania . . .
believe slavery, and the slave trade in the human species, is a
great national and moral evil . . . and ask Congress to pass
such laws as will entirely abolish slavery and the slave trade in
the District of Columbia, over which Congress has exclusive
jurisdiction." The petition with its long scroll of signatures
unrolled to the floor.

Adams noted that the petitions were not from his home state
but from Pennsylvania. "They were transmitted to me . . .
with the request that I would present them. . . . I did not
deem it proper to refuse the request, implying as it did a degree

of confidence in me, for which I was bound to be grateful. The petitioners are of the Society of Friends [Quakers], a class of people for whom I entertain the highest respect, and who, I believe, possess as much virtue, with as little guile, as any class of people on the globe. . . .

"There is a traffic in slaves in the District of Columbia which may, perhaps, require some legislation from Congress; and I move that the petition be referred to the Committee on the District of Columbia with instructions to inquire into and report upon that part relating to the slave trade. . . . In regard to the abolition of slavery here, the petitioners probably supposed that their view would receive some support and countenance from me. But I deem it my duty to declare that the proposition does not meet my approbation; and should it become a subject of discussion in this House, I shall oppose the wishes of the petitioners." His rheumy eyes lifted to his audience. "The most healing of medicines, unduly administered, becomes the most deadly of poisons."

Petitions against slavery were not new to the House, but so far they had been few. The Southern members listened to him in polite silence. The petitions were referred to the Committee on the District, of which Philip Doddridge, a Virginia slaveholder, was chairman. A week later he reported that the committee considered "it unwise and impolitic, if not unjust to the adjoining states [Virginia and Maryland] for Congress to interfere in a subject of such delicacy and importance as is the relation between master and slave."

It was exactly the response Adams had expected. Nevertheless, he wrote in his diary, he had been "listened to with great attention, and it seemed to myself I had performed an achievement." To the Puritan New Englander, slavery was "the great and foul stain upon the North American Union." Adams could never harden himself to the spectacle so common in the capital —the files of manacled Negroes, men, women and children, moving morosely through the streets to the waterfront for shipment, and the slave dealers' blatant advertisements in the newspapers, one of which was currently appearing on the front page of the *National Intelligencer*:

51

CASH FOR NEGROES. I wish to purchase from fifty to sixty likely Negroes of both sexes, families included, for which the highest prices in cash will be given. Persons wishing to dispose of slaves will do well to give me a call at Robey's Tavern on 9th St. near the General Post Office. JOSEPH W. NEAL.

One incident Adams never forgot. A slave woman, learning she was to be separated from her husband and family and carried South, broke away from her guards, ran to the attic of the Washington tavern where the Negroes were being assembled and leaped out the window. Though she failed to kill herself, she was so badly crushed that she was no longer marketable, and the slave trader had to leave her behind when he marshaled his drove of men and women, handcuffed in pairs and attached to a chain between the two ranks, and marched them away.

Adams' speech did not please the Eastern abolitionists, just beginning to feel their strength. Moses Brown, the ancient Quaker philanthropist, wrote to him from Providence, asking why he had so pointedly refused to endorse emancipation in the District. Adams replied that slavery was as abhorrent to him as it was to Friend Brown. "I believe that the spirit of the age and the course of events is tending to universal emancipation," he said. "But bound as I am by the Constitution of the United States, I am not at liberty to take a part in promoting it. The remedy must arise in the seat of the evil [the South itself]."

For three reasons, he said, he could not urge emancipation in the District of Columbia: he did not consider the inhabitants of one state competent to petition another state, or Congress acting for the District of Columbia, on a matter so important to that state or the District; he believed he was acting in compliance with the views of the majority of his constituents; and, most definitely, he was against stirring up strife between the North and South.

Opposition to emancipation was actually as strong among some groups in the North as it was in the "slavocracy," as Adams termed the South. New England industrialists and bankers, profiting from the South's production of cotton for their textile mills, did not want to disturb the *status quo*. Northern workmen resented the competition of free Negroes and opposed being put on a level with them. William Lloyd Garrison, the militant editor of the abolitionist *Liberator,* was attacked by a mob of well-dressed Bostonians, mauled, his clothes torn off, and almost lynched. A school for free Negroes in New Haven was attacked by infuriated citizens and compelled to disband.

All this only increased the ardor of the evangelists in the North and such determined crusaders as John Greenleaf Whittier, the New England Quaker poet, and the wealthy Bostonian, Wendell Phillips. Their efforts to flood the South with emancipation literature were frustrated by the refusal of Southern postmasters to handle their mail. So they turned to the avenue of propaganda that Adams held open to them, while sternly refusing to join their ranks: the right of petition to Congress guaranteed by the Constitution.

Speaker Stevenson soon saddled Adams with another legislative task. The Bank of the United States' twenty-year charter still had nearly four years to go. But Nicholas Biddle, its tough and able president, confronted with Jackson's hostility to a national bank, realized that the prospect of getting a new charter would be slim indeed if the President were reelected. He decided to apply immediately, so that Henry Clay could make rechartering a major issue for the business community in the upcoming Presidential campaign.

When Biddle's application was introduced in Congress, a hostile Representative from Georgia, Augustus Clayton, demanded that a committee be appointed to go to Philadelphia and investigate the bank's operations. In the debate Adams made it apparent that he supported the institution, and Stevenson promptly put him on the committee, taking care again to pack it with pro-Jackson Representatives.

Adams was convinced that Stevenson was trying to overload him with work. He knew something about banking—he had been a small shareholder in Biddle's bank, but had sold his stock on his way to Congress—and he preferred the assignment to the chairmanship of the Committee on Manufacturers. This time he asked the full House to relieve him of that task. "Much to my surprise," he said, "it excited considerable debate." A number of Representatives insisted his long experience in government was important to the Manufacturers Committee. Adams doubted their sincerity, but realized that his motion would not carry. So, again he withdrew it and stoically took on the added task.

He soon discovered that the Administration members of the committee knew little about commercial banking. They were concerned mainly, he decided, with making out a case against the bank. Their charges of technical violations of the charter and of practices they called usurious were patently frivolous. So Adams wrote his own minority report, 30,000 words long, in his palsied script, defending all the bank's practices. It demolished the majority's charges, and weeks later he had the satisfaction of seeing both houses of Congress pass rechartering. But Jackson's fighting spirit, so easily fueled, was by then burning bright. "The bank is trying to kill me," he told Van Buren, his candidate for Vice President, "but I will kill it!" With Van Buren's help, he wrote a blunt and emphatic veto. Yet Clay's prognosis that it would cost Jackson his reelection fell flat. When the time came, the country gave Jackson 219 electoral votes to 49 for Clay and 7 for the Antimasons' Wirt.

Meanwhile, the House no longer listened politely when Adams spoke. His first sally into debate ended all that. South Carolina had put in a claim against the government for supplies that it had bought for its militia in the War of 1812. British ships were off its coast at the time, and the hard-pressed federal government was unable to come to the state's aid. So the South Carolina legislature dug into its own treasury. The claim, which included an item of $7,600 for blankets supplied to the short-term militia, had been approved by the Committee on Military Affairs, which included two Representatives from South Carolina, William Drayton and James Blair. A motion was made to refer the bill to the Committee on Claims. There was debate about the blankets. Lewis Williams of North Carolina declared it was irregular to furnish blankets to militia serving less than a year. Drayton defended the item, explaining that, during part of the time the militia served, the weather was cold, and the troops had needed the blankets. William Nuckolls, also of South Carolina, added furiously that his state had acted in the interest of the nation and it was degrading for its representatives to have to "higgle" about repayment.

Drayton was chairman of the committee that had approved the claim. Adams disliked that. He arose and announced, in his high, strident voice, that he hoped the bill would be referred. The Claims Committee was "the committee of moral obligations." If it should approve South Carolina's claim, "I flatter myself that the state which I have the honor in part to represent will come in on the same principle [for fat reimbursement] from the treasury of the United States. As a citizen of Massachusetts, such a result would to me be very desirable."

But there was another reason he wanted the bill to go to the Committee on Claims. "We have a report on this claim from a committee the chairman of which is a subject of the sovereign state which is the claimant. . . . We are all subjects of sovereign states. He is a subject of the sovereign state of South Carolina. I am a subject of the sovereign state of Massachusetts. We all know that 'sovereign' and 'subject' are correlative terms and that wherever there is a sovereign there is of necessity also a subject. I desire the claim to be thoroughly investigated."

Charles Francis said of his father that it was his nature to attack vehemently. It was probably as much the way he said things as what he said that caused the clashes in the House. His voice grated on the nerves. His expression was pugnacious. He had a knack of ironically stressing and repeating key words—words such as "sovereign" and "subject"—until the sound of them sent his opponents into a frenzy.

When he finished, members jumped up around him, hands waved for the Speaker's attention. Stevenson recognized George McDuffie of South Carolina, who denounced Adams roundly for defaming his state and said that "if the member from Massachusetts had as much experience in the proceedings of the House as he has in another [the executive] department . . . he certainly would not have submitted the remarks just heard." Jessie Speight of North Carolina charged that Adams had "impugned the motives of the Military Committee" and the integrity of Chairman Drayton. Then Drayton himself scolded Adams. Even

John Davis and John Reed of his own state and his old friend, Everett, came to the defense of the committee. The motion to reconsider was overwhelmingly defeated.

Walking home down Pennsylvania Avenue in the winter dusk, Adams brooded over the stir he had caused. He had made a short speech and it had "brought down a swarm from all quarters, among them three members from my own state." He saw in it "symptoms of universal opposition." "Shall I not feel that my prudence and my escape from utter ruin depend upon my abstaining from taking part in all debates?" he wondered. "And is this compatible with the duties of my station?"

It was not, and Adams had no intention of retreating into prudence. Soon he was again deep in the tariff controversy, with Clay on one side and on the other the Administration members of the Committee on Manufacturers. His objective was a tariff that would reduce protective duties enough to make it palatable to South Carolina and keep her from carrying out her nullification threat, and at the same time would bring in enough revenue for the Administration to pay off the national debt and still provide funds for internal improvements. The rest of the committee divided along party lines. So he wrote his own minority report, some 20,000 words long, and saw it eventually accepted by both Clay and the Jackson forces.

One of President Jackson's strongest supporters in the House was Colonel Richard M. Johnson, the frontier barrister who had led a regiment of Kentucky riflemen in the War of 1812 and was credited with killing the Shawnee chief, Tecumseh, in the Battle of the Thames. When the House adjourned the afternoon of March 2, Colonel Johnson fell into step with Adams. "I wish to speak with you regarding the personal relations between President Jackson and you," he said. Adams, picking his way with his cane down the slushy avenue, said nothing. "I would like to see personal intercourse between you restored," Johnson went on. "I think the advance should come from the President. I have spoken to Mr. Cass [Lewis Cass, Secretary of War], and he agrees with me on this point."

Adams had not been expecting anything like this. He chose

his words carefully. "Personal intercourse between us," he said, "was suspended by General Jackson himself without informing me of the reason. I have never known the reason. I did see at the time in the [Washington] *Telegraph* an anonymous statement that it was because *he knew* I had caused or countenanced abusive charges against Mrs. Jackson in the newspapers. It is not so. But General Jackson never asked me about it, and I did not deem it necessary to notice anonymous charges in the *Telegraph*."

Johnson said he had never believed that story. It had been concocted by "scoundrel office seekers," and he thought Jackson surmised as much himself by now. "I do not speak by authority of General Jackson," he said. "But I know that his disposition toward you is now friendly, and I have no doubt that if an advance from him would be accepted by you, he would make it."

Adams thought it over. "I am disposed to receive any friendly advance from General Jackson with indulgence," he conceded.

"Would you accept an invitation to dine with him?"

"No," he answered firmly. "That is an act of ordinary courtesy usually paid to every member of Congress. I could not consider it an advance toward reconciliation." After all, Adams as a former President was no ordinary Congressman.

"Would you accept an invitation to a small and select party of friends?"

"That would be liable to the same objection."

"What do you think proper?"

"It is not for me to prescribe," Adams answered, and turned away into Sixteenth Street. "I can only say that I am willing to receive in a spirit of conciliation any advance which General Jackson might make in the same spirit."

Walking the two blocks to his house, he wondered if he had been too conciliatory. Johnson, he thought, had placed him in a delicate position. He hoped he had not said anything he would regret.

The next day Colonel Johnson's servant arrived with a letter. It was undated and unsigned, and the last sentence read: "Please destroy this when you read it." He made a copy:

57

General Jackson expressed great satisfaction that I had the conversation with you which I detailed to him, and expressed a wish that I should assure you of his personal regard and friendship and that he was anxious to have a social and friendly intercourse restored between you. There I left it and have satisfied my own mind. I shall communicate to Governor Cass the same, and there it rests, with me having done what my heart suggested. The President expressed himself as perfectly satisfied now that you never did countenance the publication to which I alluded and entertains for you the highest opinion as a man of honor.

So far so good, Adams told himself. Jackson was satisfied that he had had nothing to do with spreading the scandal that Rachel Jackson was an adulteress. He would return the letter to Johnson instead of destroying it, but let him know that he had made a copy. He would thank Johnson for his effort. He would *not* get in touch with Secretary Cass. Now that he had had the night to think about it, his mind was made up. Jackson and he had once been friends, but that was years ago. He had admired Jackson as a soldier, both in the War of 1812 and in the Seminole War. But as a statesman he held the President in cold contempt. A resumption of friendly relations would excite wide interest in gossip-minded Washington. As he wrote in his diary:

It would not fail to expose me to obloquy. The old Federal party, now devoted to Mr. Clay, have already more than once tried their hand at slandering me. They have drawn the sword and brandished it over my head. If I set foot in the President's house they will throw away the scabbard. I must walk with extreme circumspection; even that will not protect me from their malignity. Something is due to myself, and the path is narrow to avoid on the one hand the charge of an implacable temper and on the other of eagerness to propitiate the dispenser of power.

Again the dualism in Adams' character revealed itself. In his reflections, recorded in his diary, which he called his conscience, he was a man of peace, trying to steer clear of entangling controversies. In action, he courted contention.

He had no illusions about Jackson's willingness to be reconciled with him. The President, he believed, was facing a rough campaign and wanted all the support he could get. He recognized the help that Adams, with his political independence, was giving him on the tariff. Possibly he had also learned by now that Adams had been the only member of Monroe's Cabinet who had stood up for him when he invaded Spanish Florida without the government's official consent. But Jackson's antagonism toward the Bank of the United States was bringing down upon him the wrath of the business interests. His feud with the powerful states' rights champion, Vice President Calhoun, and the belligerence of Souh Carolina over the protective tariff were worrying his supporters.

Jackson's friends were, in Adams' view, more a handicap than a help to him. The Eaton affair was still the scandal of the capital. John H. Eaton, one of Jackson's oldest friends and his first Secretary of War, had had an illicit affair with a seductive brunette born Peggy O'Neill, whose father operated a tavern at the Georgetown end of the capital. Peggy was married, but her husband, John Timberlake, a Navy purser, spent most of his time at sea. Eaton, a handsome widower, boarded at the tavern, and when Peggy's father was faced with foreclosure, Eaton bought the place for him. When Peggy's husband committed suicide aboard ship, some said it was because he had been caught short in his accounts. But the story most people believed was that he had despaired when he learned of his wife's unfaithfulness.

Jackson advised Eaton to marry the girl. It did not take much persuasion. Peggy was not only good-looking; she was witty and vivacious. But it did not work out as Jackson had expected. The other Cabinet wives refused to associate with "that hussy." Jackson was furious, but helpless. Only his Secretary of State, Van Buren, a widower, and the British and Russian ministers, both bachelors, would receive the new Mrs. Eaton. Calhoun's wife, a Southern aristocrat, was the ringleader of the opposition.

Jackson brusquely told Calhoun to bring her into line. Calhoun equivocated. At a Cabinet meeting, Jackson, always the gallant toward "the weaker sex," maintained that Peggy was "chaste as a virgin." Senator Webster, hearing it, quipped, "Age cannot wither her, nor time stale her infinite virginity!"

Jackson made it appear that his hostility toward Calhoun was brought on by the Vice President's inability to explain away the charge that he particularly had wanted Jackson court-martialed back in 1818. Actually, Calhoun's failure—or disinclination—to make his wife stop snubbing Peggy Eaton started it. Early in April, Van Buren, the Red Fox of Kinderhook, cleverly solved the problem for Jackson. He persuaded Eaton to resign and then resigned himself. The rest of the Cabinet had to follow. Jackson formed a new Cabinet more to his liking, and appointed Eaton governor of Florida Territory and Van Buren minister to Great Britain. But a week later, on April 14, another of Jackson's old friends was in trouble, and Adams wrote home to his wife, who had already returned to Quincy for the summer, "I find myself trying Sam Houston for breach of the privilege of the House."

Houston, the tall, tough former Congressman, former governor of Tennessee and future President of Texas, called Co-lonneh (the Raven) among the Cherokees with whom he now lived, happened to be in the capital with an Indian delegation seeking government help. William Stanbery, a combative anti-Administration Congressman from Ohio, implied in the House that Eaton had been forced to resign from the Cabinet because he had faudulently tried to give Houston a contract for Indian rations. When Houston heard about it, he charged into the Capitol looking for Stanbery. Congressman Polk, his fellow Tennessean, grabbed him and managed to maneuver him out of the building. Houston then sent Stanbery a challenge. Stanbery ignored it, maintaining that since he did not know Houston, he could not fight him. Duels, furthermore, he declared contemptuously, were fought between gentlemen, implying he did not consider the backwoods giant one. He stuck two pistols in his waistband and hoped for the best.

Houston, on his way north, had stopped at Jackson's Hermitage in Tennessee and cut a hickory sapling which he, a habitual whittler, had made into a walking stick. He had presented it to a friend in Georgetown. Now he got it back. The evening of April 13, walking with two friends near the Capitol, he thought he recognized Stanbery in the dim light of a street lamp. Houston approached him, asking, "Are you William Stanbery?" Stanbery said, "Yes." "Then you are a damned rascal!" Houston shouted and brought his stick down on Stanbery's head. Stanbery tried to run, but Houston swung with his cane until he brought him down. He fell on top of Stanbery as the Congressman wrenched out one of his pistols and shoved it against Houston's chest. The flint sparked, but the charge failed to go off. Houston tore the pistol out of Stanbery's hand, picked him up by the heels and spanked him.

The next morning Stanbery wrote Speaker Stevenson from his bed, demanding that the House punish Houston. He also filed a charge of assault and battery in the District of Columbia court. Houston was arrested. His trial in the House of Representatives lasted a month and packed the galleries. Francis Scott Key, author of "The Star-Spangled Banner," was his counsel.

Houston appeared the first day in buckskins, a beaver collar and floppy sombrero. He sprawled in his chair, whittling a pine splinter with his hunting knife, bored with the proceedings. It was his usual mood these days. Until three years before, he had been a man of brilliant promise. One of the heroes, with Jackson, of the Battle of Horseshoe Bend in the Creek War of 1814, he had gone on to become a successful lawyer and politician. Then, during the height of his campaign for reelection as governor of Tennessee, his young bride had walked out on him. Houston had peremptorily resigned the governorship and gone back to live with his Cherokee friends.

When Jackson was told of his appearance and attitude, he angrily summoned Houston to the White House and gave him a frank talking-to. Jackson told him he was having enough trouble without having one of his oldest friends embarrassing him. He flung a purse of silver across the desk and ordered Houston to "dress yourself like a gentleman and buck up your defense."

61

It was soldier talk, the kind Houston understood. He went to the best tailor in the town, and when he returned to the House he was a model of elegance in white silk and dark broadcloth. He no longer lolled back in his chair, but took command of his defense and brought to it all his stump-speaking eloquence. The gallery loved it. One woman said she would rather be Sam Houston in jail than Stanbery in a castle.

To Adams, Houston was "that ex-Choctaw Indian." Listening to one of his perorations, in which he called to his support everything from the flag to the destiny of America, Adams wondered if Houston's silent counsel was not regretting that he had ever written "The Star-Spangled Banner."

Adams voted Houston was guilty of violating the privilege of the House. This time he was in the majority. Speaker Stevenson, in obvious sympathy with Houston, called him to the table and mildly reprimanded him. The District court fined Houston $500, which Jackson then had remitted. Houston was jubilant. "Had they taken me before a justice of the peace and fined me $10," he said, "it would have killed me, but they gave me a national tribunal for a theater, and set me up again!"

By then Adams was so busy with his committee work and daily attendance in the House, besides his copious correspondence with his supporters back in Massachusetts, that he completely neglected his diary, making no entries between March 24 and December 1. On May 16, he wrote Charles Francis that he had completed his minority report on the Bank of the United States investigation, and the *National Intelligencer* had published it. He went on, "Judge Clayton, worthy chairman of the committee, declares his determination to make a personal affair of it. But you need not be alarmed for my safety, notwithstanding the introduction of hickory club and pistol-bullet law in Congress. The judge intends only to answer my reasoning and prove himself a better poet than I am."

By July the provocative Representative Stanbery was in trouble again. This time Adams was an aggressive participant in his defense and contrived a parliamentary maneuver that influenced legislation for generations. The House was debating a joint resolution with the Senate, petitioning President Jackson

62

to proclaim a day of fasting and prayer for deliverance from the cholera epidemic. The disease, prevalent for some time in Europe, had reached the North American continent in June. From Quebec, where it was said to have arrived in a shipload of Irish immigrants, it spread to Montreal. Cases were reported in Plattsburg and Albany. Then, suddenly, it struck New York City. Now hundreds were dying there every day. Many had fled to the country. The harbor was closed to foreign passenger ships, and even coastal shipping was curtailed. Some 3,500 died there before cold weather halted the epidemic. Meanwhile, the fear that it would spread over the nation had people on the edge of panic. The Synod of Dutch Reformed Churches in New York had already asked Jackson to set a day of prayer, and the President had replied that the Constitution did not give him such authority. The House was divided, many of the minority strongly disagreeing with the President.

Unlike the Senate, whose members were chosen by the state legislatures and therefore were men of some stature, the widened franchise enabled almost any politician with a talent for stump-speaking to get himself elected to the lower house. There were few intellectuals like Adams. While most of them had read some law, many knew only the parliamentary procedure they had picked up at town meetings. The Speaker was either their mentor or adversary. Decorum collapsed with little provocation. Since the Sam Houston affair, another Congressman, Thomas Arnold of Tennessee, had been wounded with a horse pistol on the Capitol steps by an Army major he had castigated in a speech. Instead of registering a complaint with the House, Arnold knocked his assailant flat and took his pistol for a trophy.

The discussion on the resolution for a day of prayer had been proceeding decorously on the afternoon of July 9, until Representative Samuel Carson of North Carolina, a Jackson supporter, tried to read the President's letter to support his contention that the Constitution did not permit the federal or state governments to deal with religion. Members jumped up, shouting, "No!" "No!" "We've read it!" "Order!" "Order!" Speaker Stevenson ruled Carson was in order, and Carson continued reading, but only an occasional word penetrated the uproar.

When he sat down, Stanbery got the floor. He declared that Stevenson, by his ruling, had "sacrificed the privileges of the House! In England," he said, "it is not in order to refer to opinions of the King, and the same rule holds here. Never did a monarch on the British throne exercise so much power over his Parliament as the President exercises over the deliberations of this House." No other Speaker had "shaped his course to suit the executive will, with a view to getting an appointment to high office abroad." And then: "Let me say that I have heard the remark frequently made, that the eyes of the Speaker are too frequently turned from the chair you occupy toward the White House."

Speaker Stevenson declared Stanbery's "insinuations against the Chair unfounded and untrue." Representative Franklin Plummer of Mississippi called Stanbery to order and was simultaneously loudly supported and opposed, until the order of the day was moved and debate was cut off.

The next day it resumed. Stevenson, being personally involved, turned over the Speaker's chair to Clement Clay of Virginia and left the chamber. James Bates of Maine offered a resolution to censure Stanbery. Charles Mercer of Virginia defended him, pointing out that the Ohioan's words had not been formally entered by the clerk in the journal of the House, the required procedure. Stanbery, not at all repentant, said he was willing to repeat them and could prove they were true. He started to quote. Clay tried to stop him. Stanbery went on ". . . eyes of the speaker. . . . And I am prepared to show that expressions precisely similar have been used without censure in the British Parliament."

Adams got the floor. He said a principle of great importance was involved. The Constitution had provided that the House could punish its members for disorderly behavior, but it had not stipulated what constituted such behavior. By common consent it had adopted the rules of Parliament to cover situations it had not specifically defined in the *House Manual*. Therefore, the House was governed in this case by the rules of Parliament. "And what is the rule of Parliament? That the disorderly words should not be noticed until the member has finished his speech. The person objecting to them must repeat them. The Speaker must then direct the clerk to take them down in the minutes. On being read to the member, he must deny, explain or retract them."

The correct parliamentary procedure had clearly not been followed, Adams said. The resolution merely stated that Stanbery's words were "an indignity both to the Speaker and the House, and merit the decided censure of the House." It did not contain the exact words, and they had not been taken down the day they were uttered, as prescribed.

"The House has no arbitrary power of punishing without a rule," Adams went on. "What could be more odious? If the House were to be governed only by its feelings, who would be safe? And what likelihood would there be of equal justice being done? If the transgressing member happened to be a political favorite, he would . . . pass free; but if unpopular he would suffer. A member of the majority might say what he pleased, while one in the minority would be restrained even in saying what it was his right to say. What is the proposed punishment in this case? For aught that I know, it is intended to expel the member. In that case, his constituents would suffer a great wrong. The right of the people is at stake."

The debate went on. Confusion developed over the temporary Speaker's ruling on points of order. Stanbery was up again. "One motion is out of order. Then another is declared out of order," he shouted. "And appeals are out of order. I will make one motion that is in order. I make a motion that you [Clay] leave the chair!"

Clay said he was willing. There were shouts of "No!" "No!" "Go on!"

Stanbery continued: "Your conduct in that chair is a proof that you never ought to have been placed there as a judge in my case. You have spoken words which show that you are my enemy!"

George McDuffie of South Carolina arose and said, "If such disgraceful proceedings continue, I will leave the House."

The wrangle brought Speaker Stevenson back into the chamber. He resumed his chair and called for the yeas and nays on the resolution to censure Stanbery. Since he headed the list alphabetically, Adams was called on first. He waited until he had full attention, and held out a sheet of paper to the clerk.

"I ask to be excused from voting," he said, "for the reasons assigned in this paper."

The clerk read: "I ask to be excused from voting on the resolution, believing it to be unconstitutional, inasmuch as it assumed inferences of fact from words spoken by the member, without giving the words themselves; and the facts not being warranted in my judgment by the words which he did use."

The question was put: "Shall Mr. Adams be excused?" It was voted down. The speaker again directed the clerk to call the roll. Adams said, "I decline to answer."

McDuffie, an anti-tariff nullificationist who had been on the committee investigating the Biddle bank with Adams and had found the old man a provocative if unpredictable companion, tried to restore order. "I hope the gentleman from Massachusetts will be excused," he said, "and I move that he be excused."

Stevenson replied, "The House has just decided that he shall not be excused."

Adams was up again. "I did not refuse to vote from any contumacy or disrespect to the House," he said, "but because I have a right to decline for conscientious reasons, and those reasons I desired might be spread on the journal of the House."

Radliff Boon of Indiana declared that if the House accepted Adams' excuse "it would be spreading on the journal its own condemnation. The gentleman from Massachusetts might have avoided voting by going out of the House."

"I did not choose to be absent from the House," Adams answered. "I did not choose to shrink from my duty by such an expedient. Not my rights alone as a member, but the rights of all members of this House and the rights of the people of the United States are concerned in this question, and I cannot evade it. I regret this state of things, but must abide by the consequences."

Thomas Foster of Georgia said Adams' position was a serious threat to legislative procedure. "If any member may persist in refusing to vote upon important questions which come before the House, there must be an end to all legislation. If the House were not full, all that would be necessary to defeat action would be for the minority to refuse to vote, and the question could not be decided for want of a quorum."

Another vote was taken on Adams' refusal to vote, and again the Chair was upheld. Speaker Stevenson read the rule of the House, requiring that every member who was within the House when a question was put was required to vote. He again ordered the clerk to start the roll. Adams sat in his chair, his lips set tight, when his name was called.

Other members had been gathering around his desk, shouting at him, at the Speaker, at anyone who looked as if he might listen. Drayton of South Carolina moved in closer. "This is a novel and I believe unprecedented case," he declared. "Besides being a grave violation of the rules, the gentleman from Massachusetts' course may be attended by dangerous consequences. Should his example find imitations, legislative action may be defeated." He offered a resolution: "*Resolved,* That John Quincy Adams, a member from Massachusetts, in refusing to vote when his name was called by the clerk after the House had rejected his application to be excused from voting, for reasons assigned by him, has committed a breach of one of the rules of the House. *Resolved,* That a committee be appointed to report to this House the course which it ought to adopt in a case so novel and important."

Adams turned on him in savage fury. "I move that the gentleman from South Carolina is himself out of order. The rule of the House requires that a member, in addressing the Chair, must rise from his seat. The gentleman from South Carolina has just risen from a seat not his own."

Stevenson ruled Drayton was in order. But first, the roll call was resumed, passing over Adams, and the resolution to censure Stanbery was voted. By then it was time to adjourn, and action on the Adams resolution was put over.

While the commotion was going on, Adams was busy at his desk writing a letter to Louisa. It was July 11, his sixty-fifth birthday, and he would soon be joining her in Quincy. The

House was getting ready to adjourn, he wrote, as soon as it completed enactment of the tariff bill, which had passed third reading, and decided whether "to expel me or commit me to the custody of the sergeant-at-arms."

Adams had another chore to perform before leaving the House that evening. In May, when the tariff bill and his report were submitted, the Richmond *Enquirer* had published a letter Speaker Stevenson had received three years before from the former President, James Madison. Stevenson had asked the Architect of the Constitution whether the "common defense and general welfare" clause in Article I of that document gave Congress powers not particularly enumerated. Madison said it did not. Stevenson was then new in the Speaker's chair and was merely seeking guidance. A strong states' rights Southerner, he now thought Madison's answer applied to the protective tariff, which the slave states opposed and Adams, in his report, had vigorously defended.

As Stevenson retired to his office this day, Adams followed him, a bulky manuscript in the crook of his arm. He told the Speaker he had wanted to reply in the House to the letter in the *Enquirer* at the time, but had been prevented by the previous question. So he had written his reply in the form of a letter to the Speaker. He laid the longhand manuscript on the desk. He had also given a copy to the *National Intelligencer*, he said, and it would be published the next morning. Stevenson, he said, appeared "a little nettled."

The letter was 10,000 words long. It filled all but one corner of a full page of the *Intelligencer*. A classic of dialectics, it demolished from every angle any argument that Madison was opposed to the protective tariff or had ever thought it unconstitutional.

Considering that Adams' grandson, Charles Francis, Jr., said he wrote slowly and that his script by then showed he was suffering from palsy, the total of words he produced during this, his first, session in the House of Representatives, is appalling. Ten thousand words to Stevenson, 30,000 in his minority report on the Bank of the United States, and 20,000 in his report on the tariff! And he was a diligent correspondent besides, writing regularly to Charles Francis and his old associates at home. He was up daily at four and wrote until he went to the Capitol. He had no secretary. The copy of the Stevenson letter for the *Intelligencer* he made himself. Except when he was engaged in committee work, he was always in his seat throughout the daily sessions, and, toward the close, some of them lasted deep into the night.

When the House reconvened the next day, Adams was early in his seat, ready to resume the battle. But, to his surprise, as he wrote Louisa from his desk, the members had "cooled down wonderfully." Possibly they had read the morning's *Intelligencer*, which editorialized disapprovingly that "yesterday's scene of great excitement" had been one of the "most irregular and tumultuous that has been witnessed in the House of Representatives in a long course of years."

McDuffie got the floor and announced he was for tabling Drayton's resolution. "I am not at all sure," he said, "that the House could compel any of its members to vote when they scrupled the propriety of doing so. The gentleman from Massachusetts is responsible to his own constituents and not to this House, as to the question whether he will vote or not."

Charles Wickliffe of Kentucky and Everett rose to support McDuffie. Everett asked Drayton to withdraw his motion. When he declined, James Wayne of Georgia moved to table it. That motion was carried, 89 to 63.

Adams had won. He had gained acceptance of a new and powerful weapon against arbitrary majority rule. By refusing to vote, a minority could prevent a quorum and block legislation. The weapon, not always used wisely, survived for sixty years, until Thomas Reed, another New Englander, as adroit and tough-minded as Adams, became Speaker and rewrote the House rules.

Adams wrote Louisa that "the House, after trying my temper, voted by a large majority to lay Col. Drayton's resolution on the table. The pressure upon body and mind has been too much for me, but I am light-hearted."

The tariff bill, for which he had fought his own National Republican party and Clay, as well as the states' righters, was on

69

Jackson's desk, ready for his signature. Called the Adams Tariff, it was the major piece of legislation passed at the first session of the Twenty-second Congress. Adams was as exultant as anyone of his flinty nature could be. "My tariff bill, after running through half a dozen gauntlets, has passed by triumphant majorities of more than two to one in both houses of Congress," he wrote home to Quincy. "And now, after the most desperate efforts to run me down for reporting it, and to drive me from my purpose of supporting it—now, Mr. Clay's partizans are beginning to claim it as his bill, as he himself does, in his last speech before voting for it."

Charles Francis Adams, Jr., reviewing his grandfather's first session in Congress, remarked that it was an "extraordinary *tour de force.*" As it turned out, Adams was just getting up steam.

→»» IV «←

S TATES' rights, the root of the current crisis, had worried
   Adams from the beginning of his public life, and he believed—correctly—that it would sporadically plague the Union,
if the Union survived, for generations to come. Slavery was at
the bottom of the present trouble: slave states and free states
trying to live together. But the problem was much older. The
authors of the Constitution, he believed, had foreseen the difficulty, and had decided to let time solve it. But almost immediately it had risen to disturb them.

During his father's Presidency, the Federalist Congress in its
hostility toward the French Revolution had enacted the Alien
and Sedition Acts to protect themselves against the pro-French
activities of the Jeffersonians. The acts had required fourteen
years' residence instead of five for citizenship, had permitted
expulsion of "dangerous" aliens, and had forbidden critics to
speak or write against the government "with intent to defame."
John Adams had opposed them, but it was Thomas Jefferson
and James Madison who, in their Kentucky and Virginia Resolutions, had first raised the issue of states' rights, proclaiming
that the Constitution did not give the central government un-
specified powers over the states. They quoted the Tenth
Amendment: "The powers not delegated to the United States
by the Constitution, nor prohibited by it to the States, are reserved to the States respectively, or to the people."

The Federalists themselves were next to deny the government's superior powers. So unpopular was the War of 1812 in New England, whose commerce it was ruining, that a group of leading citizens met at Hartford, Connecticut, and secretly discussed a separate peace with England. Ironically, it was Andrew Jackson and John Quincy Adams who saved them from carrying out their plan. Jackson's smashing victory over the British in the Battle of New Orleans gave new hope to the American cause, and the Treaty of Ghent, signed by the commission headed by Adams, ended the war.

Five years later, Adams' good friend, Chief Justice John Marshall of the Supreme Court, established the supremacy of the national government over the individual states in a decision supporting the first Bank of the United States, predecessor of the Biddle bank, against the state of Maryland. Since the bank operated as the government's fiscal agent, he ruled, Maryland had no right to tax its Baltimore branch. Recently Marshall had strengthened federal supremacy, in its limited sphere, by declaring that the government and not Georgia had primary authority over the Cherokee Indians in that state. Both decisions confirmed Adams' rigid belief: that the Constitution was "an act of the whole people" and not merely a voluntary pact between the states. President Jackson, however, had made no effort to stop Georgia from removing the Indians from their lands. "John Marshall has made the decision," Adams heard he had said. "Now let him enforce it."

Adams had hoped that the modified tariff he had successfully presented to Congress would pacify the states' righters of South Carolina. But, instead, they took it as a sign of weakness. By the turn of the year their defiance was more belligerent than ever. The state legislature passed an ordinance declaring the Adams Tariff null and void. Governor Hayne called for mobilization of a state army to resist any effort of the government to collect duties in the port of Charleston. Calhoun had resigned as Vice President at the end of December, after Jackson named Van Buren as his next running mate, and was now back in the Senate and openly leading his home state's rebellion.

To Adams' disgust, in his annual State of the Union message

Jackson urged Congress further to conciliate the South, pointing out that the nation was in such good shape that it no longer needed protective duties for revenue. Meanwhile, the President had warned South Carolina that nullification was treason, and resistance to the collection of federal revenues would be sternly crushed.

Adams thought Jackson was knuckling under to the states' rights leaders, that being a Southern slaveholder himself he was even in conspiracy with them. The President's warning against overt resistance, he believed, was mere political bombast, as he had distrusted Jackson's sincerity, early in the controversy, when he stared down Calhoun at a Jefferson's birthday dinner and proclaimed his famous toast, "Our Union: it must be preserved!" He wrote in his diary that Jackson's State of the Union message was "in substance a complete surrender to the nullifiers. . . . More or less as I expected."

He was particularly annoyed, in January of 1833, when he read the report of a speech by a member of the South Carolina legislature, William Preston, boasting that "the protective system reels under our blows." Preston assured his confederates that the Adams Tariff was "an attempt to appease us," that South Carolina had already driven the advocates of protection "into a reduction," and he ended, "Let us go on then, and we shall get the whole debt."

The new tariff was out of Adams' hands. Instead of his Committee on Manufacturers, Speaker Stevenson had consigned the tariff part of the President's message to the Committee on Ways and Means, headed by a scholarly Northern Democrat, Gulian C. Verplanck of New York, a former professor of theology and authority on Shakespeare. It did not bode well for the Northern interests, Adams thought. Verplanck had "a gentleness in his character, unsuited to the tug of political controversy in these times."

He was feeling even more depressed than usual. His health was troubling him again, and with reason. Besides his chronic cough and rheumatism, his palsy and inflamed eyes, he woke up so feverish the morning of January 14 that he could hardly get out of bed. He had difficulty trying to stand, and was "unable

73

to read or write." It was the first time since he entered Congress, aside from occasions when he had been out of town on committee work, that he did not go to the House.

Two days later he was back in his seat, partly recovered and watching the Administration forces chip away—so he told himself—at everything he had ever fought for. The vast domain of virgin public lands, which he wanted to conserve as a source of revenue for internal improvements, Jackson in his message had proposed turning over to the states to throw open to cheap and rapid settlement. And the President wanted another inquiry into the Bank of the United States to determine whether it was a safe depository for government funds. He urged renewed pressure on the unhappy Indians to evacuate their lands and move across the Mississippi.

Early in February, the Verplanck tariff bill came up for debate in the House. It granted further concessions to the South, retaining only token protection. Adams was convinced the New England manufacturers were to be sacrificed "to the nullifiers of South Carolina and the land robbers of the West." He wrote Charles Francis that his colleagues urged him to talk on it. But because of his debilitating illness, he said, he was unprepared.

Then A. S. Clayton of Georgia took the floor to argue against retaining any protective duties on manufactures. Clayton announced he was particularly qualified because he owned one of the few textile plants in the South. The Southern plantation owners, he said, produced $45,000,000 annually in cotton, rice, tobacco and sugar, and the Northern capitalists were sapping their profits with the protective tariff. It was "robbing the Southern planter of one-half he earns to swell the profits of the Northern manufacturers." Since the slaves raised and harvested the crops that supplied the Northern mills and factories, he said, it was "the slaves that sail the Northern ships and run the Northern spindles." He drove home his point with a metaphor: "Their [the South's] slaves are their machinery, and they have as good a right to profit by them as the Northern men have by the machines they employ."

Adams heard him with indignation. So that was how the South regarded the black people they held in bondage? Hu-

74

man machines! To be driven until they broke down, and then, if so inclined, sold off for junk! His Puritan instincts were thoroughly revolted by Clayton's cynical correlation. He might not be properly prepared, but there were a few things he was obliged to tell the slavocracy concerning its "peculiar institution." He bided his time while the South Carolina contingent moved in behind Clayton and slashed away at the "tyranny" of protection. Then, on February 4, he took the floor to move that the enacting clause be stricken out of the Verplanck bill, since the Southern opponents had made it clear they would no longer submit to "this system of oppression."

He began with what sounded like a mild defense of protection under the Constitution. Protection, he said, was the right of the citizen and the duty of the government. "Do the words 'We the People' mean nothing?" The Constitution was the work of the "People of the United States." He assumed the government was bound to protect "the great interests, all the great interests, of the citizens." He went on: "In the southern and southwestern portion of the Union there exists a certain interest which enjoys under the Constitution and law of the United States especial protection peculiar to itself; protection first by representation."

He reminded the slave interests that Article I of the Constitution provided that representation in the House "shall be determined by adding to the whole number of free persons . . . three-fifths of all other persons [slaves]." Since the number of representatives allowed each state was proportioned to its population, "there are on this floor upward of twenty members [from the South] who represent what in the other states has no representation at all," he said.

Except for a copy of the Constitution, Adams' desk was clear. He spoke without notes, but he was no longer intimidated by the sound of his own voice. He was not, and never would be, in the class of the great orators: dramatic, compelling, posturing. His face was flushed, his voice abrasive. Tears riveted down his cheeks from his inflamed eyes. But his words were clear, precise, and devastating:

"I have heard it declared by the gentleman from Georgia

[Clayton] that the species of the population he alluded to constituted the *machines of the South.* Now those *machines* have twenty-odd Representatives in this hall, Representatives elected not by the *machines,* but by those who own them. Is there any such representation in any other portion of the Union? Have the manufacturers asked for representation on their *machines?* Their looms and factories have no vote in Congress, but the *machines* of the South have more than twenty Representatives on this floor.

"I could show that decisions here have been effected in general by majorities less than that. Nay, I might go further and insist that *that* representation has ever been, in fact, the ruling power of this government. Is this not protection at the expense of another portion of the community? Yes, this very protection has taken millions and millions of money from the free laboring population and put it into the pockets of the owners of those Southern *machines.* I do not say that is not all right. What I say is that the South possesses a great protected *interest*"—he waved the copy of the Constitution over his head—"an *interest* protected by this instrument. I am for adhering to the bargain, because it is a bargain. Not that I would agree to it if the bargain were now to be made over again.

"This *interest* is further protected by another provision of the Constitution so contrary to the feelings of the people of the North." He read the clause requiring fugitive slaves to be returned to their owners: 'No person held to service or labor in one state, under the laws thereof, escaping into another, shall, in consequence of any law or regulation therein, be discharged from such service or labor, but shall be delivered up on claim of the party to whom such service or labor may be due.'

"What," he asked, his voice at its harshest pitch, "what is this but protection to the owners of the *machines of the South?"*

He hurried on: "This Constitution contains another clause extending still further protection to this *interest.* It guarantees to every state protection against domestic violence. This, to be sure, is a general provision, but everybody knows that where this sort of *machinery* exists there is more liable to be violence than elsewhere, because the *machinery* sometimes exerts a self-moving power. Such a power has been exerted. Very recently."

Now he was on incendiary ground. The members in the back rows had already moved down the aisles. They crowded in closer. The Southerners were glowering at him. He glowered back. They recognized the reference: the Nat Turner rebellion of two years before, which had chilled the North as well as the South. Turner, a Virginia Negro who saw himself as the messiah, had gathered a band of sixty fellow slaves in Southampton, near the North Carolina border, and led them on a rampage, slaughtering fifty-five whites, among them twenty-four children and eighteen women, before the U. S. Marines from Norfolk came to the rescue. Turner and sixteen of his followers were eventually hanged, but since then many Southerners lived with the fear that their captive work force would turn on them. It was not the first such rebellion—there had been the Denmark Vesey conspiracy in 1820 and, before that, the Haitian revolt—and who could say it would be the last? Slaveholders were locking their doors by night and looking to their firearms. Overseers were tightening their vigilance. The whips swung harder, while Southern politicians angrily accused the abolitionists of having inspired Turner.

"That same *interest* [the slaveholding interest]," Adams went on, "is further protected by the law of the United States. It is protected by the existence of the standing army. If none of the states of the Union possessed any of this *machinery* and another portion of the Union were not exposed to the danger of Indian tribes, I believe it would be difficult to prove to this House the necessity for a standing Army. The Army has been protecting this very *interest*. Of what use to my district of Plymouth is the Standing Army of the United States? Not one dollar's use, and it never has been. I would go further. The Army is not of one dollar's worth to the whole manufacturing *interest*."

There was, he said, still another branch of the nation's service that protected, at a cost of two or three million a year, the *interest* of the South: the Navy, policing the waters that the ships traveled with their cargoes of cotton from the South.

"So, disband the Army. This would go as far as four or five million dollars toward reducing revenue to the wants of the government. Next, abolish the Navy, for why should commerce and navigation continue to enjoy protection when it is withdrawn from the other *interests* of the country? Well, when this has been done, and Congress has been so very generous as to give away all the public lands, what would remain for the general government to do? Nothing. The members then might withdraw *protection* from themselves by abolishing their pay, and there would be one more step: dissolve the government.

"My constituents," he concluded, "have as much right to say to the people of the South, 'We will not submit to the protection of your *interest*' as the people of the South have to address such language to them."

The gage was down. He was against any further reductions in the protective tariff. He was against the Verplanck bill, against any more concessions to the forces of nullification.

In the melee that followed, Drayton of South Carolina was first to get the Speaker's attention. He replied angrily to the "inflammatory remarks of Mr. Adams." He said Adams had threatened that "protection would be withdrawn from the slave properties of the South unless the freemen of the North and East were protected by the tariff." Adams, he said, had "thrown a firebrand into the House!" For three days Adams sat in studied silence while the counterattack raged. Then he responded briefly, "It is not I who have thrown the firebrand, but the forces of nullification."

Word of his speech had meanwhile gotten out, and the *National Intelligencer* was flooded with requests to publish it. The *Intelligencer* did, in full. Northern newspapers picked it up. The influential *Niles Register* of Baltimore, a weekly with national circulation, responded to appeals with a reprint. In Boston, William Lloyd Garrison hailed it in his *Liberator*.

With practically no preparation, without notes, Adams had made the most eloquent speech of his career so far. Calling it "my *chiffon* of a speech," he wrote his son Charles that he could not have imagined it would be the most popular thing he had ever done or said. But from then on he was never again reluctant to wield his dialectical broadsword against the forces of black bondage.

His motion to strike out the enabling clause of the Verplanck bill was voted down. But it mattered little. Henry Clay had done a complete about-face in the Senate, and with Calhoun had worked out a compromise tariff bill that satisfied the Administration and the South Carolinians. It provided for a twenty percent *ad valorem* duty on all protected articles at the outset, to be reduced five percent on some and ten percent on others annually until the net return did not exceed the revenue needed to operate the government. Jackson, meanwhile, got his Force Bill adopted, authorizing him to use the Army and Navy if the Palmetto State persisted in its defiance. He signed both bills the same day, and South Carolina rescinded its nullification proclamation. The first big crisis between the North and South was averted.

Before the Twenty-second Congress adjourned, on March 4, Adams again gave the abolitionists a helping hand. William Heister of Pennsylvania presented a petition signed by 1,000 citizens of his state, against slavery in the District of Columbia, and the Southerners moved to table it. Adams promptly challenged them. He was not in favor of the sentiments expressed in the memorial, he said again, but tabling it was "disrespectful of the petitioners." The privilege of petition, he repeated, was guaranteed by the Bill of Rights, and nothing but very extraordinary circumstances should induce the House to treat one with disrespect. He moved that the petition be referred, as had those he had presented in the first session, to the Committee on the District. The House supported him, 98 to 75.

Then Adams did something that appeared curious to those who knew his attitude on slavery. Mason of Virginia called for the yeas and nays on referring. Adams quickly pointed out to him that this would open the subject of the petition to debate. He advised Mason to withdraw his motion, which Mason did.

While others might be confused about his position, Adams was not. He was a Northerner and morally against slavery, but public opinion in the North, even in his own Plymouth district, was not ready to support abolition; meanwhile, he would help all he could within the Bill of Rights.

In April he went back to Quincy, still worried about his physical deterioration. "The state of my health, I fear, is irretrieveable," he wrote one day; but then, on another, in a more objective mood, "My present infirmity serves me only as an apology for wasting my time in idleness." On July 11 he observed that it was "the sixty-seventh birthday of my age and I am approaching very close upon the limits alotted to long life."

Time was accordingly more precious than ever. He meticulously set down how he spent it, from his rising at four until his bedtime at around nine:

1. In the morning, the minutes of Thomson's translation of the Septuagint Bible.

2. In teaching my granddaughter to read, a task to which I devote from two to three hours a day.

3. In the exercise of my garden and nursery, an average of two hours more.

4. My diary, one hour.

5. Correspondence, two hours.

6. Miscellaneous reading, two hours.

There are twelve; seven in bed [later he reduced it to six], three at and after meals, and two wasted, I know not how. This wasted time, I have found by constant experience to be as indispensable as sleep. It cannot be employed in reading, not even in thinking upon any serious subject. It must be wasted upon trifles—doing nothing. The string of the bow must be slackened, and the bow itself laid aside.

To his six-year-old granddaughter, Louisa Catherine, sitting for her daily lessons, Grandfather was not the martinet he pretended to be. His study was to become a cherished memory, with its tumblers inverted over caterpillars, its two big celestial globes in their mahogany stands, the miniature bronze busts of Cicero, Caesar, Demetrius, Aristotle peering out from the clutter on the work table and mantel. Grandfather was having trouble teaching her. "She seems to make no progress," he complained, "though not deficient in intelligence." In the hope that it might help him understand her difficulty, he tried to put himself in her place by studying Hebrew. Charles Francis, driving out from Boston to escape the heat, found his father's study even more stifling, with all the windows tightly shut.

In mid-June, Adams' old friend, President Quincy, came to tell him he would be invited to Harvard to confer an honorary degree of doctor of laws on Andrew Jackson, who was coming to Boston on a tour of New England. Adams was sardonically interested when Dr. Quincy said he would address the President in Latin, but he refused to take part in the ceremony. "My personal relations with Jackson are such," he said, "that I could hold no intercourse of friendly character with him." His indignation mounting, he went on: "As an affectionate child of our Alma Mater, I would not witness her disgrace in conferring her highest literary honors upon a barbarian who cannot write a sentence of grammar and can hardly spell his own name."

The next month a delegation of Boston Antimasons asked him to stand for governor. He consented with the stipulation that no party tag be attached to his candidacy. It was about time to heal the breach between his old party, the National Republicans, and the Antimasons, he thought, and—consulting his aches and pains—if he could do that it would be a nice final gesture. Besides, Antimasonry did not appear so important any more. More immediate was the rising tension over abolition, of which nullification was only a symptom, and Jackson's threat to pull the government funds out of the United States Bank and distribute them among his "pet" state banks, his "spoils system" of discharging competent government workers to make room for enrolled Democrats, and the Administration's determined egalitarianism.

The state of his health was troubling Adams more and more. He was not sleeping well. His cough hung on. He was depressed. Too often, now, his walks led him among the slabs in the village churchyard, to the graves of the Adamses, from the early Puri-

81

tan farmers of Braintree to his illustrious father and mother, John and Abigail, and his son, George. Soon the proud old name would die out, he told himself, since his grandchildren were all girls.

Then, on the evening of September 30, while in the parlor playing whist with his wife and daughter-in-law and a neighbor, a message came from Boston, and his spirits abruptly brightened. "My health is partially recovered," he wrote. "A blessing of Heaven sheds a last ray upon my hopes of the future as regards the present world. There is now one son of the next generation, and my hopes revive!" Charles Francis' wife had given birth to a boy, and he was named John Quincy Adams II!

Again, Louisa and her entourage preceded him to Washington for the December opening of the Twenty-third Congress. Adams went by stage and steamboat as far as Amboy. There he boarded a train of the newly opened railroad across the New Jersey flatlands to Bordentown. The cars were oversized stage coaches on flanged wheels, whose passengers sat in two compartments, four to a side, on parallel benches. The baggage was stacked on a wagon in the rear, covered with an oilcloth.

Adams, chronometer in hand, checked off the mileposts. For the first ten they barreled along at a mile every two minutes. They stopped, and the trainmen oiled the wheels. Five miles farther, clicking off a mile in a minute and thirty-six seconds, a wheel of the coach Adams was in caught fire and slipped off the rail. The coaches buckled and slid 200 feet along the right of way. Adams' coach righted itself, but the one behind it was stove in. It was "the most dreadful catastrophe that ever my eyes beheld," Adams said. "Blessed, ever blessed be the name of God that I am alive and unhurt."

Walking among the fifteen victims lying beside the road, "men, women and a child, bleeding, mangled, groaning, writhing in torture, and dying," he shuddered at the thought that his wife and grandchild could have been among them. One passenger was dead, and another dying. The child would not live. He sought out the coroner and had him hold an inquest on the spot. Three hours later a relief train arrived and he was on his way again.

In Washington he learned that his fellow Congressman, John Davis, had outpolled him for the Massachusetts governorship. The National Republicans had refused to accept Adams as compromise candidate of the Antimasons. Boston—State Street Boston—was as hostile to him as ever. The mercantile men had appreciated his defense of the protective tariff, but had soured on him again when they read his corrosive assault on Clayton and the slave interests. Mayor Otis, voicing their solid adherence to the *status quo,* warned that offending the Southern states could lead them to boycott Northern products and completely upset trade relations. They would stoutly approve and pass around clippings of an anti-abolitionist editorial in the New York *Herald* saying, "The merchants, men of business and men of property . . . should frown down the meetings of these madmen if they would save themselves."

But the crusade of "these madmen" was on the march. Besides Garrison's violent *Liberator,* the Quaker agitator, Benjamin Lundy, was publishing his weekly, *The Genius of Universal Emancipation,* in Washington, and the Reverend Elijah Lovejoy his antislavery *Observer* in St. Louis. John Greenleaf Whittier, a better poet than Adams and soon to become a good friend, had left his Haverhill, Massachusetts, farm to establish in Philadelphia the headquarters of the new American Anti-Slavery Society. In New York, the wealthy dry goods merchants turned philanthropists, Arthur and Lewis Tappan, were spreading the gospel of emancipation through the New York Anti-Slavery Society. The seeds sown by the Presbyterian evangelist, Charles Finney, in western New York, were bearing a bumper crop of abolitionist missionaries, his prize fruit the rugged, hard-fibered and completely dedicated propagandist, Theodore Weld, now leading the Lane Seminary campaign in southern Ohio for "gradual emancipation, immediately begun." From Charleston, South Carolina, the patrician Grimké sisters, Angelina and Sarah, daughters of a slaveholding state Supreme Court justice, had migrated North to join the campaign, taking as their inheritance a number of family slaves and liberating them. And on August 28 of that year, 1833, Great Britain encouraged them all by ending slavery in her West Indies colonies.

Northerners who ventured below the Mason-Dixon Line and were caught with abolition literature on them were publicly flogged or sentenced to hard labor. By now state laws in most of the South forbade teaching the Negroes to read or write. Educated blacks could be dangerous, as witness Toussaint L'Ouverture, Denmark Vesey, Nat Turner. Prevent unrest by keeping the blacks illiterate. The Southerners seldom called them slaves. Harriet Martineau, in her travels through the South, said she never heard the word used. They were "our Negroes," "our force," "our people," "the hands."

The abolitionists were troublemakers. They did not deny it. Even Adams would say, in 1839, that they were "pouring oil into the summit of a smoking crater." Meanwhile, the sprawling cotton plantations of the newly opened Deep South required more and more slaves. A prime male Negro, once worth $260, now brought $1,000. Parts of Virginia, where the land was exhausted by the years of cotton growing, turned profitably to breeding slaves for the new market, using their sturdy males for stud, with the slaveholder and his sons helping out.

The twenty-four states were equally divided between slave and free, and the three-fifths ratio authorized by the Constitution for the South's slave population gave it, as Adams had pointed out in his answer to Clayton, a powerful voice in government.

With the mails barricaded against their literature, the abolition societies, under the leadership of Weld, Whittier and Henry Stanton of Rhode Island, turned increasingly to enrolling citizens on petitions to Congress for emancipation or prohibition of the slave trade, or both, in the District of Columbia. Abuses had become particularly flagrant there. Free Negroes were arrested on the trumped-up suspicion of being fugitives and sold back into slavery by their jailers, who pocketed the money, because the victims could not pay the "expenses" of their imprisonment. Most Northern Congressmen sided with the conservative mercantile interests. But one of them, a former President of the United States, insisted it was his constitutional obligation to present petitions and demand that they be respectfully received. And to him the antislavery petitions came, first from the Quakers, eventually even from his own Plymouth constituents.

-»»- **V** -«««-

THE lead item under Deaths in the *National Intelligencer* of Washington on October 25, 1834, read:

> Thursday morning, the 23rd, John Adams, Esq., son of the ex-President. Family and friends are respectfully invited to attend the funeral of the deceased from his late dwelling, on Saturday at 3 P.M.

The second son of John Quincy and Louisa Adams was thirty-one and married to Mary Hellen, a first cousin on his mother's side. Their romance and wedding had taken place in the White House, where Mary came to live with the then President's family after her mother's death.

John's health had been declining for two years. His father had blamed the malarial climate of Washington and had urged him to give up managing the family's struggling grist mill in suburban Rock Creek and retire to Quincy. But John had refused. When the news that he was bedridden reached his parents in Quincy, his father hurried to Washington and arrived there the night he died. Louisa, who had been too ill to make the journey with her husband, came a month later in the care of Charles Francis.

John Quincy was heartbroken, blaming himself for having

been so absorbed in his congressional interests that he had not fully realized the seriousness of his son's decline. If he had only insisted that John leave Washington while his health could still be saved. Adams read his Bible with fierce concentration.

His father's mood worried Charles Francis. It was depressing to see the old man so burdened with grief. He had withdrawn more than ever, shutting himself away mornings and evenings in his study, walking, walking the days away, alone.

Washington was quiescent during the summer and autumn absence of Congress. An occasional Negro-driven cart wandered down the wide and dusty emptiness of Pennsylvania Avenue. Most of the stalls of the Centre Market at Eighth Street were bare. The hotels—Gadsby's, Brown's, Fuller's—and the brown brick boarding houses between Capitol Hill and the White House drowsed behind shuttered windows. Adams paced the steep paths around the empty Capitol, putting off as long as he could his return to the house of his dead son.

Every room of the Sixteenth Street dwelling held poignant memories for Louisa and himself. They still owned the house they had occupied when Adams was Secretary of State under President Monroe. A large brick house with four rows of windows and a low stoop, it filled two lots on F Street at Thirteenth. Louisa brightened when her husband announced they would move back into it, together with Mary and her daughters, Louisa Catherine, seven, and Georgiana Frances, four. They had spent their happiest years there. Adams' $6,000 a year as Secretary, unlike the relative pittance the young country had paid him abroad, had been ample for all their needs. They had entertained, even lavishly on occasions—several hundred guests at the ball in 1815 honoring Andrew Jackson for his victory in New Orleans—and the boys had been young and carefree.

The trying years in the White House had been ahead of them then. Louisa's spirits had still been high, her mood romantic: playing old English love songs on her harp winter evenings in the drawing room, writing brittle little poems. Now another poem came from her pen, entitled "John's Grave."

Softly tread! For herein lies
The young, the beautiful, the wise.

For Adams, the very intensity of his grief appears to have shortened it. When Congress reconvened early in December, he was back at his desk in the House, presenting a stack of antislavery petitions that had come to him during the recess. So far he was still having them referred to the Committee on the District of Columbia. But he saw that the resentment of the Southern contingent was growing, believing as they did that the petitioners were irresponsible troublemakers threatening their way of life, even endangering their security by goading their slaves to insurrection.

Of greater concern to him at the moment was Jackson's latest entanglement—this time with France. The President's blustering quarrel with America's former ally was approaching a crisis. Whether the action Adams felt compelled to take in the days ahead averted a destructive and unwanted war, a war that could have become unavoidable, is necessarily speculative; but it did enhance the young republic's prestige before the world. All in all, it was the most curious and enlightening episode in Adams' stormy career in the House.

As the country's most distinguished living statesman, next to Jackson, Adams had been chosen to deliver the oration at the nation's memorial service for General Lafayette, who had died May 24. The ceremony honoring the American war hero and French liberal was to be held in the House chamber on December 31. Adams had worked on his address most of the summer, collecting data from Revolutionary records, from George Washington's nephew, his own diary and his father's papers. On Christmas Eve he was still rewriting, and had "yet work for three or four more days."

His own career, he realized, was involved in the ceremony. Jackson's dispute concerned the settlement of claims for French depredations on American shipping and property during the Napoleonic Wars. The President was threatening reprisals against France unless she began paying the indemnity. The claims had been hanging fire for a quarter century. Adams as President had been unable to collect. Jackson had got nowhere with the conservative King Charles X. Then, in the July Revolution of 1830, Louis Philippe had come to the French throne. The "citizen king" had spent a number of his expatriate years in America, teaching school, and he was a protégé of Lafayette. Jackson's minister to France, William C. Rives of Virginia, negotiated a settlement treaty with Louis Philippe. France was to pay $5,000,000, in six annual installments. In return, the United States would pay $300,000 in French counterclaims going back to the American Revolution, and reduce the tariff on French wines.

When the first payment came due, the Treasury sent the draft to the Bank of the United States. It bounced, and Nicholas Biddle had the pleasure of charging Jackson's government the usual fifteen percent penalty. The French legislature had not appropriated the money.

Temporarily disciplining his flinty temper, Jackson sent his most persuasive diplomat, Edward Livingston of New York, to replace Rives. Livingston's smooth approach worked no better at the French court. The King was pleasant, the deputies indifferent. They doubted that America would become genuinely troublesome over a paltry 25,000,000 francs, which they could use conveniently themselves. But they did not know Andrew Jackson. He was convinced America was in the right, and he vowed he would get the money if he had to take it out of France's hide. In his State of the Union message to Congress in December of 1834, Jackson asked for "a law authorizing reprisals upon French property" if the Chamber of Deputies delayed much longer.

This amounted to a threat of war, and the opposition Whig party, led by Webster and Clay, decided Jackson had blundered politically, that the country would never support him in a war against an old ally over claims dating back twenty-five years. The part of the President's message threatening reprisals was referred by the two houses of Congress to their Committees on Foreign Affairs. The Senate committee, headed by Clay, denied the President's request. It advised that "nothing should be done to betray suspicion of the integrity of the French government." The House committee stalled.

So the matter stood as Adams polished the periods on his memorial address. Meanwhile, he had one ear cocked toward the State House in Boston. Daniel Webster's colleague in the United States Senate, Nathaniel Silsbee, had retired, and the Whig-dominated Massachusetts legislature was about to vote on a successor. One group favored John Davis, now governor, the man who had originally asked Adams to stand for the House of Representatives. The other group *wanted John Quincy Adams!* The Davis faction predominated in the lower house, the Adams faction in the Senate.

Nothing would have pleased Adams better than to be advanced to the United States Senate, to the forum of Webster, Clay, Calhoun and Benton. As the combative challenger of Jackson's Democracy, all he needed do was insert in his speech a few pointed words of defense for Lafayette's France. The Massachusetts Whigs would understand his intent.

On the appointed day, Adams was escorted with solemn ceremony to the Speaker's rostrum in the House chamber. In the front row sat President Jackson and his Secretaries of State, Treasury, War, Navy and the Attorney General. Conspicuous among the notables behind them was Daniel Webster. The two aging gamecocks, Jackson and Adams, exchanged frigid glances. Adams began to speak. He spoke for two hours and fifty minutes. Webster, his dark eyes alertly expectant, waited to send the message to the State House in Boston that Adams had adroitly used the occasion to pillory Jackson for his imprudent blustering toward the homeland of Lafayette. Jackson listened with equal attention.

Adams talked on and on. It was a dull review of the Revolution and Lafayette's part in it, spiced with none of the biting dialectic of his extemporaneous speeches. He described Lafayette's career from the day he joined Washington's shabby army to his death as his country's most venerated statesman. Not a word about the present French crisis. When he finished, the distinguished audience applauded politely. And Webster sent word to the Whigs in Boston that John Quincy Adams might not be the man to represent Massachusetts with him in the Senate; they should await further instructions.

If any other member of the Massachusetts delegation in Congress had been involved, Webster would have bluntly asked him where he stood on the issue that the Whigs hoped would win the next Presidential election for them. But the former President could be testily aloof about his prerogative to keep his own counsel. And Adams' Whig colleagues could not enlighten Webster.

Meanwhile, Adams had become impatient to hear from the House Committee on Foreign Relations. Churchill Camberleng of New York, an Administration leader and close friend of Vice President Van Buren, was chairman of the committee. Adams talked with him, and learned that Camberleng had no immediate intention of reporting on the President's proposal. The Democrats were no more inclined than the Whigs to support a war with France. Departing from his practice of keeping to himself, Adams sounded out his fellow Representatives, Democrats and Whigs alike. Each party, he decided, was treating the problem as a purely political issue. The Whigs were "chuckling at the prospect" that the French Chamber would indignantly refuse the appropriation and the blame would fall on Jackson. The Democrats, on the other hand, were positive the country would blame the Whig-dominated Senate for not backing the President. And from the Paris press poured furious denunciations of Jackson.

Adams now took matters into his own hands. In a House speech he called on Secretary of State Forsyth to submit the latest dispatches from Minister Livingston in Paris, together with a copy of the President's annual message. Forsyth complied, and Adams then moved that the documents be referred to the Committee on Foreign Affairs "with instructions to report forthwith on that part of the message of the President which relates to this subject."

France, he reminded the House, had failed to honor a treaty formally signed with the United States. "I am governed," he went on, "by the persuasion that it is inconsistent with the interest and honor of the nation to leave the subject longer unacted upon. Mr. Livingston [in his last dispatch] said he is now far from sanguine. Let the House . . . say to the nation and to the world whether they will sustain the President in . . . maintaining the interests, the rights and honor of the nation. I hope the House will not suffer itself to appear in a contrasting character with that of the President of the United States by shrinking from the responsibility incumbent upon them as representatives of the people."

Adams added that he had not yet committed himself to support any action of the committee which might tend "to produce war. . . . What I wish is that the House should deliberate; and for the very reason that the measure of the President, or some other measure which the honor of the country may require, may possibly eventuate in war. It does not follow because the House deliberates it must either declare war or authorize reprisals. . . . Possibly at the end of the discussion they may come to the same conclusion as the other branch of the Congress. . . . The Senate has taken up the subject. Their committee has considered and reported upon it. The Senate, too, has deliberated, and their deliberations have ended in the determine to dodge the question. May not the House come to a like conclusion, and *dodge the question,* as the Senate has done."

Speaker John Bell of Tennessee sharply called Adams to order. It was not permitted, he said, to speak disparagingly of any act of the other branch of Congress. Adams apologized with a mock show of contrition. He had merely wished to make it clear, he explained, that the object of his motion was not to advocate war, but to persuade the House to deliberate the President's request.

The rule of order he had violated was rudimentary, and Adams knew it. But he had made his point before the Speaker could stop him. It was a trick he employed more and more as time went on, to the frustration of his opponents.

William S. Archer, a Virginia Democrat, protested that instructing the committee to "report forthwith" implied that the House shared Jackson's belligerent attitude toward France.

"Is the House in this disposition?" he asked. "Does it partake of the fervor manifested by the gentleman from Massachusetts? I, for one, do not. I confess I should have great regret in being driven into war, and especially for so small a subject of interest, with our ancient friend and early ally."

The debate grew noisy. Joel B. Sutherland of Pennsylvania said that "while I approve the elevated and patriotic feelings of the gentleman from Massachusetts, I am not quite ready to go along with him." Neither was Camberleng, nor Augustus Clayton of Georgia. Even Adams' old friend, Edward Everett, sitting next to him, opposed him with measured eloquence, and then wrote home that Adams had made "a furious war speech, in defense of Jackson!"

Robert Lytle of Ohio warmly supported Adams. "Since I have had the honor of a seat upon this floor," he told the chamber, "it has never been my good fortune to listen to a speech . . . in which I felt the sensations produced upon me by the appeal made by the venerable member from Massachusetts.

"There was in it to my mind a degree of moral grandeur and sublimity which as an American citizen I was proud to see and hear. The former President, now a Representative, sustaining with the candor and undisguised patriotism of an American freeman, the spirit and proposition of his successful rival. And upon what proposition? That the people of this country should vindicate their national pride and honor.

"What is the proposition of the gentleman from Massachusetts? Does it amount to a declaration of war? No, sir! It merely calls upon the Committee on Foreign Affairs to make a report to vindicate the House from the imputation of pusillanimously cringing to the juggling and caprices of a foreign potentate!"

A murmur of approval, then shouts of "Hear!" "Hear!" swept the hall, crowded now as word had reached the lobbies and cloakrooms and even across the rotunda into the Senate that John Quincy Adams was *supporting* Andrew Jackson! The debate ended with Adams agreeing to an amendment to his motion, striking out "forthwith" and setting February 20, two weeks away, for the committee to report.

Walking down Capitol Hill, Adams wondered how the legislature in Boston would receive the news that he had come to the support of the President. Would the Whig leaders understand that his feelings toward his old enemy in the White House had nothing to do with the position he had taken? That he disliked and distrusted Jackson as much as ever? But in controversies with foreign powers he had to stand by the government when he knew, as now, that the Administration was in the right.

Instead of the Massachusetts legislature, Adams might better have speculated on Daniel Webster's reaction to his diatribe. Webster had come into the House chamber toward the end of Adams' speech. Edward Everett and Levi Lincoln, another Representative from Massachusetts, had walked with him to his rooms at Mrs. Bailiss' boarding house on Pennsylvania Avenue at Eighth Street. After they left, Webster sent a letter to the Whig leaders in Boston.

Adams, he wrote, had demonstrated again that he just was not politically dependable. Appointing him to the Senate would weaken the Whigs' control. Give the seat to Governor Davis. To replace Davis in the governorship, he suggested Everett. There was a man you could count on.

As the mails moved up the coast, carrying the next editions of the Washington *Globe* and *National Intelligencer,* the reports of Adams' speculation on the possibility of war with France alarmed shipping and business circles in New York and Boston. Merchants swiftly took inventory of their French imports and marked up the prices. Insurance brokers rushed to their ledgers. Charles Francis' wealthy father-in-law, Peter Chardon Brooks, was "greatly alarmed." Charles Francis was as indignant as a young man of his studied poise could be. He had earnestly hoped to see his father elevated to the Senate. But the old man had no one to blame but himself, Charles said, when he learned that Davis had been chosen.

Adams, however, took the news philosophically. He told himself he preferred the House, anyway. There he had his constituency solidly behind him—he had been reelected without opposition. If he knew, or suspected, that Webster was responsible for his rejection, he did not admit it, even to the privacy of his diary. In a brief speech a few days later, he chided the mercantile interests for their reaction. He asked the women of the country to forgive him for causing prices to go up on "the silks and ribands" of their fancy dresses. "God forbid," he told the House, "that I should be instrumental in taxing the ladies for the ornaments of their beauty."

Not until February 26, five days before adjournment, did the Committee on Foreign Affairs bring in its report. In the meanwhile, the French government, realizing that Congress was apparently unwilling to support Jackson, had grown more militant. Paris recalled its minister to Washington and told Livingston he was no longer welcome there. Livingston, however, declined to budge until he heard from his government. There was talk of sending an American frigate to bring him back along with his legation staff.

When Camberleng presented the committee's majority report, he did not please Adams. The report said that "it would be incompatible with the rights and honor of the United States further to negotiate in relation to the treaty entered into with France, . . . and that the House will insist upon its execution, as ratified by both governments."

"When a nation says it will no longer negotiate," Adams replied, "the only alternative compatible with its honor and interest is war." He reminded the House that the next Congress would not meet until December. The President's hands should not be tied during the nine-month interim. If further negotiation was possible, and he believed it was, he wanted the President to be free to do so. He emphasized once again that he was concerned not about the claim, but about the question of France honoring its treaty with the Administration. "In that determination . . . I adhere, and I hope the House is willing to adhere. I have no hesitation," he went on, "in saying that if, together with negotiation, this determination is not sufficient to preserve the peace of the country, I, for one, am willing to take the hazard of war. . . . The interest and honor of the country are at stake. Where would we be if we did not take a ground to compel France to do—what? Justice! Justice! . . . What will be

95

the consequence if we consent to any compromise or concession? Every nation in the world will violate its engagements with us!"

At first he had not been in favor of Jackson's aggressive action, he said. "I considered the measure recommended [for reprisals] as imprudent, and if I had been of his councils at the time, I would have advised him against it. But there was no injustice in it. . . . What I deemed imprudent was only bold, and boldness itself can be the profoundest prudence."

He presented a substitute resolution phrased to support the Administration if it should consider further negotiation advantageous. This was heatedly debated. Edward Everett was a minority member of the committee. He was against any resolution at the start, and then came around to supporting an amendment asserting that the treaty should be executed "at all hazards." Another Massachusetts representative, Benjamin Gorham, denounced Adams' course as "not in accord with the sentiments of Massachusetts."

"If such is the fact," Adams retorted, "I can only regret it. I have only to say it was in accord with the dictates of my heart."

As the debate continued, he was up and down in his chair more than any other member. The oldest there, he was the most active, the most wary. Congress was now close to adjournment. The sessions dragged deep into the night, but Adams was at his desk punctually, even early, every day. At dusk, when the huge brass chandelier with its thirty whale oil lamps was lighted, he ate the slice of bread he had brought from home wrapped in a page of the *National Intelligencer*. The session was to end on Tuesday, March 3. On Monday Camberleng moved that Adams' much-debated resolution read "that in the opinion of this House the treaty of the 4th of July 1831 should be maintained, and its execution insisted upon." Adams accepted the change and, at midnight, the yeas and nays were called for. An outburst of applause, joined in by the gallery, greeted the Speaker's announcement of the vote: 212 yeas and no nays!

Adams went home tired but happy. "His resolution" had won unanimous support. It was the greatest parliamentary victory of his career, he wrote his son. And Charles Francis agreed.

This was "the first great triumph of Mr. Adams in the House," he declared years later, when he edited his father's diary. The *Register of Debates* twice referred to it as "Mr. Adams' resolution, as modified at the suggestion of Mr. Camberleng." Samuel Flagg Bemis, the distinguished Yale historian, on the other hand, says in his book, *John Quincy Adams and the Union,* that it was no longer Adams' resolution, but a compilation. Adams himself apparently did not consider the distinction important. What concerned him was that he had, single-handedly, forced the House to back the President in a foreign dispute when the Administration was plainly in the right.

For the sixty-seven-year-old statesman, it *was* a momentous achievement. As he said, he had started with everyone against him. He listed his opponents: the Administration party, the nullifiers of South Carolina and Georgia, Archer and the "Virginia hairsplitters," the Clay and Webster Whigs, "and conceive my astonishment, Baylies and Gorham from my own state." And he had bested them all!

⇢⇢⇢ VI ⇠⇠⇠

ADAMS' pleasure over a personal triumph never lasted long. Before he and the family returned to Quincy for the summer of 1835 he was again deep in misgivings about the future of both the country and himself.

The last day of the Twenty-third Congress—at almost the last hour—the Senate retaliated against the House for backing the President in the French dispute. The Adams resolution gave the Administration only moral support. No provision had been made for financing a war if one should occur before the next Congress convened in December. So Representative Camberleng proposed a special defense fund of $3,000,000 for the President if he "should deem it expedient for military and naval service." Camberleng offered it as an amendment to the annual bill to support the nation's fortifications and naval fleet. It passed the House, 109 to 66. But the Whig-dominated Senate opposed it. Calhoun led the attack. He was not ready, he said, to assume "a war with France before Congress meets again." "Preparation for war may lead to war," Clay pontificated. Webster called the amendment a dangerous grant of power to the President.

In conference, the Senate then whittled the fund down to an additional $300,000 for fortifications and $500,000 for the Navy. By then the Capitol lamps had long been lighted; weary

98

legislators were clearing out their desks. Webster wanted more than ever to make Jackson's "irresponsible aggressiveness" the main issue of his campaign for the Presidency. He contrived to delay approval of the conference report until the midnight hour set for the adjournment of Congress had passed.

By then some seventy house members who were not returning for the next session assumed their term had expired at midnight. Speaker Bell tried to round up a quorum, and failed. The House adjourned at 3:30 A.M., and not only the special fund, but the entire fortifications bill to which it was attached, was lost.

Webster was confident the blame would fall on the House, and on his cantankerous old colleague who had created the issue in the first place by refusing to "dodge the question." Webster and Adams thoroughly disapproved of one another. Webster was everything that Adams was not: noble in appearance, outgoing, persuasive. Born poor, he had used his talents to become prosperous and distinguished. He was a staunch party man, first a Federalist and now a Whig; at the same time, he openly mixed his law practice and politics, and his corporation clients paid him handsomely. He relished good food and vintage wines; John Gadsby's hotel bar was his favorite in Washington. Attractive women stimulated the actor in him. He considered Adams' inflexible righteousness narrow and old-fashioned. Adams, on the other hand, found his declamations often hollow when stripped of their rhetorical ornament. And Webster's theatrics repelled him.

Dawn was gray on Adams' back as he let himself into his house after the long night of adjournment. Behind the closed shutters of his room, he spent a few restless hours in bed, then arose and walked the emptying town. Crowded stages were pulling away from the Pennsylvania Avenue hotels, their roofs piled with baggage. Saddled horses and carriage teams waited at the hitching posts in front of the boarding houses.

In his dark afterthoughts on the closing session, his victory of a few days before seemed empty to him. The Senate Whigs had had the last word, after all. With no appropriation to sup-

99

port his resolution, all he had accomplished was to alienate his Whig colleagues. His position was the same, he told himself, as it had been back in 1808, when the Massachusetts Federalists had appointed him to the Senate and he had supported the Embargo Act of the Republican President, Thomas Jefferson. "My conduct then expelled me from the Senate," he reminded himself, "and it has excluded me from it now."

Back in his study, he envisioned "nothing before me but the prospect of a desperate struggle and political ruin. . . . The French Chamber will reject the bill for payment of the five million," he wrote. "Some rash act of President Jackson will follow, and if the two countries should be saved from war, it seems as if it could only be by a special interposition of Providence. Standing alone as I do, disconnected from all parties . . . what can save me from destruction at the next session, if the French question should continue, but an unseen protecting power?"

Now that there were no daily House sessions, he finished settling his son John's estate and looked into the operation of the Rock Creek grist and flour mill that had absorbed most of his savings. Thanks to John's stubborn labors to the end, the mill was making a small profit now under the management of one of Louisa's brothers-in-law.

Washington was settling down for its long summer siesta, but the issues confronting the nation could not be postponed. Of chief concern to Adams, besides the French crisis, was the growing dissension between the North and South, aggravated now by the rebellion of the Texas frontiersmen against Mexican rule and the pressure of the slave states on Jackson to absorb the territory into the Union.

During his own Presidency, Adams had tried to purchase Texas from Mexico, but slavery had not been a political issue then. Recently Mexico had outlawed slavery, but the Texans, many of whom had migrated to the rich wilderness from the exhausted cotton lands of the old South, had defiantly kept their Negroes. To the Southern leaders there was no question that the territory, large enough to make several states, would retain slavery, and the South's representation in Congress would consequently be immensely strengthened.

So matters stood late in May when Adams, delayed by the convalescence of his youngest granddaughter from a fever, finally left for Quincy. As usual, he traveled alone by public stage, leaving Louisa to bring the rest of the household and the baggage in the family carriage. Reports to the newspapers from Paris had indicated no softening of France's defiance of Jackson. But while he stopped over in Philadelphia, a ship arrived with the news that the French legislature had suddenly voted the funds to execute the treaty.

Whether they had been influenced by the support the House had given Jackson, Adams had no way of knowing. But he saw that the problem was as far from solution as ever, for the French government had stipulated that no payment would be made until Louis Philippe received an apology from the American President for his threatening action. Adams could easily predict the old duelist's reaction to that.

In Quincy, the Boston newspapers and the *National Intelligencer* from Washington kept him abreast of developments. He read that Jackson had flatly rejected the French demand and ordered Minister Livingston home. Since the French minister had already left Washington, diplomatic relations were virtually ended. Each side waited for the other to make the first overt move.

If one came, Adams wondered what the Administration would do, with not even a fortifications fund to fall back on. It was fortunate, he thought, that Louis Philippe had troubles at home. His cabinet was known to be shaky. While he had come to the throne as the "citizen king," the well-to-do were benefiting more under his rule. Both the old aristocracy and the masses were restless. Revolutionaries were active. One, named Giuseppe Fieschi, tried to assassinate the King late in July. Then, too, Adams surmised that France, together with her ally, Great Britain, was concerned over Russia's recent alliance with Turkey and her attempts at expansion in the Balkans. The greatest danger, he decided, was Jackson's quick-burning temper.

At the same time, the antislavery agitation was causing new violence at home. In the rural county of Madison in central

Mississippi, two itinerant quacks called "steam doctors" were reportedly discovered conscripting slaves to rise up and "wipe out the entire white population." The two strangers were hunted down by posses and lynched, together with three other whites suspected of helping them, as well as a number of Negroes, variously reported as ten to fifteen.

Then, too, a botany teacher from the North had come to Washington to lecture, bringing with him specimens wrapped in newspapers. When a fellow lodger at his Georgetown boarding house discovered that some of the wrappings were from abolitionist publications, he reported that the botanist was an agent sent to stir up local Negroes. The arrest of the teacher started a riot. Several hundred whites roamed the Negro quarters in Georgetown, chasing and clubbing Negro freedmen, demolishing their huts and their schoolhouse. The half dozen ward constables were overrun, and Mayor Bradley had to call on the militia to put down the rioters. A remnant of the mob invaded the business district of the nation's capital and wrecked a popular restaurant because it was owned by a mulatto, Beverley Stone. A "Black Code" was quickly enacted: Negroes caught with a copy of Garrison's *Liberator* or any other abolitionist publication would be publicly flogged; thereafter, they could drive carts and hackneys, but could no longer operate taverns or eating houses.

The white working class of the North, Adams realized, was as antagonistic to the evangelical appeals of the abolitionists as the Southerners. Emancipation to them meant that the freed blacks would compete for their jobs and drive down their already low wages, and, worse still, would move in around them. An abolitionist meeting in Philadelphia touched off a riot in which forty Negro homes were destroyed. Hoodlums in the New Hampshire village of Canaan dragged an academy from its foundation because fourteen of its students were Negroes.

In the predawn quiet of his study in Quincy, the whale oil lamp lighting the clutter of papers and books on his work table and the bay fog graying the windows, Adams filled his diary with forebodings over "the great fermentation upon this subject . . . in all parts of the Union." In spite of the hostility of

Northern workmen and the well-dressed gentlemen of the cities, he believed "the theory of the rights of man has taken deep root, . . . allied itself with the precepts of Christian benevolence. We are in a state of profound peace and over-pampered with prosperity," he wrote, "yet the elements of exterminating war seem to be in vehement fermentation, and one can scarcely foresee [how] it will end."

The abolitionists, determined to draw Adams into their ranks, pressured him increasingly. Prominent among them was the editor Benjamin Lundy, now preparing to move his aboli-tionist press from Washington to Philadelphia, in search of a more dedicated audience. Others were the poet Whittier, Gar-rison, and the Quaker followers of Moses Brown in Rhode Is-land.

Meanwhile, the old New England Federalist and recent mayor of Boston, Harrison Gray Otis, was saying, "I cannot find in the Christian Scriptures any prohibition of slavery." The editor of the pro-Webster *Atlas* in Boston proclaimed, "Let there be a meeting called forthwith in Faneuil Hall, and let the Websters and Otises and Adamses and Storys, and Spragues and Austins and Choates and Everetts [a roster of Bay State aris-tocracy] be invited to vindicate the fair fame of our city. Let a manifesto go forth proclaiming our sentiments for the rights of the South and our abhorence of the conduct of those encourag-ing *a civil and a servile war!*"

Adams did not attend the meeting. Nothing he could say would influence the New England mercantile and banking families whose new mill towns depended on slave-produced cotton and whose banks were profiting from loans to Southern planters for crop and land expansion and slave buying. Their vested interest, he thought, was as large as or larger than that of the New York merchants who, according to *Niles Register,* held mortgages on Southern plantations and slaves amounting to $10,000,000. Nevertheless, he believed as firmly as he had at the time of the Missouri Compromise, fifteen years ago, that slavery was "a foul stain upon the North American Union" and had to end eventually.

Yet he could not openly support the abolition crusaders.

They were morally right but politically naïve and irresponsible. They offered no workable solution. Adams feared intuitively that when the crisis came, "the planters of the South will separate from the Union, in terror of the emancipation of their slaves." He hoped that "this consummation may yet be remote." But as he watched the South become steadily more belligerent and the abolition leaders more determined, his misgivings mounted.

Historians maintain that, while Adams considered himself a Man of the Whole Nation, he was at heart a sectionalist. It would be surprising if he were not. For, even though he had spent much of his life abroad and in Washington, he came from wholly New England stock. In his day, the people of the North and South were far apart in culture, mores and manners. Even their accent was so different that Adams' father had written home from the Continental Congress in Philadelphia that he had difficulty understanding some of the Southern delegates. And conditions had not changed much since then. The Massachusetts constitution, drafted by John Adams, had abolished slavery in 1783; the other New England states had followed within a few years. The occasional visitor from the North found Southern households something to write home about. Their only incentive being the whip, the black servants were shiftless, "slow as molasses." Southern food was usually overcooked and cold by the time the slave girl brought it to the table from the outside kitchen. Housewives carried heavy rings of keys on their wrists, since they were convinced that everything had to be kept locked against the thieving proclivity of their slaves. Southerners showed amazing patience waiting for things to be done. It was said that two white men were required to make a black man work.

Freed from manual labor, Southern gentlemen devoted themselves to sports, to riding, hunting, gambling. Courage and honor were highly esteemed. Duels were frequent. One of the rowdiest in Adams' recollection was between Andrew Jackson and Thomas Hart Benton, who fought up and down the hallway of a Tennessee hotel, Jackson taking a bullet in his shoulder and Benton pitching down a flight of stairs. Both were considerably younger then and had since become great friends. Henry Clay fought the erratic wit and statesman, John Randolph of Roanoke, but both smooth-bore pistols missed their marks. Only a few months back, another touchy Southerner, Representative Henry Wise of Virginia, had quarreled with his predecessor in the House, Richard Coke. They met in a clearing outside Washington, and Wise shattered Coke's arm in the first exchange.

Adams considered most of the planter-statesmen overbearing and arrogant. Although living in a democracy, they still regarded themselves as old world cavaliers. Their quickness to quarrel, their injustice-collecting, intimidated some of the Northern legislators, who had not been brought up to enjoy exchanging shots on the field of honor.

It was entirely apparent to Adams that the North and the South had practically become two different cultures, the one increasingly industrial, the other permanently agrarian. Somehow, their Union had to be preserved until the immoral institution that threatened to separate them could be discarded. He did not foresee emancipation in his lifetime. But while he lived, he had to do all his conscience would permit to hurry it along.

T HE Twenty-fourth Congress convened on Monday, December 7, 1835. The returning members dropped their papers on their desks and drifted down the aisles, to shake hands with their former President. Nearly all of them had at one time or another traded angry words with Adams; nevertheless, they had by now a sincere regard for their cantankerous colleague.

Among the first was John Bell of Tennessee, who hoped to be reelected Speaker. Although Bell had reprimanded and called Adams to order time and again (he was a faithful Whig, dedicated to the leadership of Clay and Webster), Adams considered him "on the whole a good Speaker and impartial as far as he dares." Following him came Churchill Camberleng, short, portly, affable, a knowing politician and successful New York merchant, but to Adams "an unscrupulous Jackson deputy sheriff." From the North Carolina contingent came Speight, Bynum, Graham, nullificationers all; from Virginia, Claiborne, Mason, and tall, lean-limbed young Henry Wise, as handy with ironic, baiting adjectives as Adams himself.

Unlike the Senate galleries, the semicircular, red-velvet-hung House balcony was empty. Long before the ceremonial hour of noon arrived, the galleries of the upper chamber on the north side of the rotunda were filled, the ladies' gallery in the center a showcase of fashion. Attending the Senate, particularly on opening day, was the leading diversion of genteel Washington. Besides the Senators' wives and relatives, visiting ladies and their escorts came to the sessions regularly during their stays. The thrill of hearing the heroic statesmen debate shared attraction with seeing and being seen by the capital's best people.

Below them on the elevated rostrum with its figured red carpet and mahogany desk, they saw Vice President Martin Van Buren, dapper, pink-faced, his red hair freshly barbered. Facing him from the first of the three crescent rows of desks sat Henry Clay, tall and bony, fingering his snuffbox, his cravat carelessly tied, his frock coat open, hanging away from his knees. The women loved Clay. He had a way with them, as he did with cards and oratory. His manner was back-fence casual; the soft climate of Kentucky was in his drawl. Thomas Benton of Missouri, on the other hand, had the taut manner of a bull about to charge, and the same bulky build. John Calhoun of South Carolina was old for his fifty-three years. A gaunt, sharp-featured dignitary, he wore the drawn, pallid look of the esthete. A contemporary wit observed that he had never been young.

Daniel Webster's chair was empty. He was still in Boston, conferring with Whig leaders on the coming election and studying the reports from the Webster-for-President rally in New York City's Masonic Hall the evening of December 4. "Liberty and Union, now and forever, one and inseparable," from his famous reply to Hayne, had been the watchword, and there had been a good turnout of merchants and professional men, who generally distrusted the Jacksonian Democrats, New York's Van Buren included. Unless he could carry New York State, with its forty-two electoral votes, Webster knew his chances were slim.

His co-leader of the Senate Whigs, Henry Clay, had arrived back in Washington only a few hours before Congress convened. Walking to the Capitol that morning, Adams passed Clay's carriage still hitched to the post before his lodgings on F Street in the next block. The wheels and the horses' shaggy winter coats were mud-caked, the dirt of wilderness roads overlaid with the red clay of F Street.

Adams thought he recognized Clay's wife at one of the upstairs windows. She was an amiable creature who usually preferred to remain behind at Ashland, managing the big Kentucky estate with its colony of slaves and her brood of six daughters and five sons. Adams remembered a New England matron's remark to her at a Washington tea: "Isn't it a pity your husband gambles so much?" While Adams agreed in principle, he liked Mrs. Clay's answer: "Oh, I don't know. He usually wins."

Winter had not yet come down from New England. The trees stood bare against the sky, except for patches of rusty leaves on sheltered branches, but the air was still soft, and brown rain water filled the wagon ruts. Early as always, Adams picked his way around the puddles, past the procession of carriages moving up the steep roadway of Capitol Hill. Few among the women visitors at the carriage windows recognized the elderly pedestrian in the black frock coat and woolen muffler.

The opening routine in the House included choosing a Speaker. Adams voted for Bell, but the Administration forces, 132 to 84, elected Bell's fellow Tennessean, James K. Polk, a friend of Jackson. The next day, the President's State of the Union message was read to each of the two houses. Although the reading consumed nearly two hours, the message was solidly constructed and provocative. Adams let the opening sentences slide over his head. "A period of profound interest to the American patriot . . . The unexampled growth and prosperity of our country . . . The career of freedom is before us." But his interest sharpened when the President came to the controversy with France. The cause of the trouble had been rehashed so often that both houses were familiar with it, but Jackson summarized it for the country at large. During the Napoleonic Wars, he explained, France had captured American ships and cargoes on the high seas, burned American vessels and confiscated others in the ports of nations ruled by her armies. Besides the damage to American shipping, the property seized had brought France more than 25,000,000 francs ($5,000,000) at forced sale.

Twenty-five years of negotiation had finally brought about a settlement. The claims had been acknowledged by the French legislature. "But the payments, I regret to inform you, still are withheld." In words that the simplest among the electorate could understand, he told of the surprising French demand that he, Jackson, apologize for having asked Congress to support him in reprisals, if the $5,000,000 was not paid.

The next sentence had been carefully worded with the help of Van Buren, Secretary of State Forsyth and Minister Livingston, *and secretly of the British embassy.* "The concept that it was my intention to menace or insult the government of France is as unfounded as the attempt to extort from the fears of that nation what her sense of justice may deny.

"But the American people," he went on, "are incapable of submitting to an interference, by any government on earth, however powerful, with the free performance of the domestic duties which the Constitution has imposed on their public functionaries. The discussions between the several departments of our government belong to ourselves. . . . The principle which calls in question the President for the language of his message would equally justify a foreign power in demanding explanation of the language used in the report of a committee or by a member in debate.

"The honor of my country shall never be stained by an apology from me for the statement of truth and the performance of duty; nor can I gave any explanation of my official acts, except such as is due to integrity and justice, and consistent with the principles on which our institutions have been framed. This determination will, I am confident, be approved by my constituents."

The American chargé d'affaires, Thomas Barton, had remained in Paris after Minister Livingston's withdrawal. Jackson revealed that Barton had been ordered to make a final demand upon the French government for payment, "and in the event of their refusal, without further explanation, to return to the United States."

By now the spectators in the Senate galleries were listening as attentively as the lawmakers. The only person whose interest might have strayed, since he had read it all beforehand, was Van Buren (called the Little Magician and the American Talleyrand), sitting behind his raised desk looking affably polite and self-confident as always. His concern at the moment was to watch the Senate Whigs' reaction to the next paragraph:

"Much loss and inconvenience have been experienced in consequence of the failure of the bill containing the ordinary appropriations for fortifications, which passed one branch of the national legislature at the last session, but was lost in the other. This failure was the more regretted, not only because it necessarily interrupted the progress of a system of national defense, . . . but also because it contained a contingency appropriation inserted in accordance with the views of the executive in and of this important object and other branches of the national defense, . . . some portions of which might have been usefully applied during the past season."

In the House of Representatives, Adams wondered what the Administration's next move would be if Barton's effort failed. He believed that, once the newspapers had carried the message, popular opinion would be behind Jackson. He could order reprisals, and the Congress would have to back him.

"Parties founded in sectional interests, . . . represented by candidates for the Presidency," Jackson went on, "are constantly prone, in the zeal of party and selfish objects, to generate influences unmindful of the general good."

That was aimed at Webster, Adams thought, and it was well deserved. The remainder of the message did not please him. He always had regarded as inhuman the Administration's indifference to the suffering of the Indians being driven off their lands in Georgia and Alabama. Now Jackson was trying to justify it by saying, "It seems . . . an established fact that they cannot live in contact with a civilized community and prosper. . . . The plan for their removal and reestablishment [west of the Mississippi] is founded upon the knowledge we have gained of their character and habits."

And, finally, there was the request that Congress pass a law prohibiting Northern abolitionists from using the mails "to circulate inflammatory appeals addressed to the passions of the slaves and calculated to stimulate them to insurrection, and to produce all the horrors of a servile war."

Unconstitutional, Adams thought. Plainly unconstitutional!

Newspaper reaction to the message was prompt. In Washington, the Democratic *Globe* vigorously supported the President's French policy. The Whig *National Intelligencer* denounced the message as "artfully contrived to fan the sparks that kindle war"; it doubted that France would accept the President's disavowal of an intended insult. The Democratic New York *Post* and Boston *Post* enthusiastically approved the Administration's course; the *Tribune* in New York and *Courier* in Boston, both anti-Jackson, deplored it. The Jacksonites and their press were particularly emphatic in their condemnation of the Senate for failing to pass the fortifications bill.

On December 15, Daniel Webster was back in his seat. Including himself, he counted four Presidential candidates in the Senate. Martin Van Buren had been nominated by the Democrats at their national convention in Baltimore in May. The Whigs had not held a national convention. Massachusetts had nominated Webster. The party leaders in South Carolina had named Senator Willie (pronounced Wylie) Pierson Mangum, a former Jacksonian Democrat who had broken with the President over the removal of the government deposits from the Bank of the United States. Senator Hugh Lawson White, a former Tennessee superior court judge and comrade of Jackson in the Indian wars, who had also broken with the President over the bank issue, had been named by Whig caucuses in Tennessee and Alabama.

Still another Whig in the field was William Henry Harrison of Ohio, former governor of Indiana Territory and one of the better generals in the War of 1812 (he had fought Tecumseh at Tippecanoe and taken Detroit from the British).

In stature Webster knew he overshadowed his three Whig rivals. As far as he could tell from the press, the country's reaction to Jackson's message was divided along party lines. The turnout for the Webster-for-President rally in New York and his conferences with New England party leaders had persuaded him he had a good chance against Van Buren, too.

Alarm spread in the capital when it was learned that Barton, the chargé d'affaires who had delivered Jackson's final demand to the French government, was back home. However, the men of the President's "kitchen cabinet"—Amos Kendall, the journalist, Taney, the jurist, and Van Buren among them—appeared unperturbed, even better spirited. Soon rumors circulated that the British foreign office had interceded and persuaded the French government to come to terms with Jackson. It was said that the paragraph in the President's message to Congress denying that he had intended to insult the government of France had been drafted with the help of the British minister in Washington, and that Louis Philippe's ministry was expected to accept it. Support for the rumors came when the mail from abroad brought copies of the Paris *Moniteur,* which regularly reflected French policy. A lead article said, "There exists, at the moment, no legitimate cause of war between France and the United States, and in no case shall the aggression come . . . from France."

Jackson's pugnacity had paid off! Even the *National Intelligencer* said, "We sincerely congratulate our readers on the general aspect of the news from France." Webster was in a funk. The attacks on the Whigs, and particularly on himself, were beginning to hurt. They had to be answered, and convincingly. He found his chance when a new fortifications bill came up in the Senate on January 14. Rising and smoothing the lapels of his brass-buttoned blue frock coat, he addressed the Chair and waited for the stillness that dutifully followed.

"Sir, a charge has been sounded all over the land and now again renewed." That charge was that the loss of the previous bill and the special defense fund was the fault of the Senate. Under their craggy brows, his eyes roved around the chamber and returned to the rostrum, occupied by Senator William King of Alabama, sitting in for Van Buren. "Sir, my object is to tell the story of this transaction, and to exhibit the conduct of the Senate fairly to public view. I owe this duty to the Senate, and I hope I may be permitted . . . to say a few words defending my own reputation."

That previous Senate, he went on, had disposed of all business brought before it "with uncommon despatch and promptness. . . . Owing to the state of business in the House of Representatives toward the close . . . several measures did not receive attention, so as to be agreed to or rejected." One was the fortifications bill.

The parliamentary rule prohibiting criticism of the other branch of the legislature applied to both houses, but it was more sternly enforced in the larger and less dignified House, the "popular branch." Moreover, Webster was careful to emphasize that he was not blaming but explaining.

Several times, he declared, the Senators, including himself, had helped House committees correct errors in their proceedings. Through an oversight, for example, the House had failed to include funds for street paving and repairs to the Capitol in the proper appropriation. In joint committee this had been taken care of in the bill *for diplomatic service.*

"There was also the President's gardener," he went on. "His salary had not been provided, and there was no way to remedy this important omission but by giving him a place in the diplomatic service bill, among the chargés d'affaires, the envoys extraordinary and ministers plenipotentiary. There he now stands, and should I see him mornings overlooking the workmen on the lawns and walks . . . which adorn the grounds I should expect to see at least a small diplomatic button on his working jacket."

He let his audience enjoy this, then went on to the fortifications bill.

When the Senate received the original bill, he said, it contained no mention of a special fund for defense. A few minor revisions were made by the Senate, and it went to joint committee. The Senate heard no more from the House until the evening of adjournment, when it received the message that the House had tacked on the $3,000,000 special fund.

"I heard the message with great surprise and astonishment, and I immediately moved to disagree, as a member of the Committee on Finances. I stand here today ready to defend the part taken by me. The Senate rejected the grant. The President had asked for no such grant. No emergency had happened. . . . How, sir, were we to know that the appropriation 'was in accord with the views of the executive?' He had not told us so."

In joint conference, Webster's committee had provided the compromise: $300,000 additional for fortifications and $500,000 for equipment and repairs of ships of war. This was duly sent to the House.

"The House never acted on the report of the committee," he said. "The bill therefore was lost. *It was lost in the House of Representatives. It died there, and there its remains are to be found!*"

His voice reached effortlessly to the velvet-hung galleries, crowded now that word had spread: "Webster is speaking!"

"Why was not this appropriation recommended to the Congress by the President? Are we ready to say that the power of fixing places for fortifications, the power of ordering new ships to be built, the power of laying out money to raise men for the Army; in short, every power great and small respecting military and naval service, shall be vested in the President without specification of objects or purpose, to the entire exclusion . . . of Congress? For one, I am not so prepared.

"The honorable member from Ohio, near me"—he pointed to Senator Thomas Ewing—"has said that if the enemy had been on our shores he would not have agreed to this vote." His voice soared. *"And I say if the proposition were now before us, and the guns of the enemy were battering against the walls of the Capitol, I would not agree!*

"It was a false necessity. There was no enemy on our shores; there were no guns pointed against the Capitol; we were in no war, nor was there reasonable probability that we should have war, unless we made it ourselves.

"I think I see, in all the brightness and sunlight of broad noon, that it is this career of personal confidence, along this beaten track of man-worship . . . that our own system [of republican government] is making progress toward its end.

"A personal popularity achieved first by military achievement, and sustained by party, by patronage, which looks for no ills, seems to render men willing to gratify power long before its demands are made, and to surfeit executive discretion even in anticipation of its own appetites. If it had been the purpose of both houses of Congress to create a military dictator, what formula would have been better suited to their purpose than this vote of the House? The whole war power would have been in the hands of the President.

"Sir," he concluded, "if the power to make reprisals and this money from the Treasury had both been granted, is there not great reason to believe we should now [be] up to our ears in a hot war? I . . . believe this."

He stood beside his desk, suddenly silent, his great dark eyes flashing. Then he sat down, and the chamber resounded with hearty applause—from the jubilant Whigs.

The speech appeared four days later in the *National Intelligencer*, after Webster had proofread it. In the meanwhile, a few Administration supporters in the Senate had attempted to reply, but their efforts were ineffectual. Adams gave the text a careful reading. Stripped of its soaring rhetoric, he saw it as a clever distortion of the proceedings, subtly aimed at repairing Webster's prestige. At the same time, he regarded it as an attack on himself, aimed at discrediting him with his Plymouth Rock constituency for compelling the House to support the Administration. For the record, it should be answered, and he ached to do it, but the House rules stood in the way.

Then, on January 22, Churchill Camberleng, who had originated and led the defense appropriation through the House, took the floor to complain that he and the House had been maligned in that morning's *United States Telegraph*. In discussing Webster's speech, the newspaper had insinuated that the fortifications bill had been lost because of faulty leadership in the House. "The members," he said, "will vindicate the proceedings of the House in relation to that bill from the attacks of the other body."

Speaker Polk stopped him.

"It is not in order to allude to the other body."

Adams stood up to propose appointment of "a select committee to inquire into the causes and circumstances of the failure of that bill."

The House had just convened for the day. Since members had to have a good excuse for not attending if they wanted to collect their daily $8, most of them were on hand. Some lolled in their armchairs, legs stretched out or hooked over a corner of their desks, reading newspapers or their mail. Groups stood talking in the aisles, their heads turning occasionally to take aim at the nearest spittoon. Broad Southern drawls mingled with the nasal voices of the New Englanders and the slurred accents of the western frontier. Camberleng's complaint got little attention, but the Southerners were alert for the high-pitched voice of "the old curmudgeon," Adams: it usually meant trouble. Several Whigs shouted objections to his proposal, but they were overruled.

Adams waited for quiet, and went on. He wanted the committee to report on the "loss of the $3,000,000 appropriation bill in consequence of what has occured in another place on this subject, in which not only the facts stated by the President in his message have been denied—"

"Allusions to proceedings of the Senate are not in order," Polk reminded him. "It is indispensable that this rule be observed to preserve harmony between the two houses of the legislature."

"I am well disposed to observe the rule," Adams answered. "I have offered the resolution in consequence of what has occured in another place. I did not say that place was the Senate. I did not refer nominally to anything that took place in the Senate, but to what took place elsewhere."

Charles Mercer, a good friend of Adams, called him to order. Mercer, a Virginia lawyer, was a leader in the movement to colonize freed slaves in Africa; he was also a devoted Whig.

"The gentleman from Massachusetts has not nominally alluded to the Senate, but he has intentionally done so," he protested. "The meaning of the gentleman is what I take exception to."

"As I understand the rules," Adams said tartly, "exception must be taken to words of a member, not to any meaning which any gentleman may think proper to attach to his words."

Polk wavered. He had high respect for Adams' parliamentary experience—too high, said some of his Southern colleagues. So

116

far, he decided, the old gentleman was within bounds. By now the newspapers had been thrown aside, the mail forgotten. Legs came off desks. The groups broke up and moved down the aisles around Adams.

Whether he had nominally or intentionally referred to the Senate, Mercer insisted, he was equally out of order.

"I cannot anticipate what the gentleman from Massachusetts intends to say," Polk answered. "The moment he makes a remark in violation of the rule, the Chair will enforce observance of it." He held up the *House Manual*. "I have the authority before me."

"I will endeavor, so far as my humble ability will permit me," Adams said, "to avoid any collision not only with the letter but with the spirit of the rule to which the gentleman from Virginia has appealed, and I will transfer the location of the 'place' where these things have happened from the Senate of the United States—if the gentleman thinks the Senate the place to which I allude—to the office of the *National Intelligencer*. If the gentleman from Virginia has any objection to that—"

"I object to any quibble calculated to produce a collision between the House and the Senate," Mercer shouted to Polk.

"Order!" "Order!" came from some of the Congressmen closing around Adams, and "Go on!" "Go on!" from others. Polk was interested in Adams' stratagem, but his fingers worried the pages of the manual. He again overruled Mercer.

"In the *National Intelligencer*," Adams went on, "there is published a report of proceedings which have taken place in a certain quarter; and in that paper I find it charged not only that the statement in the message of the President was untrue, but that failure of the appropriation was not caused in the Senate, but in another house."

His audience had become so noisy, taking sides among themselves and shouting at Adams, that James Parker of New Jersey appealed to Polk to restore order. "It is impossible," he complained, "to understand what is going on."

Adams stood, head bent, hands braced on his desk, while

117

Polk pounded his gavel. No notes were before him; he had not expected to speak until Camberleng's mention of the innuendoes in the *Telegraph* had inspired him.

He heard young Henry Wise of Virginia say, "I hope the gentleman from Massachusetts will be permitted to proceed whether he is in order or out of order. If ever there was a case where members should be permitted to speak frankly on both sides, that the whole truth may be elicited, this is one."

He was loudly supported, and opposed.

Emphasizing still that it was the *Intelligencer* account he was discussing, Adams took up Webster's complaint that the House had waited until late on adjournment day to present the $3,000,000 amendment to the Senate. How could the House have acted sooner? he asked. The fund had been voted to implement the resolution supporting the President in his dispute with France (the "Adams resolution") and that resolution had been approved only the night before. There had been some opposition to the amendment, of course. Debate had delayed passage until late the next day, and Webster's committee had been told that. As to the bill dying in the House, "the Senate sent the message [on the compromise] at two o'clock in the morning, when it was known both in the House and the Senate that no quorum could be found."

Elisha Whittlesey, a Whig from Ohio, tried to silence Adams by calling for the order of the day. This brought on another outburst for and against. When quiet was restored, Polk ruled Whittlesey's motion out of order.

"It is difficult to reconnect my train of thoughts after so many interruptions," Adams complained. But he was soon back on the attack.

"One charge [by Webster] was that the House of Representatives voted the fund without a recommendation from the President. That was the great offense on which was founded the burst of indignant eloquence which would rather see the enemy battering down the walls of the Capitol than agree to such an appropriation for the defense of the country!"

He was charging full tilt now, his usually bloodless face

118

flushed with indignation. "Am I to be told that the House must not appropriate money unless it is recommended by the Executive? Why, sir, the Executive has told us that that appropriation was perfectly in accord with his wishes. Yet here an unconstitutional conspiracy and man-worship are imputed to this House on account of that appropriation. Where was the possibility of a *recommendation* from the Executive when the resolution had been passed but the day before? That resolution was itself passed in consequence of a communication from the Executive. Then why was the charge of man-worship made? I will appeal to the House to say *whether I am a worshipper of the present Executive.*

"I voted for that appropriation, and I glory in the vote. . . . I had not approved the special measures which were recommended by the Executive at the commencement of that session of the Congress. Neither had the House of Representatives. But the House, and, thank God! the people of the country, did homage to the spirit which urged the recommendation.

"I again repeat, why is it that the House must be charged with man-worship and unconstitutional conspiracy because they passed an appropriation of $3,000,000, *for the defense of the country* at a time when imminent danger of war was urged?

"Observe, sir, the terms, objects, conditions of that appropriation. It was to be expended under direction of the President of the United States, the executive head of our nation, sworn to the faithful execution of the laws, sworn especially and entrusted with superintendency of all the defenses of the country against the ravages of a foreign invader. It was to be expended for the military and naval services, including fortifications and ordnance, and to increase of the Navy. Not one dollar of it could have been applied to any other purpose by the President without a violation of his official oath and of his official trust. Not one dollar of it could have been applied by him to any other purpose without making himself liable to impeachment.

"Nor was that all It was to be expended only in event that it should be rendered necessary *for the defense of our country* prior to the then next session of Congress, an interval of nine months during which no other provision could have been made to defend your soil from a sudden invasion or to protect your commerce floating upon every sea."

He had a silent audience now, crowded deep around his chair, and beyond him the rows of desks were empty.

"And this, this is the appropriation following close upon the unanimous vote of 217 [*sic*] that execution of the treaty of 1831 should be maintained and insisted upon. This is the appropriation so tainted with man-worship, so corrupt, so unconstitutional, that the indignant and patriotic eloquence of the *National Intelligencer* would sooner see a foreign enemy battering down the walls of the Capitol than agree to it.

"Sir, for a man uttering such sentiments, there would be but one step more, a natural and easy one to take, and that would be, with the enemy at the walls of the Capitol, to join him in battering them down!"

"A spontaneous burst of feeling and applause," was how a House reporter described the demonstration that followed. Polk had to use his gavel to restore order. And someone in the group around Adams' desk—his identity is lost—coined a new name for him that day, lifted from one of John Milton's poems. Thereafter, John Quincy Adams was known as "Old Man Eloquent."

As for Webster, he had not only been answered; his chance of succeeding Jackson in the White House the next year had vanished. Only the Massachusetts Whigs remained faithful to him. But then, they never did care much for Adams.

→»» VIII «←

WHILE Adams was helping the Administration in the French crisis, the abolition movement headed toward eruption onto the floors of Congress. President Jackson's proposal that the government bar antislavery literature from the mails was rejected by the Senate. But postal authorities in the South and in New York City were already doing it on their own, even letting a mob burn the "incendiary" publications in Calhoun's South Carolina. So the poet Whittier directed the field workers of the American Anti-Slavery Society to concentrate instead on sending petitions to Congress for emancipation in the District of Columbia.

In the House, several Northern Representatives beside Adams, including George Briggs and William Jackson from his home state, were now willingly presenting the petitions. The most outspoken was William Slade of Vermont. Slade, a lawyer and former newspaper publisher from the town of Cornwall, was an aggressive and outspoken abolitionist. Adams still hoped to keep the movement from arousing the House, where the Southerners and their Northern supporters, Whigs as well as Democrats, predominated. Until abolition sentiment in Congress grew much stronger—a day still remote, he knew—the petitions should be respectfully submitted, respectfully received and no more. Yet Slade, whose dedication Adams shared but whose lack of political discretion he deplored, could not be restrained.

When John Fairfield of Maine presented a petition from his constituents, he followed the pattern set by Adams: he did not endorse its contents, he said, but moved that it be referred to the Committee on the District. The House voted instead to table it, which theoretically at least made it available for future consideration. Fairfield was agreeable, but Slade was not. He demanded that the petition be printed, "to the end that [it]may receive the attention which the importance of the question and character of the memorial demand."

He had petitions, he said, and he knew the signers. Many of them "feel deeply . . . the right and duty of Congress to abolish slavery and erase from the national escutcheon the foul blot of the slave trade within the limits of the district."

Speaker Polk ruled Slade out of order for going into the merits of the petition. Slade was silenced, but the Southerners were aroused. When Jackson offered a petition from Massachusetts, James Hammond of South Carolina moved that it not be received. "I will not sit here," he shouted, "and see the rights of the Southern people assaulted by the ignorant fanatics from whom these memorials proceed." Balie Peyton of Tennessee denounced "these firebrands cast upon the House."

Francis Thomas of Maryland was on his feet. "As one of the Representatives of a slaveholding state, I would never provoke examination here calculated to create false hopes in the minds of an ignorant and stupid population [the slaves]. Is it not madness, worse than madness? . . . These fanatical crusaders . . . pour their poison into that national chalice from which the whole people of the United States have so long quaffed the sweet waters of concord and union."

For two days the Southerners held the floor, except for occasional barbed interruptions by Slade. That night, December 18, Adams finished a long letter to his son Charles, a letter started early in the week and interrupted by the uproar in the House.

"We have had two days of debate," he wrote, "on the petitions for the abolition of slavery and the slave trade in the District of Columbia. Of debate, I say, but it was all on one side. The voice of freedom has not yet been heard, and I am constantly urged to speak in her name. She will be trampled under foot if I do not—and I shall be trampled under foot if I do. . . . What can I do?"

On Monday, December 21, the Southerners resumed the offensive. Henry Wise led off with a philippic against "those misguided meddlers" and demanded "that the House not receive any further memorials on this subject." He was followed by another Virginian, John Patton, who called for "a distinct vote that the House is opposed to such interference."

Now Adams arose. His was the manner of the elder statesman counseling directly out of his long experience. The petitions, he said, should be handled as he had done "in my first act as a member of this House. . . . Petitions were transmitted to me . . . with the request that I present them. . . . Sir, I did so in homage to the sacred right of petition, a right which, in whatever manner it may be treated by other members of this House, shall never be treated by me other than with respect. . . . I then declined to support the petitions, . . . to keep discussion of the subject out of the House. From the moment petitions are referred to the Committee on the District of Columbia, they go to the family vault 'of all the Capulets,' and you will never hear of them again."

His voice sharpened. "If you come to the resolution that this House will not receive any more petitions, sir, you will have discussion, a discussion upon the merits of slavery. Speeches of my colleagues, probably of myself, will be incendiary, because if discussion is thrust upon us"—his head went back as it habitually did under the compulsion of "speaking my mind"—"I might make a speech as incendiary as any pamphlet upon which such torrents of denunciation have been poured . . . *in derogation of the sublime merits of slavery!*"

But it was too late to stop Wise and his Southern coterie, or, for that matter, Slade. The contentious Vermonter went on to demand that all abolition petitions be referred to a special committee for investigation, "and let it [the committee's report] go out to the country."

Christmas came on Friday, bringing an intermission in the debate. It also demonstrated vividly the separation between the two cultures, North and South. The Virginia statesmen were by the middle of the week, riding or driving back to their plantations, to carol singing and yule logs; tall candles lighting the windows, roast venison and turkey, suckling pig, plum pudding on the table; fox hunts over hoar-frosted fields; mulled wine by the fireplace. Christmas in the Old Dominion was a jovial memory of ancestral England. In Washington, the homes and boarding houses of the Southerners—Episcopalians from the Carolinas, Maryland Catholics—made a brave if less ebullient show of saluting the holiday behind candlelit windows framing swags of laurel and holly wreaths.

The houses of the New Englanders stood somberly apart. There Christmas—so long suppressed by the Puritan forefathers as a remnant of "popery"—was not observed. (Except in the parlors of a few homesick Germans, Christmas trees were still unknown; and Clement Moore's *A Visit from St. Nicholas* had not yet popularized the Santa Claus legend.)

Adams spent the holiday in his study, examining the bundles of abolition petitions that had been piling up there since his return to Washington. Their salutations and prayers were brief and to the same point: that Congress abolish slavery and the slave trade in the District of Columbia. Many had copied the standard form sent out by the American Anti-Slavery Society. Women's names predominated in the long list of signatures. The scrolls had come to Adams from villages and rural communities in New England and New York State, Pennsylvania and Ohio; none was from a city.

One petition particularly pleased him. It was signed by 366 inhabitants of Weymouth, no more than an hour's walk from Quincy. During his first term in the House a small petition had come to him from Cohasset, but this was the first since then from his Plymouth district. He smiled over the names, many of them of people he knew well. Nevertheless, he realized that the majority of his constituents were still opposed to freeing the Negroes.

Monday was the regular day for presenting petitions in the

House, and on the first Monday after New Year's, Adams' desk was cluttered with scrolls, the overflow on the floor around him. His motion that they be referred to the Committee on the District of Columbia was voted down. He went on, quoting the prayers: "trade in the human species," "great national and moral evil." Southern tempers snapped again. Thomas Glascock of Georgia broke in angrily, and Adams called him to order. Speaker Polk clashed with Adams. Patton of Virginia called the petitioners "misguided meddlers." The women signers were "frustrated old maids." The acoustics in the high-domed chamber were poor even on orderly days. Now the jumble of voices rose to an uproar.

The House adjourned without deciding whether to table or reject the petitions. The next day, action was put off to take up more urgent business. Postponement followed postponement, while the Southerners and their Northern supporters looked for ways to stop the crusade.

At the same time, in the other wing of the Capitol, an Ohio Senator, Thomas Morris, caused a heated, though more orderly, debate over slavery. Morris was a Democrat but a long-time abolitionist, the son of Baptist pioneers. Now sixty, he had spent his life on the frontier. His youth was strikingly similar to that of another statesman from the backwoods, then twenty-six and working obscurely in a little general store in New Salem, Illinois. Like Abraham Lincoln, Senator Morris had had little formal schooling, had read Blackstone by the cabin fireplace, practiced country law and served in the state legislature before coming to Washington. He was as thoroughly opposed to slavery as Adams, but lacked the former President's ready combativeness. His manner was diffident, and it was with diffidence that he presented to the Senate two petitions from his home state. His motion to table them was opposed by Calhoun, who scathingly denounced the abolition movement.

The Senate should arbitrarily reject all these petitions, Calhoun declared. "They are a foul slander on nearly one half of the states of the Union . . . gross, false and malicious." Slavery, he reminded the Senate, was strictly a state institution. "Congress has no jurisdiction, no more in this district than in the state of South Carolina. Receiving the petitions will give them importance. We must turn them away from our door."

The Fifth Amendment to the Constitution, he proclaimed, was an "insuperable barrier to abolition." He quoted: " 'No person shall be . . . deprived of life, liberty, or property, without due process of law.' Are not slaves property?" he asked. "And if so, how can Congress any more take away the property of a master in his slave, in this district, than it could his life and liberty? They stand on the same ground. The one in the eyes of the Constitution is as sacred as the other."

But the majority doubted the wisdom or necessity of Calhoun's extreme proposal. Even his fellow Senator from South Carolina, William Preston, supported the more tolerant procedure: to receive the petitions and refer them to the Committee on the District of Columbia. "The committee room," said Preston, "is the lion's den from which there are no footprints to mark their return."

The method succeeded in the upper chamber, since many of the Northern Senators, even Whigs "trucking to the aristocratic lords of the slaves," ignored the petitions.

Calhoun, however, continued to denounce the abolitionists. Slavery, he insisted, was "a good—a positive good!" The primitive Negroes were far better off under their paternalistic masters than "the millions of white slaves" working in the mills and factories of the North. He only provided additional ammunition for the Northern agitators, who thereafter concentrated on the House of Representatives and, if the petitioners' Congressman was known to be unsympathetic, directed the scrolls to Adams.

Calhoun's alter ego in the House, Henry Wise, meanwhile, declared, "The war is now commenced. Nothing can satisfy the South but a bold, direct and manly vote upon this question. . . . Any attempt . . . to legislate upon the subject will be not only unauthorized but dangerous to the union of the states."

Adams continued to present his petitions, including the one from his own district and another "from 158 ladies, citizens of the Commonwealth of Massachusetts, for *I have not brought myself to doubt whether females are citizens."*

They were added to the stack awaiting disposition while the House debated. Leonard Jarvis, an anti-abolitionist from Maine, argued that all petitions pertaining to slavery should be "laid on the table without being referred or printed." Wise, like Senator Calhoun, wanted nothing less than their outright rejection. Meanwhile, another Southerner had been earnestly seeking a procedure that would be acceptable to North and South alike.

Henry Laurens Pinckney was an able statesman, a descendant of a famous South Carolina family that had fought in the Revolution, helped frame the Constitution and supplied ministers to France and England. Pinckney himself had been active in South Carolina politics for a long while. He had published a Charleston newspaper, the *Mercury*, and had been an early protégé of Calhoun.

The resolution he proposed provided that "all the memorials which have been offered, or may hereafter be presented, . . . be referred to a select committee with instructions to report that Congress possesses no constitutional authority to interfere in any way with the institution of slavery in any of the states . . . and that, in the opinion of the House, Congress ought not to interfere . . . with slavery in the District of Columbia, because it would be a violation of the public faith, unwise, impolitic, and dangerous to the Union, assigning such reasons for these conclusions as, in the judgment of the committee, may be best calculated to enlighten the public mind, to repress agitation, to allay excitement, to sustain and preserve the just rights of the slaveholding states and of the people of this district and to reestablish harmony and tranquillity amongst the various sections of the Union."

Pinckney pleaded with the defenders of slavery to go along with his proposal "for the peace and preservation of the Union." The Southern extremists protested, but the resolution was carried, 174 to 48.

Adams voted with the yeas. He could not have been more

127

pleased if he had written the resolution himself, he said. It promised to preserve the right of petition and at the same time put a stop to the debate. He wrote to his friend Solomon Lincoln in Hingham that this was what he had "urged again and again, . . . but [it] would have been rejected if moved by me." He concluded with one of his rare displays of optimism: "And there is a truce in the servile war for the remainder of this session, at least."

Weeks went by while the select committee, appointed February 8 and headed by Pinckney, worked on its presentation. Adams let the petitions gather in his study and turned his attention to developments on two other fronts. The Creek Indians on the Alabama–Georgia border were steadily resisting state and federal efforts to transplant them beyond the Mississippi. While there had been only sporadic disturbances so far, it was feared that an uprising might be brewing. The big news of the moment, however, was the Texas revolution.

The colonists, who had been lured south of the border by cheap land grants, had become increasingly restive under Mexican rule. The virgin soil was ideal for cotton, and many of the settlers were Southerners who, abandoning their worn-out farms, had brought some 5,000 slaves with them and defied the Mexican authorities' emancipation edict. When the Mexican dictator, Santa Anna, prohibited further immigration and attempted to disarm some of the settlers, they revolted.

On March 2 the colonists declared their independence. Four days later Santa Anna's army stormed the Alamo in San Antonio and massacred its garrison, including the courageous frontiersmen, Davy Crockett, Jim Bowie and Bill Travis. Jackson's Tennessee protégé, Sam Houston, took command of the Texas army, and in a dramatic attack, glowingly recounted in the American press, destroyed the main Mexican force at San Jacinto and captured Santa Anna.

The Texans promptly adopted a constitution—a constitution that, to Adams' deep dismay, restored slavery. The young republic sent an emissary to petition the Jackson Administration for recognition, although the Mexican regime that had succeeded Santa Anna showed no willingness to accept the loss of its northern domain. Moreover, Adams learned that the emissary was also empowered to propose annexation to the United States.

Adams' friend, Benjamin Lundy, had meanwhile returned from Mexico, where he had gone to establish a plantation colony for freed Negroes. The revolution had frustrated his plan and had also provided him with material for a series of articles he was now publishing in the Philadelphia *National Gazette*. In them he charged the revolution had been secretly promoted by General Houston and the slavemaster President, Jackson, to create a great new slave state and so greatly enlarge the Southern representation in Congress.

Adams had complete confidence in Lundy's sincerity. There was no more zealous and upright apostle in the abolition movement than the warm-mannered, cheerful Quaker. Lundy's articles were, however, a small voice lost in the country's cheering for the intrepid Texans. Editorials saluted their courage and spirit. Sam Houston was the man of the hour. Reports that he was to be the first President of Texas were met with delight. And petitions began arriving in both houses of Congress for immediate recognition of the new republic. To Adams, recognition of Texas was one thing. But its annexation to the United States, he was convinced, would mean war with Mexico. He watched anxiously for developments.

An infection on Adams' leg kept him restive at home for a week. So unusual was his absence from the House that the *National Intelligencer* considered it worth a news item. The morning walks had to be discontinued for the rest of the session. He rode to the Capitol and back in the family barouche, his young granddaughters, Louisa Catherine and Georgiana Frances, usually sharing the morning ride. Spring, he noted, was three weeks later than usual; it was May 1 before the peach and cherry trees blossomed. By then muddy Pennsylvania Avenue had dried to red dust that powdered the drab fronts of the boarding houses and awninged shops. But the steep hill at its eastern end stood lush against the sky, its gravel paths winding through green shrubbery and flowering trees and around the ponds stocked with gold and silver fish, to the white Capitol at the summit. The ponds and ornate drinking fountains were considered an engineering marvel: the water came in pipes from a spring on the farm of John Smith two miles away.

From the carriage drive, Adams limped up the long flight of steps to the rotunda, helped along with his cane. His leg still wore a poultice, and his chronic cough and rheumatic pains tormented his nights; the palsied entries in his diary were brief and days apart. The one for May 8 read: "Reflecting on our relations with Mexico, the prospects of more momentous discussion, and my own condition so infirm, so helpless, so nearly hopeless . . . I shall henceforth speak in the House of Representatives at the hazard of my life."

No word had yet come from the committee on Abolition Petitions. Adams heard that the members—five of them from the North, the other four from the South—were unable to agree. Finally, on May 18, Chairman Pinckney announced that their report was ready.

There were three resolutions. The first denied that Congress had the power to abolish slavery in any of the states. Adams was willing to agree to that, for the time being at least. The second declared that slavery *ought* not to be interfered with in the District of Columbia. That, too, he approved, since the citizens of the District would have no voice themselves in any such action. But then came the third one: all petitions or papers relating in any way to abolition should, "without either being printed or referred, be laid upon the table, and no further action whatever be had thereon." *That* the son of John Adams, the protégé of Washington, intimate of Hamilton, Madison, Monroe and Jefferson would never agree to. Freedom of petition had been ruled sacred by the Founding Fathers. No misguided demagogues should infringe it now. He was out of his chair, gesturing for the Speaker's attention, his sore leg and all his other aches and pains forgotten.

Polk recognized instead one after another of his Southern colleagues, who endorsed the first and third resolutions but wanted the second one revised: "ought," they protested, implied that Congress *did* have the authority to interfere with slavery in the District, which they denied.

Adams was determined now to oppose all three resolutions; furthermore, to prove them untenable, which he had hoped he would not have to do. But his shrill "Mr. Speaker!" was shouted down by the organized and forewarned opposition. When Polk again looked past him and recognized George Owens of Georgia, a member of the Pinckney committee, Adams shouted, "I am aware that there is a slaveholder in the chair!" This brought angry protests. Polk ordered him, "Sit down!" and pounded his gavel until he did.

Owens said, "I move the main question be now put." This maneuver, known in parliamentary procedure as "the previous question," would choke off debate. The House supported him, 95 to 82.

"Mr. Speaker, am I gagged or not?" Adams demanded.

"The motion is not debatable," Polk reminded him. He ordered the roll called on the first resolution. When the clerk came to Adams' name, he was up again. "If the House will allow me *five minutes,* I pledge myself to prove that resolution false and utterly untrue."

"Order!" "Order!" "Sit down!"

Polk still ignored him. The resolution was carried, 182 to 9, only eight Northern Whigs being willing to go along with Adams.

By now it was one o'clock, the time set for taking up the scheduled business of the day. Polk postponed the other two resolutions, and the House converted itself into committee of the whole to act on an appeal for help from the settlers on the Alabama–Georgia border. The resistance of the Creek Indians against their forced transplant had blossomed into a savage uprising. Homesteads had been pillaged, families massacred. Stagecoaches on the road between Columbus, Georgia, and Montgomery, Alabama, had been waylaid and their occupants scalped. Settlers who had been warned in time had sent their women and children into the villages. Some 1,200 were now crowded into the small settlement of Columbus, reported Representative Dixon Lewis of Alabama, among them children whose parents had been tomahawked, wives whose husbands had died holding off the raiders. The refugees had lost their livestock and provisions and, said Lewis, "in some instances even their Negroes." They were out of food. A joint resolution from the Senate was on the agenda, authorizing the President to rush emergency rations to them.

Sitting as a committee, the House could facilitate action, since the stringent rules of parliamentary practice did not apply. Among these was the previous question. Adams got the floor and twisted in and out of the Indian uprising to make the hostile majority listen to what he had to say on the slavery resolution. Instead of the five minutes he had previously pleaded for, he spoke for an hour and a half, loudly called to order time and again, but always staying close enough to the subject of debate to prevent the Chair from silencing him. He had never been in better form.

The victims of "the law of scalping knife and tomahawk," he said, deserved help, but since the ration funds would come out of the public treasury, he had to justify his position to his New England constituents. It was a reasonable premise, and even the Deep South contingent was politely attentive. But then: In voting to help the refugees, he went on, Congress would be resorting to its war power, "to that common defense and general welfare declared to be among the purposes for which the Constitution itself was ordained by the people. . . . In the authority given to Congress by the Constitution . . . to declare war, all the powers incidental to war are by necessary implication conferred upon the government. The powers incidental to war are derived . . . from the laws and usages of nations."

This started an undertone of mumblings. Voices reached across the desks: "What's the old curmudgeon getting at?" "What's war got to do with this?"

"In your relations with the Indian tribes, you never declare war," Adams continued, "although you do make and break treaties with them, whenever [it] happens to suit the purposes of the President and the majority of both houses of Congress."

That brought shouts of "Order!" "I protest—" "Mr. Speaker—"

In committee of the whole, the Speaker left the rostrum and appointed a substitute. Augustine Shepperd of North Carolina, now in the chair, warned Adams against speaking disrepect-fully about the Administration or Congress. Adams promised, "I shall be more prudent."

Congress and the President possessed two kinds of power, he went on, "altogether different . . . and often incompatible. . . . The war power, limited only by the laws and usages of nations, . . . is tremendous. It is strictly constitutional, but it breaks down every barrier so anxiously erected for the pro-tection of liberty, of property and of life. This is the power which authorizes you to pass the resolution now before you, and in my opinion there is no other."

Now the words came fast.

"And this is the reason I was not permitted to give this morn-ing for voting . . . against the first resolution . . . on the abolition petitions. As I was not permitted to give a reason be-fore, I rejoice that the reason for which I shall vote for the resolution now before the committee is identically the same."

He had hoped to keep to himself the concept which he was now to expound. It had far-reaching implications, and in the quiet of his study he had told himself it was better left unsaid; the time was not ripe. But his enemies had provoked him to combat.

"Suppose a civil war. Suppose Congress were called to raise armies, to supply money from the whole Union, to suppress an insurrection, would they have no authority to interfere with the institution of slavery? . . . By war . . . it may become nec-essary for the master to recognize his [the slave's] emancipa-tion by a treaty of peace. Can it for an instant be pretended that Congress, in such a contingency, would have no authority to interfere with the institution in any way? It would be equiva-lent to say that Congress has no constitutional authority to make peace. From that instant that your slaveholding states become the theater of war, civil, servile or foreign, . . . the war power

133

of Congress extends to interference with the institution of slavery in every way by which it can be interfered with."

This concept, presented by Adams to a hostile House that spring day in 1836, was precisely the one used by President Lincoln twenty-six years later for his Emancipation Proclamation.

By now the members were crowding around Adams' desk. Visitors on their way to the Senate had heard the shouting and, for a change, turned into the House galleries. Word reached the upper chamber that Adams was launched on one of his diatribes, and Senators crossed the rotunda to listen.

Adams turned to the Texas revolution. Did the House know, he asked, that the country was being piloted into war with Mexico? That President Jackson and General Houston were conspiring to annex the territory to the United States in order to create a new slave state?

"The war in Texas is a Mexican civil war, and a war for the reestablishment of slavery where it was abolished. It is a war between slavery and emancipation, and every possible effort has been made to drive us into the war on the side of slavery."

He shook his finger at the Southerners in front of him—Wise, Bynum, Mason, Haynes. "Do not you, slaveholding exterminators of Indians, from the bottom of your souls, hate the Mexican-Spaniard-Indian emancipator of slaves? . . . And do you think that your hatred is not cordially returned? And this is the nation with which, at the instigation of your executive government, you are now rushing into war—a war of conquest."

Did they presume to think that England, having three years before emancipated the slaves in its West Indies colonies at a cost of $100,000,000, would let a neighboring foreign territory be conquered by a rival power for the restoration of slavery? Why did they need Texas? "Have you not enough Indians to expel from the land of their fathers? Are you not large and unwieldy enough already?"

His strident voice was at top pitch. "Are you ready for all these wars? A Mexican war? A war with Great Britain? . . . A general Indian war? A servile war? And as an inevitable consequence of them all, a civil war? For it must ultimately terminate in a war of colors as well as of races. And do you imagine that, . . . while in the very nature of things your southern and southwestern states must be the Flanders of these complicated wars, the battlefield upon which the last great conflict must be fought between slavery and emancipation, do you imagine that your Congress will have no constitutional authority to interfere with the institution of slavery in any way? . . . From the instant that your slaveholding states become the theater of war, civil, servile or foreign, from that instant the war powers of Congress extend to interference with the institution of slavery in every way!"

He ended, "I shall vote for the resolution."

By now the oil-lamp chandeliers had been lighted. It was nearing eight o'clock, and the members had been sitting since ten in the morning. The Southerners' response lacked its usual fire. Haynes of Georgia protested that Adams had "discussed everything but the subject under consideration." Waddy Thompson of South Carolina and Henry Wise put in a few edged words, and help for the settlers was approved. The House adjourned for the day.

Adams "came home much exhausted and soon sought my bed." But he was soon awake again and wondering how the nation would react. He had said more, much more, than he would have if his temper had not been aroused by the obvious conspiracy to silence him. The speech was, he realized, "one of the most hazardous I have ever made, and the reception, even by the people of my own district and state, is altogether uncertain."

Next day the House resumed the roll call on the Pinckney proposals. On the second resolution, that slavery ought not to be interfered with in the District, Adams asked to be excused from voting. He was not ready to go on record either for or against it. Passage was peremptory. The roll started on the third resolution, that all antislavery petitions should be tabled "with no further action whatever thereon." When the clerk came to Adams, he shouted, "I hold the resolution to be in direct violation of the Constitution of the United States, of the rules of this House, and of the rights of my constituents!"

Polk told him debate was out of order. The clerk went on with the count, and the resolution was passed, 117 to 68. The Pinckney gag rule was in effect.

Adams brooded at his desk. Of the 144 Representatives from the free states, more than half had voted with the South to silence him! He was tired and discouraged.

"This is a cause upon which I am entering at the last stage of life," he wrote in a memorandum that evening, "and with the certainty that I cannot advance it far. My career must close, leaving the cause at the threshold. To open the way for others is all that I can do."

This was still his mood on Sunday, as he led his family into their pew at the Second Presbyterian Church. Over the years he had acquired an almost mystical faith in divine guidance. A transcendental force, he believed, pervaded the atmosphere of a church, a force that had seldom failed to provide "a pointed application to my own situation and circumstances. . . . Support, encouragement. Sometimes warning and admonition." He listened carefully to the sermon but could find in it no application to himself. Then the minister opened the song book and called for Number 129, a hymn by the English cleric, Isaac Watts, and Adams, singing loud and earnestly, felt he had been given his answer:

> Just in the last distressing hour
> The Lord displays delivering power.
> The mount of danger is the place
> Where we shall see surprising grace.

As time went then, it did not take long for Adams' home district, and the nation, to respond to his long speech. The *National Intelligencer* printed it in full. Gales, one of the publishers, told Adams that there was such a demand for copies that he was bringing it out in pamphlet form. He already had 2,500 orders. Reading proof on the galleys, Adams found it disjointed, badly organized. He wrote his friend, Robert Walsh, in Bordentown, New Jersey, that it was a hodgepodge of material he should have made into three or four speeches. But it was the only way he could circumvent "the absurd rules of the House, construed as they are by a slaveholding Speaker."

The Washington correspondents of the out-of-town newspapers had missed Adams' performance, but they quickly mailed the text to their editors. The abolitionists were jubilant, the Southerners outraged. The part that alarmed the North was Adams' charge that the Administration might bring on a war with Mexico by taking Texas into the Union. Until Adams spoke, that possibility had not been discussed in the press. "My speech comes back with echoes and thundering vituperations from the South and West," Adams said, "and with one universal shout of applause from the North and East."

In Boston, his son Charles Francis, reading the newspapers, observed, "My father seems to have taken the lead in a tremendous battle about the question of slavery," and concluded, naïvely, "which ended in his being strictly silenced."

⇛ IX ⇚

ALONG with Charles Francis, the proslavery majority in the House believed that John Quincy Adams had been "strictly silenced." Henry Wise even presented a petition from Halifax County, Virginia, proposing that Congress now "provide husbands at public expense to all female petitioners, thereby giving direction to their minds."

The volatile young Virginia lawyer stopped beside Adams' desk one evening during their dispute over recognition of Texas, and ridiculed Adams' contention that the President was conspiring to annex Texas as a slave state. "Jackson is a bad man," Adams told him frostily, "and so are you. You have some bad principles, as that one man may hold another in bondage. You are bad so far as your principles are bad. . . . Jackson is a bad man because he has no principles."

Yet, a few weeks later, while debating admission of Arkansas to statehood, Adams gratuitously complimented Wise. "However much I differ . . . from him," he told the House, "I will do him the justice and say his course is straightforward, and you may always know where to find him. . . . In the intercourse of public or private life, I hold in high esteem an adversary of such character."

The bill to make the Territory of Arkansas a state brought a new flood of petitions to Adams' desk. Under the Missouri Compromise, the Territory, lying south of 36° 30', the lower border of Missouri, would enter the Union as a slave state. A companion bill gave statehood to Michigan in free territory. The abolitionists were aroused because the Arkansas constitution prohibited its legislature from ever interfering with slavery.

On Monday, June 6, Adams took the floor to present the petitions: twenty-two from Massachusetts, Ohio and Pennsylvania. With studied deliberation—while the Southerners chafed—he summarized each one in turn:

"Memorial of George Atkinson and 94 citizens of Harrison County, Ohio, praying that Congress will take measures to obtain repeal of the Constitution of Arkansas, which allows slavery, before admitting that state into the Union.

"Petition of Francis B. Bacon and 327 inhabitants of Massachusetts, remonstrating . . ."

Speaker Polk applied the new gag rule, tabling each without further consideration, but he was powerless to cut off Adams or hurry him; the gag did not prohibit the presentation of antislavery petitions.

Since the roll call for petitions each Monday started with Maine and proceeded geographically down the list of states—Massachusetts was third, following New Hampshire—the clerk seldom reached the slave states, whose representatives also had memorials from constituents praying for various favors.

Adams went on to explain that he did not endorse the petioners' opposition to granting Arkansas statehood; he had originally approved the Missouri Compromise, hoping but doubting even then, fifteen years before, that it might solve the slavery problem. Given the opportunity again, he would not be so gullible, he said, but it was now the law and he would stand by it.

He offered an amendment to the Arkansas bill, "that nothing in this act shall be construed as assent by Congress to the article in the constitution of the state in relation to slavery and emancipation of slaves."

This brought on a disorderly debate that lasted from ten o'clock the morning of June 9 until eleven the next morning. The Southerners, led by Wise, interrupted Adams constantly with shouts of "Question?" "Point of order!" They in turn were challenged by Adams' partisans, including Briggs, Cushing and Hoar of Massachusetts and Slade of Vermont. At suppertime Adams unwrapped his slice of bread at his desk while other members drifted out to eat and drink at Gadsby's or Brown's Hotel or, more sumptuously, across Pennsylvania Avenue at Boulanger's or the Epicure House, the latter a cellar rendezvous favored for its canvasback duck.

Tempers became progressively more frayed as the night went on. Jesse Bynum, a rabid anti-abolitionist from North Carolina, and Daniel Jenifer, a new member from Maryland, quarreled and, under the Southern code, agreed to meet with pistols. Members sampled one another's flasks or slipped out to refortify themselves at nearby taverns. Twice after midnight the House, sitting as committee of the whole, lacked a quorum, and the delinquents were brought back in custody of the sergeant-at-arms.

At five in the morning, Adams made a final plea for his amendment. He spoke for three hours, sternly reviewing the details of the Louisiana Purchase, which had included the Arkansas Territory, and the Missouri Compromise and incidentally, complimenting his chief adversary, Wise. As for his other opponents: "Dromgoole [George Dromgoole of Virginia] was drunk with whiskey and Bynum drunk with slavery," he said. They "used insulting language which I demanded should be taken down by the clerk, but which the chairman would not notice."

Wise alone had the endurance to hold the floor after Adams. Although buoyantly healthy and thirty-eight years younger than Adams (he drank sparingly, rode hard and had the effortless gait of an Indian), he admitted at ten o'clock in the morning that "I am in unfit condition to continue, but, . . . so help me, God, I will persevere [against Adams] if I die by it!"

An hour later Adams' amendment was put to a teller vote, and defeated, 90 to 32; the bills admitting Arkansas and Michigan were reported favorably, and the House finally adjourned. Stephen Phillips, of the Massachusetts delegation, gave Adams a lift home in his carriage. Adams fell into bed, "much exhausted."

In the Senate, meanwhile, Henry Clay presented a memorial from Kentucky for recognition of Texas independence, and John M. Niles, a new Senator from Connecticut, offered one from his state praying for support of the "gallant Texans . . . contending for their rights against the barbarians."

The Senate Committee on Foreign Relations, to which the petitions were referred, reported back favorably. Its resolution for immediate recognition was debated before crowded galleries by Calhoun, the champion of slavery and states' rights, and Webster, defender of the Union, and Calhoun won. Jackson, however, moved with diplomatic caution—to Adams' surprise. The President let it be known that he wanted further information on the stability of the young republic before he decided.

As the first session of the Twenty-fourth Congress moved to its July 4 adjournment, it appeared to Adams that the aroused South was fastening slavery on the country more securely than ever. Its Representatives had beaten him down on the gag rule and on Arkansas, and with the White House secretly on their side, he expected they would soon bring Texas into the slavery fold despite anything he could do. But he had no intention of subsiding.

His charge that Jackson and General Houston might embroil the country in war with Mexico was arousing wide concern in the North, which was still predominantly anti-abolitionist but unwilling to fight over Texas. Benjamin Lundy's articles, on which Adams had based his charges, had been reprinted in the *Emancipator*, the weekly of the American Anti-Slavery Society. Now they were brought out in pamphlet form, and Adams ordered 100 copies, which he turned over to Abbot Lawrence of the Massachusetts contingent to distribute among the Northern Congressmen. He was amused at an editorial in the *Emancipator*:

We hold John Quincy Adams, though no special favorite of ours, in high honor for his bold and fearless defense of the

141

rights of New England and the Union while truckling politicians of the North dare not say their souls are their own. We honor him for showing the blood of his ancestors, . . . for dauntlessly meeting at the threshold the ephemeral despots of the day and for standing up almost single-handedly against advocates of gag law and chains.

The two Southern Congressmen, Bynum and Jenifer, now met on the dueling ground beside the Bladensburg Road. Adams learned that they exchanged six rounds without damage to either. On the last round, Bynum fired before the command and left himself at the mercy of Jenifer, who then had all the time he wanted to aim his smooth-bore, muzzle-loading pistol but magnanimously missed anyway.

Upon adjournment of Congress, Adams left on his annual pilgrimage back to Quincy. As usual, he stopped in Philadelphia to visit with Nicholas Biddle, still president of the embattled Bank of the United States. Biddle's neo-Grecian mansion stood on a landscaped slope beside the Delaware. A bathhouse projected out over the river, where Biddle and his house guests swam at high tide. Adams, up as always before or with the sun, found the tide out and the house on dry land. Public bathing and bathing suits were still in the future. He took off his shirt and pantaloons and trotted naked down to the water for a leisurely swim under the wide river's morning mist.

A delegation called upon him later in the day to invite him to attend a joint meeting of the Pennsylvania Society for Promoting the Abolition of Slavery and the Philadelphia Anti-Slavery Society. Adams sternly refused. "I believe the cause itself will be more benefited by such service as I can render to it in the discharge of my duties in Congress than in supporting your societies," he told them.

That day, July 11, was his sixty-ninth birthday. "With praise and prayer to God," he said, "and a solemn sense of my earthly condition, and hopes of a better world, I enter upon the seventieth year of my pilgrimage."

Benjamin Lundy, preparing to start his new antislavery publication, the *National Enquirer,* in Philadelphia, came by to ask Adams to contribute to it. He declined, but accepted an invitation to a party that evening of Quakers engaged with Lundy in the abolition movement. The party was large, men and women sitting around tea tables in the North Ninth Street home of James and Lucretia Mott, all deep in earnest discussion. (The Quakers were the only sect that permitted women an equal voice with their menfolk.) Adams thoroughly enjoyed the party. His hostess, he thought, was particularly attractive: "sensitive and lively, and an abolitionist of the most intrepid school."

His opponents in the House, where he kept his own counsel and communicated rarely even with his Northern colleagues, and then tersely, would have been surprised by his behavior that evening. He could be an entertaining, even amusing guest, and among these people whose sincerity and lack of guile he admired, he put aside his habitual reserve, joining heartily in their discussion of "the sin of slavery."

He approved their dedication to the gradual achievement of emancipation, he said, but he would not, could not join them. As a member of Congress, sent there by the voters of his Plymouth district, he was compelled to abide strictly by the Constitution, which not only condoned slavery, but made it the responsibility of the states. He thought the pamphlets and fiery oratory of the Northern abolitionists were doing the movement more harm than good. William Lloyd Garrison in *The Liberator* was giving the crusade a radical complexion by his bad-tempered attacks on the South, on the Constitution: "a covenant with death and an agreement with hell"; on the "black-hearted clergy" for not rallying solidly behind him; on the churches: the Methodists, "a cage of unclean birds and a synagogue of Satan," the Presbyterians, "the most implacable foes of God and man."

Lundy smiled his agreement. Six years before, in Baltimore, he had briefly turned over the editorship of his earlier publication, *The Genius of Universal Emancipation,* to Garrison, who had swiftly involved the paper in a libel suit and been sent to

143

jail for castigating a New England ship captain who accepted a cargo of slaves.

Asked about the gag rule, Adams discarded his affability. The House majority's action was sheer sophistry, he declared. It was ridiculous to contend that the Constitution guaranteed merely the right to present a petition, that procedure after that was up to the discretion of Congress. Petitions were entitled to proper consideration, and he would fight for that consideration to his last breath.

When he left, it was going on midnight, long past his usual bedtime. Lundy accompanied him back to Biddle's and came in "to discuss with me nearly another hour." The next day Adams was full of misgivings. Reviewing the evening, he deplored "the undue proportion of talking assumed by me, and the indiscretion and vanity in which I indulged myself."

The House majority that had forced through the gag rule might better have taken stock of *their* indiscretion. To the people of the North, proscription of the right to petition their government for redress of grievances was something that directly affected their own liberties. They might be lukewarm about the injustice of slavery, might even have been influenced to oppose abolition by the intemperance of Garrison and his followers or the prospect of free Negro migrants competing with them for a living. But there were still plenty of old men among them who, like Adams, remembered the bitter opposition to the Constitution until it included the Bill of Rights. And to the younger, it was still fresh history.

The abolition societies, led by the American Anti-Slavery Society, were quick to recognize and take advantage of the North's awakening concern. By the time Adams returned to Washington for the second session of the Twenty-fourth Congress, the 60 societies scattered through the North had increased to more than 1,000.

Canvassers, some paid by the American Society but the majority of them women volunteers, carried petitions from door to door across New England and the Middle Atlantic States. Indoctrinated by a group of dedicated evangelists known as the Seventy—missionaries from Lane Seminary at Cincinnati, early

144

hotbed of abolition—they collected signatures among village church congregations, at lonely farmhouses, from the Saturday-night customers in barbershops and country stores.

Masterminding the campaign were Adams' friend, John Greenleaf Whittier, and from the American Society the abolitionist journalist, Henry Stanton, and Theodore Weld. Of these, the self-effacing Weld was the most charismatic. A rugged, craggy-faced zealot, he had started out to be a minister, had come under the spell of the revivalist, Charles Finney, and had dedicated his life to freedom for the slaves. He took no pay for his work, only the bare expenses of keeping alive and replenishing the rough clothes he wore. He lived in an unplastered attic in the farmhouse of a Negro family two miles upriver from New York City. He accepted no titles. He wrote anonymously, even the bestseller, *Slavery as It Is, Testimony of a Thousand Witnesses,* a devastating factual indictment based on case histories which provided Harriet Beecher Stowe with much of her material for *Uncle Tom's Cabin.* He was a Grahamite, eating nothing but graham crackers and milk, bread made from unbolted flour and vegetables. He became known as "the most mobbed man in America." Gangs of ruffians repeatedly tried to break up meetings where he spoke, but he outfaced them all. And from the platform his resonant voice wove a hypnotic spell. "Logic on fire," Lyman Beecher called him. "As eloquent as an angel and powerful as thunder!"

Weld saw to it that the canvassers were effectively indoctrinated against any show of indifference or opposition. To the leaders of the campaign the most vulnerable objective was slavery and the slave trade in the District of Columbia. But if this failed to interest, there were other petitions, against annexation of Texas, or for repeal of the gag rule, or against admission of new slave states, or for abolition of the interstate slave trade.

Adams had by now made himself the undisputed champion in Congress of the right of petition, and it was through him thereafter that most of the petitions were funneled.

H E stood, a stiff little figure in gray frock coat and white
neckcloth, on the stage of the old Federal Street Theater
in downtown Boston. Behind him sat Mayor Armstrong and the
Common Council. Out front, he was pleased to notice, every
seat was occupied and latecomers lined the walls. This was
the day he had been preparing for all summer. James Madison,
the fourth President, had died on June 28, and soon after Adams' return to Quincy, a Boston delegation had called on him
to deliver a eulogy on the life and character of his old friend.

Many hours of research, of writing and revising had gone into
the speech, reaching back into the records of Madison's partici-
pation in the Continental Congress and the Constitutional Convention, his fight for the Bill of Rights and against the Alien
and Sedition Acts, his two terms in the White House, and the
sectional conflicts of the War of 1812.

For Madison's relations with Jefferson, who had made him
Secretary of State and then his successor, Adams had read deep
into Jefferson's correspondence, just published by his grandson.
To Adams, Jefferson was a devious man, anything but the self-
less idol that the Republicans, who now called themselves
Democrats, were making him out to be. Adams' father and Jef-
ferson had clashed often over policy before and during their
Administrations. John Adams had eventually made his peace

146

with Jefferson—during their last years their letters to each other had been warm with old memories—but John Quincy never would. A sentence in one of the letters from Monticello that particularly irritated him, while it pertained to John Adams, might have as readily applied to his son. "I think it part of his character," Jefferson wrote one of his friends, "to suspect foul play in those of whom he is jealous, and not easily to relinquish his suspicions."

Charles Francis had had to prune out whole pages to reduce his father's speech to two and a half hours' length. The date was September 27. Adams had driven in from Quincy that morning and changed his clothes at his son's home. From the State House the procession had marched to the theater under a darkening sky. The first hour had gone well. The only light came from the glass ceiling over the stage, but it was sufficient to allow Adams to read the precise script of his son's final copy— although he did wish Charles Francis would use better ink.

Then the storm broke. The rain beating on the skylight forced Adams to strain his voice, and still he saw hands cupped to ears in the back rows. At intervals it was so dark that he could not decipher the script at all; he had to depend on memory or to improvise. His throat burned. His voice faltered. His rheumy eyes dripped tears on the manuscript. He wondered if he would be able to finish, but he managed to go on for another hour and a half, every moment of it torture, his voice at the end a hoarse whisper.

His audience applauded loudly, although they had heard only fragments of his laboriously polished eulogy. They had come to pay homage to the last of the old regime, the little group of brave and earnest men they called the Founding Fathers. And the old former President behind the lectern was at the moment a symbol, the brittle link to that heroic yesterday.

Adams rode home sick and tired. "I must never again engage to address such an oratory," he told himself. "My voice is now gone; my eyes are in no better condition."

As requests for copies of his speech arrived from the newspapers, he realized that he had again offered himself for partisan denunciation, particularly from "the Jeffersonian school.

147

. . . It will be specially unpalatable in Virginia." This because he had defended Madison's scholarly protest against the Alien and Sedition Acts passed by Congress during John Adams' Administration, and had criticized Jefferson for his extreme hostility in advocating nullification if they were not repealed.

While this was all long ago and would seem by now academic, Adams had demonstrated that it was curiously linked to the South's confident position on slavery. Jefferson's resolution had inspired the nullification proclamation of the Calhoun states' rights forces in South Carolina. Nullification had been halted then by Jackson, but it had not been forgotten. To the slave states it was the shotgun that protected their rights. If federal legislation should ever interfere with slavery, their lawmakers could nullify that legislation, and invoke the next step if necessary: secession.

"If controversy is made," Adams concluded, "I shall have an arduous and probably a very unthankful task to perform, and I may sink under it, but . . . I will expose some of the fraudulent pretenses of slaveholding democracy. I pray for temper, moderation, firmness, and self-control; and, above all, for a pure and honest purpose; and if it so please Heaven, for success."

There were repercussions, but by the time they appeared, Adams was on his way back to Washington and interested in a more immediate issue: the coming national election.

As he traveled south, the country's growing interest in politics was in vivid evidence: torchlight parades in New York, Philadelphia, Baltimore; noisy partisan rallies. Everywhere he stopped, the topic, and not always restrained, was the qualifications of the five candidates for the Presidency. In Madison's time, such discussions had been confined to the clubs and parlors of respected citizens. The franchise had been limited to men of property. But the new Western states had changed that, giving the vote to all male citizens provided they were white and twenty-one and over; the Eastern states had had to conform. Now everybody felt he had an equity in the November election. The most discussed candidate was the Democrats' nominee and Jackson's protégé, Martin Van Buren. The leading Whig appeared to be General William Henry Harrison, the hero of the Battle of Tippecanoe, now living quietly in Ohio.

After Adams left Massachusetts he found little support for Daniel Webster, which did not displease him. Actually, he felt, all the candidates were "at most third-rate men—men whose pretensions rest neither upon high attainment nor upon eminent service, but upon intrigue and political speculation."

For the first time, slavery played a part, although small, in a national election. Garrison in his *Liberator* and the abolitionist press in New York denounced Van Buren, charging he had assured the Southern Democrats he would not tamper with their "institution." Unfortunately, none of the Whig candidates, even Boston's Webster, was supporting abolition, so they had no substitute to recommend. The local abolition societies, meanwhile, kept their sights on the drive for petitions to Congress.

When Adams got back to Washington, the pile of scrolls delivered to him from the post office was by far the largest it ever had been. He methodically unwrapped and entered them in his ledger: name and address of the sender, the date it was sent, the number of names inscribed. Mainly their prayer was for abolition immediately in the District of Columbia. Some came from as far away as Michigan, Ohio, and Maine. Several, he was delighted to discover, were from the Massachusetts twelfth congressional district, his own Plymouth constituency.

The early snow did not keep him from resuming his solitary morning walks. In the past he had occasionally crossed paths with another early riser, Jackson, on horseback, both the President and former President staring sternly ahead. But now the old soldier was keeping to his bed chamber. Adams learned he had been coughing blood again and was more emaciated than ever. The House met on December 6 and sat for an hour and a half, while the clerk read the President's final State of the Union message. To Adams it "teemed with glorification upon the prosperous condition of the country, with a considerable spice of piety." He wondered how much longer prosperity would last. In New York and Philadelphia he had found prices soaring and the merchants straining for credit. Hard money had become scarce since Jackson's Specie Circular in midsummer, directing that settlers' payments for the government's vast western lands must be made in gold or silver.

Jackson's pronouncement on Texas was more to Adams' liking. The President reiterated that Congress should postpone recognition until the new republic was firmly established. Adams did not have to be reminded that his speech had played a signal role in that decision.

Returns were now in from the states and revealed that Van Buren had won the Presidency. The tabulation gave him 170 electoral votes, William Henry Harrison of Ohio a surprising 73; Hugh Lawson White of Tennessee, 36; Daniel Webster, 14, and William P. Mangum of North Carolina, 11. Webster had carried only his home state of Massachusetts, and that by a bare fifty-five percent. When Jackson defeated Adams, the total vote had been 361,120. This year it was 1,498,205.

The two halls of Congress immediately provided the capital's best entertainment and the country's liveliest reading. In the Senate, Jackson's one-time gun-brawl opponent and now bosom friend, Thomas Hart Benton, pleaded long and eloquently to expunge from the Senate's *Journal* Henry Clay's resolution of two years before censuring the President for removing the government's deposits from the Bank of the United States. As always, Benton, next to Adams the most erudite man in Congress, staged a good show.

In the House, Adams' counterirritant, Henry Wise, took angry issue with the President's message, particularly the passage praising the executive departments for "their prosperous condition and the ability and integrity with which they have been conducted." Integrity, indeed! said Wise, reminding his audience that the departments had been staffed by the "spoils system" of rewarding the faithful. He proposed the appointment of a select committee to investigate their operation.

Wise had Adams' talent for savage ridicule and a carefree readiness to use it. He hoped that "he who conquered the conquerors of Napoleon at New Orleans . . . may live long to witness the effects of his errors [while] in his 'palace of power.'" Jackson's message, he said, was "vanity and egotism, sophisticated nonsense." It was "the worst as well as the last annual message which Jackson ever wrote."

On Monday, January 9, Adams started presenting his petitions for abolition in the District. The first, from Dorchester, Massachusetts, was signed by 150 women, "wives and daughters of my immediate constituents." He told the House he hoped their supplication would be respectfully received and referred to the Committee on the District of Columbia. This, he assured the members, was all he asked: that their right to petition their government not be "treated with contempt as at the last session [when] all discussion, all freedom of speech, all freedom of the press on this subject [had been] violently assailed in every form in which liberties of the people can be assailed." He knew many of the petitioners personally. To the son of Abigail Adams they were "a class of citizens as pure and as virtuous as the inhabitants of any section of the country."

The Southerners tried to stop him, led by Thomas Glascock of Georgia, who demanded that Adams' motion to receive the petition be tabled. He wasn't interested in the "purity and virtue of the signers," Glascock said contemptuously. "Their petitions are creating an excitement which ought to be put down."

Francis Pickens of South Carolina invoked the Pinckney gag and was quickly challenged by Adams. That rule, Adams declared, had died with the last session. Speaker Polk was uncertain. Adams quoted the *House Manual,* and in the argument Polk called him to order several times for his biting asides, but the House supported the old statesman. Now, Adams continued, he had a petition from 228 women of South Weymouth, "and as part of my speech I intend to take the liberty of reading the petition."

Glascock shouted an objection. The House rules specified that the contents of a petition had to be briefly summarized. Adams' penetrating voice cut through Glascock's: " 'Impressed with the sinfulness of slavery and keenly aggrieved by its existence in a part of the country over which Congress—' "

Henry Pinckney of South Carolina, author of the previous gag, rose to a point of order. "Has the gentleman from Massachusetts a right under the rules to read the petition?"

Polk was struggling to remain judiciously calm in his black morocco armchair. "The gentleman has a right to make a statement of the contents of the petition," he said.

"But has he the right to read the petition?"

"I am reading the petition as part of my speech," Adams retorted. "I take this to be one of the privileges of a member of the House. At the time my friend from South Carolina—"

Polk ordered him to proceed with the contents of the petition.

"I am doing so, sir," said Adams.

"Not in the opinion of the Chair," Polk told him.

"I was at the point of the petition: 'keenly aggrieved by its existence in a part of the country over which Congress possesses exclusive jurisdiction in all cases whatever—' "

Cries of "Order!" "Order!" came from all parts of the hall. Adams' dry voice rose.

" 'Do earnestly petition your honorable body—' "

John Chambers of Kentucky cut in with a point of order. Adams ignored him.

" 'Immediately to abolish slavery in the District of Columbia—' "

"Mr. Speaker! Mr. Speaker! A point of order!" Chambers yelled.

"The gentleman from Massachusetts will take his seat," Polk ordered.

Adams' words came faster and sharper: " 'And to declare every human being free who sets foot upon its soil.' "

The House was in uproar. Polk, calm no longer, pounded his gavel and pointed it at the former President.

"Take your seat!"

Chambers stated his point of order: House Rule 45 provided that in presenting a petition a member should state briefly its contents. "Can the rule be evaded by any gentleman who chooses to read the petition as part of his speech?"

Polk consulted the rules and decided the petition should not be read.

Adams appealed to the House. Could it afford to support a decision establishing that a member should not have the right

152

to read what he chose? "I have never heard of such a thing. If this practice is reversed, let the decision stand upon the record, and let it appear how entirely the freedom of speech is suppressed in this House. If the reading of a paper is to be suppressed, so help me, God, I will only consent to it as a matter of record."

He went on, "The petition is only five lines, so I cannot give verbally a more brief statement of its contents than the petition itself gives." Picking up the scroll again: "The petitioners 'respectfully announce their intention to present the same petition yearly before this honorable body, that it may at least be a memorial in the holy cause of human freedom.' "

This brought a renewed outburst. By now only the members sitting near Adams remained at their desks. The others were clustered in the aisles and in the well, the Southerners gesturing and calling furiously for the Speaker's attention. Polk finally managed to quiet them and accepted a motion to receive the petition. It was voted. Then Charles Haynes of Georgia moved that it be tabled. Adams demanded that it be sent to the Committee on the District. The House voted to table it.

Adams was immediately up again, this time with a petition from forty inhabitants of Dover, Massachusetts. The debate carried into the next day. A motion by John Davis, an opposition member from Indiana, for suspension of the rules to vote on restoring that Pinckney gag was narrowly defeated by the slavery coalition's failure to have the required two-thirds majority in attendance.

Adams' Dover petition was still the unfinished business of the House the next Monday. By then the Southerners had their ranks on hand, and Albert Hawes of Kentucky offered a resolution to reestablish the gag. Adams fought back furiously, his face livid to the fringes of his white hair, knuckles pounding the desk. ("A bruiser, an old roué who cannot live on slops but must have sulphuric acid in his tea," was how Ralph Waldo Emerson saw him at times like this.)

In a rasping peroration he denounced "this mockery, to receive petitions, then refuse to hear them read." He went on, "For aught I know, ere long any member who should dare to raise his voice on abolition of slavery will be expelled from this House. Sir, I am ready to be that member whenever the House shall come to that decision."

He was still virtually alone. The resolution carried, 129 to 69, and of the Northern members who voted nay not one had come close to joining the battle by his side.

The Democrats and anti-emancipation Whigs now had a new name for Adams. The New York *Times,* voice of that city's merchant society, headed an editorial "The Massachusetts Madman":

> Monday is playday for Mr. Adams in the House of Representatives, and our readers may expect in every report of Monday's proceedings an account of time wasted and business deferred through the waywardness and obstinacy of this strange being. Petulant, irascible and exhibiting almost childish obstinacy, he makes himself an object of pity and a laughing stock to the House.
>
> [He] ought to retire to his paternal Braintree, . . . his slippers and nightcap. . . . His years, his services, his undoubted talents do not avail . . . to save him from derision. . . . His infirmities of temper are such that they who know him best attribute his course less to the independence he boasts of, less to a conviction that he is right, than to mulish obstinacy and wrong-headed determination to have his own way. . . . He permits no man to be his political friend. . . . Well has he been called "The Massachusetts Madman." He boasts that he places all his glory in independence. If independence is synonymous with obstinacy, he is the most independent statesman living.

The Albany *Argus,* organ of the Van Buren hierarchy in New York State, promptly echoed the *Times.* "If there is a single American citizen who doubts the application of the phrase, 'The Massachusetts Madman,' to John Quincy Adams," it said, "we beg leave to refer him to the congressional proceedings."

James Paine of the Boston *Advocate* clipped the editorials and mailed them to Adams. "I am not an abolitionist in the remotest degree," Paine wrote, "but am in favor of free discussion." Adams thanked him warmly and tucked the clippings in his letter book. His mornings were occupied in writing a long report to his Plymouth constituents, telling them why and how he was fighting for the right of petition. He wanted them to understand that he did not intend obstructionism, as his enemies charged, but was defending the Constitution against the growing arrogance of the slave states. The fireplace in his study drew poorly, and frequently the embers from the night before were cold when he arose these predawn winter mornings. He still used his tinderbox in preference to the new friction matches with their phosphorus stink (as he favored old-fashioned goose quills over the new steel pens) and, rather than waste time building a fire, he ended his morning walks at his desk in the House.

A young Washington correspondent arrived there early "on a dreary morning in January" and found him sitting alone under the gray skylight of the empty hall, wrapped in his greatcoat, writing. The journalist, an Old Colony man himself, knew better than to interrupt the former President. He walked silently to the reporters' table and went to work on the speech he was copying and polishing for a congressional client. After a while, Adams appeared beside him. "You are a very industrious young man," he said.

"I cannot keep pace with you, sir," the reporter answered, "for I found you already here when I came in."

Adams looked up at the glass ceiling, still thinly washed with daylight. "I believe I was a little early, sir."

Washington's interest at the time was focused on Benton's campaign to expunge the censure of Jackson from the Senate *Journal.*

"Do you think the expunging resolution will be disposed of today?" the young journalist asked.

"Oh, certainly. And [it will pass] by a decided majority. I hope so, at least. It has already absorbed more time than should have been devoted to it."

But how, the reporter asked, could the Senate get around the constitutional requirement that Congress keep a correct and complete journal of its proceedings?

"The Constitution is a sacred document," Adams answered.

155

"There are some men . . . who make a great parade of their devotion to"—with sarcastic emphasis—"*the dear Constitution, who nevertheless are perfectly reckless of its violation if the ends of party are to be accomplished.*" As for the expunging, he went on, it was simple—a procedure established by the British Parliament during the reign of James I. Black lines were drawn around the resolution, a diagonal line through it, and "Expunged" written across its face. Thus the *Journal* remained physically intact.

Late that afternoon the reporter found Adams standing outside the bar of the Senate, listening to the debate. At nine that night the debate was still on (the resolution was passed the next day) , and he met Adams leaving the Senate chamber.

"I am somewhat weary," Adams said. "I think I shall go home."

They walked together down the dark steps of the Capitol into a raging snowstorm. The snow was a foot deep in Pennsylvania Avenue and the reporter looked in vain for a hansom cab. He asked if he might accompany the old gentleman on the mile walk to his house.

"I need not the service of anyone," Adams told him. "I am somewhat advanced in life, but not yet, by the blessing of God, infirm." He quoted, his voice piercing the wind:

> "For in my youth I never did apply
> Hot and rebellious liquors in my blood."

The reporter watched him "draw his Boston wrapper closer around him, hitch up his mittens and with elastic step stride off into the darkness."

The long letter Adams had been composing that morning went into the mail a few days later, addressed—as many more were—"To the inhabitants of the twelfth congressional district of Massachusetts." The Quincy *Patriot* would receive and publish it, and the other village newspapers of the district would follow. So would *The Emancipator* in New York, and in good time Hezekiah Niles would reprint generous extracts in *Niles Register*. So, although national wire services were still far in

156

the future, Adams kept his constituents and a good part of the country informed of his fight for his convictions.

The restored gag categorically tabled all antislavery petitions without their being either referred or read. But it could not bar their presentation. On January 23 "The Massachusetts Madman" had the floor again and announced he had several petitions from New Hampshire containing 900 signatures. He added gratuitously, "It has been said that in New Hampshire there was no one in favor of the abolition of slavery, but this is—"

The entire New Hampshire delegation, including the future President, Franklin Pierce, was on its feet, shouting "Order!"

"Much confusion," observed the factual *Register of Debates*.

"The gentleman from Massachusetts is out of order," Polk told him.

"I bow with submission, sir."

But a moment later he was detouring the gag rule again. This next petition was from "137 citizens of Plymouth. . . . Yes, sir! From the spot where our forefathers landed, from the land of the Pilgrims. I hope the House will allow it to be read. . . . Its contents will make a deep and salutary impression."

Instead, there was another chorus of protests and a stern ruling by the Speaker: "The petition will not be read!"

Not even the great actor, Edwin Forrest, could register pleased surprise better than Adams did as he glanced over the petition he picked up next. Surely, he exclaimed, here was one he should be permitted to read. Signed by fifty-four ministers and members of the Lutheran Church of New York, it called on Congress to secure to the inhabitants of the District of Columbia the protection of the law and the rights inherent in the Declaration of Independence. He assured the House, "There is nothing about slavery or abolition of slavery in it. I move it be referred to the Committee on the District of Columbia and that it be printed."

Polk suspected Adams was again employing evasive tactics. Although a Southerner and slaveholder, Polk was a man of moderate principles and attempted to rule objectively. He was convinced Adams was as interested in promoting abolition, within the precepts of the Constitution, as he was in the right of petition.

"The gentleman from Massachusetts knows the contents of the petition," he said, "but the Chair does not. If the petition relates to slavery, it must be laid on the table."

Said James Parker of New Jersey: "The only way to arrive at the nature of the petition is to read its contents."

"But the order of the House declares the petition should not be read," Adams protested.

"Then," said Polk, "the gentleman admits it relates to slavery."

"I do not admit any such thing. I have presented the petition in the form required by the rule, by giving a brief statement of its contents."

Polk asked to see the petition.

"In my opinion it falls clearly within the meaning and intent of the resolution," he said.

Pinckney interrupted, "Half the states are eternally prevented from presenting their petitions by the discussion on this subject," he complained. He moved the previous question.

"How can the previous question be taken," Adams asked, "without the House knowing on what it is to be taken?"

Polk said it was "on the memorial presented by the gentleman from Massachusetts."

"And what is that memorial?"

Polk told him to take his seat. "The gentleman has no right to propound such a question."

The House was in disorder again. William Shepard of North Carolina, unable to get Polk's attention, shouted that "Southern men are compelled to sit and hear their constituents insulted, and the House denies them all opportunity to reply."

Samuel Hoar, a quiet-mannered member of the Massachusetts delegation so far rarely heard from, got the Speaker's nod. "I ask that the petition be read in order that I may understand on what I am about to vote."

"It would be out of order," Polk told him.

"Will it then please the Chair to tell me on what I am about to vote?"

The Speaker finally gave in. Adams triumphantly read the petition. In truth, it never mentioned slavery. Instead, it appealed to Congress "to pass such laws as justice and the character of our nation require . . . to secure their inalienable rights [for] more than six thousand inhabitants of the District . . . deprived of all personal rights . . . by others to whom they are said to *belong as property*."

The House loudly voted to table the petition while Adams sat smiling at his desk.

James Mercer Patton was a member of one of the first families of Virginia. He was tall, good-looking, forty, a prosperous lawyer and solid family man, a moderate Democrat. His seat was next to Adams'. On February 6 the former President's desk again held a stack of petitions. Patton tried several times to get a look at them, but Adams had them covered with other papers. When Massachusetts was called, Adams announced he had thirty petitions to present. Each was peremptorily tabled. He came to the twenty-ninth. This one, he announced, was from "nine ladies of Fredericksburg, Virginia," praying like the others for abolition in the District.

A petition from *ladies of Virginia?* It seemed impossible!

"I will not name them," Adams said, "because from the disposition prevailing in the country I do not know what might happen to them."

The petition appeared genuine, he said, but whether it was or not, he felt it was his duty to present it.

The majority quickly voted to table it.

Now, Adams said, he had another petition from Fredericksburg on which, before he presented it, he wanted the decision of the Speaker. "It is a petition from twenty-two persons declaring themselves to be slaves. I wish to know whether the Speaker considers such a petition as coming within the order [gag rule] of the House."

A crescendo of rumblings. Polk tapped his gavel. He could not tell, he said, until he had the petition in his possession.

"If the paper is sent to the clerk's table, it will be in the possession of the House," Adams protested. "I wish to do nothing except in submission to the rules of the House. This paper purports to come from slaves. . . . It is signed partly by persons who cannot write [and] make their mark and partly by persons whose handwriting would manifest they had received the education of slaves. . . . I will send it to the Chair."

Joab Lawler, a preacher from Tuscaloosa, Alabama, jumped up. "I object to its going to the Chair! I want it to appear on the *Journal* that I objected!"

Polk said the circumstances were so extraordinary that he would take the sense of the House. But before he could do so, Charles Haynes, a country doctor from Georgia, was up, shouting mad. He was astonished "that the gentleman from Massachusetts or any other gentleman should ever make a question on a paper of this kind."

"I call the gentleman from Georgia to order," Adams answered, "on the ground that he is making personal reflections."

Haynes, cautioned by Polk, said, "I will not trust my feelings to pursue the subject further under its present aspect." Breathing hard, he sat down.

Dixon Hall Lewis of Alabama demanded the House "punish severely such an infraction of its decorum and its rules. . . . I call on the members from the slaveholding states to come forward *now* and demand the punishment of the gentleman from Massachusetts. . . . If the House will inflict no punishment for such flagrant violation of its dignity, it would be better for the Representatives of the slaveholding states to go home at once!"

Julius Alford of Georgia said, "The moment it [the petition] is presented I shall move, as an act of justice to the South, that it be taken from the House and burned."

"Along with the member who presented it!" a compatriot shouted.

Patton of Virginia had meanwhile gone to the clerk's table and was examining the petition from the "ladies of Fredericksburg." He announced indignantly that "the name of no lady is attached to that paper." Fredericksburg was his home town, he said. He recognized only one name and that was "of a free mulatto of the worst fame and reputation.

John Quincy Adams.

John Quincy Adams in 1847. The last life portrait. Engraved from a daguerreotype by Mathew Brady.

Mrs. John Quincy Adams.
Portrait attributed to
Charles Bird King.

*Courtesy of the Smithsonian
Institution National Collection
of Fine Arts*

Charles Francis Adams at
the age of twenty-two.
Portrait attributed to
Charles Bird King.

*Photograph by George M.
Cushing. Courtesy of the
Adams National Historic Site,
U.S. Department of the Interior*

A contemporary artist's sketch of the Quincy Mansion in the years when John Quincy Adams came home to it from Congress for the summer months.

Adams' Washington swimming hole. The bank
of the Potomac below the White House in the
early 1830's. Engraved from a sketch by W. H.
Bartlett.

CASH FOR 500 NEGROES, INCLUDING both sexes, from 12 to 25 years of age. Persons having likely servants to dispose of, will find it to their interest to give us a call, as we will give higher prices, in Cash, than any other purchaser who is now, or may hereafter come into the market. PRANKLIN & ARMFIELD,

mar 8—d&ctf. Alexandria.

CASH FOR 300 NEGROES.—The highest cash price will be given by the subscriber for Negroes of both sexes, from the ages of 12 to 28. Those wishing to sell, will do well to give me a call, at my residence, or at A. Lee's Lottery Office, five doors east of Gadsby's Hotel. Letters addressed to me, through the Post Office, shall receive the earliest attention. WM. H. WILLIAMS,

feb 25—dtf Washington.

CASH FOR 400 NEGROES, including both sexes, from twelve to twenty-five years of age. Persons having servants to dispose of will find it to their interest to give me a call, as I will give higher prices, in cash, than any other purchaser who is now in this market.

I can at all times be found at the MECHANICS' HALL, now kept by B. O. Sheckle, and formerly kept by Isaac Beers, on Seventh street, a few doors below Lloyd's Tavern, opposite the Centre market. All communications promptly attended to. JAMES H. BIRCH,

feb 29—dtf Washington City,

the 5th day of March
cluded from all benef
Given under our ha

mar 7—w3w

POWER'S A ring the years Esq. in two vols.

The Rev. William ness of God, as manif their history, habits, a copper-plate engravin The American Jou Feb. 1836. Subscrip Just received l

mar 4

DRAKE'S P EMS.—New day received from De

Also, beautiful edit pears, Croker's editi riety of the most sple

mar 14

"Children for Sale!" was the way Adams
angrily described advertisements such as these
which appeared regularly in the Washington
newspapers. From the March 28, 1836, issue
of the *Daily National Intelligencer*.

The House chamber in Adams' time, now Statuary Hall. An attendant lights the thirty oil lamps in the great brass chandelier for an evening session.

Samuel F. B. Morse's "The Old House of Representatives" in the collection of the Corcoran Gallery of Art

Cinqué, the capable young leader of the *Amistad* captives. Painted from life by Nathaniel Jocelyn of New Haven.

The capture of the schooner *Amistad* off Montauk Point, Long Island, August 26, 1839. Painted by an unidentified artist of the time. The United States coastal survey brig *Washington* (at left) bears down on the schooner, while a Mendi landing party trades with local citizens for water and food (lower right).

The Adams Mansion at Quincy, Massachusetts, as it appears today.

The Adams study in the Quincy Mansion. It is far more orderly today than it was when John Quincy Adams occupied it.

"It is regrettable," he went on, "that the gentleman from Massachusetts did not think it proper to permit me to see that paper before he presented it." He reiterated that the mulatto signer was "a woman of infamous character." The others, he believed, were free Negroes, all bad.

But it was the slaves' petition that had the House in uproar. Polk tried to get his hands on it, but Adams now refused to send it up to him.

Waddy Thompson of South Carolina ended an angry outburst by suggesting that a District of Columbia grand jury ought to indict Adams for the crime of inciting slaves to rebellion. "There is a point at which forbearance ceases to be proper," he shouted. "The sanctuary of age is not lightly to be violated, but when the sanctuary is used to throw poisoned arrows, it ceases to be sacred."

The supporters of slavery were convinced that Adams had finally exposed himself to retribution. They descended on him: Wise and James Bouldin of Virginia, Lawler and Lewis of Alabama, Jenifer of Maryland, Haynes of Georgia—and Churchill Camberleng and Francis Granger of New York joined them.

Abijah Mann, Jr., a former justice of the peace and village postmaster in Herkimer County, New York, almost thirty years younger than Adams, looked benignly across the desks at him. "It becomes us to respect his gray hair, his old age, his long public services," he expostulated, "and to excuse if possible the obstinacy and ebullitions of temper he so often exhibits." A pause. "Would it be charitable to attribute it [Adams' behavior] to disappointments of individual ambition? Seeking revenge? . . . Attempting to ruin that which he could not rule?" Another, longer pause. "It would be unjust to believe that in the prime and vigor of manhood the honorable gentleman would adopt the course of action which at this late period of his life seems to control him."

Adams let that pass as if he hadn't been listening. He did not have to be reminded that he was old and burdened with infirmities. But at the moment, assailed from all sides, he had never felt more vigorously alive. He listened silently while Thompson offered a resolution to call him to the bar of the House for censure, and Haynes amended it because he declared it wasn't strong enough, and Lewis amended it to make it still stronger.

The debate raged undiminished through the next day. The resolution as finally phrased read that "John Quincy Adams, a member from the state of Massachusetts, by his attempt to introduce into the House a petition from slaves, for the abolition of slavery in the District of Columbia, committed an outrage on the rights and feelings of a large portion of the people of the Union; a flagrant contempt upon the dignity of this House; and, by extending to slaves the privilege belonging only to freemen, directly invited the slave population to insurrection; and that the said member be called to the bar of the House and be censured by the Speaker."

Virginia's Patton tried to caution his colleagues not to move too fast. While the memorial from the Fredericksburg women had been included in the censure resolution, the signers, he pointed out, were free Negroes. As for the petition from the slaves, he warned that "neither the one fact nor the other assumed in the resolution" might be true. But they refused to listen. Adams gave him a quizzical look, remembering that Patton had shown a strange interest in the petitions on his desk the morning before.

Shouts of "Expel him!" "Expel him!" pelted the old warrior as he stood up. He addressed himself to Patton.

"Let the petition be as the gentleman from Virginia has stated, from free Negroes—prostitutes, as I suppose, for he says there is one such on the paper and he infers that the rest are of the same description."

"I did not say they were prostitutes," Patton protested. "As for the infamous character of the women in question, I wish to wipe away the stain from the *ladies* of Fredericksburg, as these women have been called 'Ladies of Fredericksburg' by the gentleman from Masssachusettts."

"I am not sure whether I called them 'Ladies' or the petition so stated," Adams answered. "I am not in the habit of using that term. The word 'woman' is much dearer to my heart."

Glascock hurried to the clerk's desk and picked up the petition. Triumphantly he pointed to the notation on the back. It was endorsed, he announced, in Adams' handwriting: "From nine ladies of Fredericksburg."

Cries of "Order!" "Order!"

Adams spoke louder. "I do not know that they are infamous, as the gentleman has said."

"I did not say that I knew these women," Patton, now as agitated as his colleagues, called to the Speaker.

"I am glad to hear the honorable gentleman disclaim knowledge of them," Adams answered, "for I had been going to ask: if they are infamous women, who was it that made them infamous? Not their own color but their masters. I have heard it said in proof of that fact, and I am inclined to believe it is the case, that in the South there exists great resemblance between the progeny of the colored people and the white men who claim possession of them. Thus, perhaps, the charge of infamous might be retorted on those who made it, as originating from themselves."

That brought the Southerners loudly out of their chairs. "Great confusion," said the *Register of Debates*, which used the term sparingly.

By now the Washington dailies, particularly the *National Intelligencer*, were reporting the debate in detail, and the newspapers around the country were following as quickly as the horse-drawn mails permitted. To Adams' detractors who scoffed at his dedication to the right of petition his challenge now came with the jarring clarity of an anvil clang:

The character of the "ladies of Fredericksburg" did not concern him, he said. "Where is your law which says that the mean and low, and the degraded, shall be deprived of the right of petition? . . . Where in the land of the freemen was the right of petition ever placed on the exclusive basis of morality and virtue? Petition is supplication. It is entreaty. It is prayer. And where is the degree of vice or immorality which shall deprive the citizen of the right to supplicate for a boon or to pray for mercy? Where is such a law to be found? It does not belong to the most abject despotism. There is no absolute monarch on earth who is not compelled by the constitution of his country to receive the petitions of his people, whoever they may be. The sultan of Constantinople cannot walk the streets and refuse to receive petitions from the meanest and vilest in the land. That is the law even of despotism."

Thursday afternoon the debate, which had begun Monday morning, was still on. Adams' voice was beginning to crack, but he was otherwise in top form, parrying, dodging, stabbing slaveholder sensitivities to the quick. "He possessed," said Rufus Choate, "the instinct of the wild animal for the jugular," and Choate, one of Massachusetts' great trial lawyers, was with him in Congress.

As the House finally prepared to vote on the censure, Adams addressed the Chair.

"I suppose I shall not be struck dumb by the previous question before I have the opportunity to say a word or two in my own defense. But, sir, the gentlemen are consuming the time of the House in such a manner that I think the obligation rests upon me to modify their resolve, . . . so that when I come to the bar I may not, in one word, put an end to their resolution.

"The gentlemen who have such a laudable zeal for the slaveholding portion of the confederation charge, first, that I attempted to present a petition from slaves, and, second, that that petition was for their emancipation from slavery. I did not attempt to present the petition. . . . I said I had a paper, purporting to be a petition from slaves. . . . I asked the speaker whether he considered such a paper as included within the general order of the House [the gag rule] that all petitions relating to slavery should be laid on the table."

Now, Adams played his incendiary trump card: "As to what the petition was for. If the House should choose to read the petition, . . . they would find it . . . the reverse from that which the resolution states it to be. My crime has been for attempting to introduce the petition of slaves *that slavery should not be abolished!*"

The petition was clearly a hoax, aimed at discrediting Adams; but instead he had deftly contrived to embarrass the Southerners with it. Adams believed it had been drafted by a Fredericksburg slavemaster who had compelled his slaves to scrawl their signatures or crosses on it, and that Patton had been forewarned.

Waddy Thompson, the fiery young South Carolina nullificationist, expressed the indignation of the proslavery faction. "Is it a mere trifle to hoax, to trifle with the members from the South on this subject?" he demanded. "Is it a light thing for the amusement of others to irritate almost to madness the whole delegation from the slave states?"

The censure resolution was withdrawn and a new set of *Resolves* hurriedly drawn up:

> 1. That any member who shall hereafter present any petition from the slaves of this Union ought to be considered as regardless of the feelings of the House, the rights of the Southern states, and unfriendly to the Union.
>
> 2. That slaves do not possess the right of petition secured to the people of the United States by the Constitution.
>
> 3. That the Hon. John Q. Adams, having solemnly disclaimed all design of doing anything disrespectful to this House in the inquiry he made of the Speaker as to the petition purporting to be from slaves, and having avowed his intention not to offer to present the petition if the House was of the opinion it ought not to be presented—therefore, all further proceedings in regard to his conduct do now cease.

Adams was as inflexibly opposed to the new resolutions as he had been to the previous one. The third made it appear that he had apologized for his action. He had not. The Democrats were now weary of the whole proceedings. Aaron Vanderpoel of New York, a Democrat from Van Buren's Kinderhook, moved the previous question to cut off further debate. Adams asked him to withdraw it. "I would like an opportunity for a full hearing in my own defense," he said.

Another Democrat, William Kennon of Ohio, tried to put an end to the embarrassing subject by moving to table it. But for the first time in his petition battle, Adams had a majority of the members on his side. They voted, 144 to 50, against tabling. The chandeliers had been lighted, but a Southern move to adjourn was also defeated.

The resolutions were called up separately. The first one, denouncing any member who presented a petition from slaves, was defeated, 104 to 92. The second was passed over to take up the resolution on Adams. He was on his feet, angry and defiant. "I here say that I have not done one single thing that I would not do over again in like circumstances. Not one thing have I done that I have not done under the highest and most solemn sense of duty."

Only 21 members voted for the resolution, and 105 against. It was a tremendous victory for Adams, who had started out with the House almost solidly against him.

At the same time, he did not miss the significance of the ballot on the first resolution. Only 15 Democrats from the Northern states had voted with their Southern colleagues to proscribe petitions from slaves. On slavery, sectional sentiment had proved stronger than party loyalty.

The second resolution came up two days later, and was overwhelmingly carried, 163 to 18, although Adams reiterated that petition was the privilege of all mankind, "under God." The slaves still had no rights.

The country's dailies and weeklies had kept their readers informed on Adams' latest battle, shaping their accounts to their editorial policy. The Southern press fumed. To the anti-abolitionist papers in the North it was another example of the "Massachusetts Madman's" outrageous behavior. The abolitionists sent the old former President warm letters of praise for his humanitarian courage. Another letter, from Pittsburgh, Pennsylvania—the first of many such that he was to receive—bore a hand-drawn letterhead: "Vengeance is Mine, says the South" and a raised arm holding a hunting knife. Signed "Dirk Hatteraik," it warned that the sender "and others" were on their way to Washington to drag him from his seat in the House and lynch him. Adams filed it along with the friendly letters and continued his early-morning walks through the sleeping streets of the capital. He had something more important to worry about.

The republic of Texas, having voted overwhelmingly to join the United States, had sent an aggressive diplomat, William

Wharton, as minister to persuade the Administration, first, to recognize the new republic, as Congress had authorized, and then to start proceedings to annex it. Wharton and Waddy Thompson, who had led the fight for recognition of Texas in the House, were frequently seen together. What concerned Adams more was that Wharton appeared to have ingratiated himself with Jackson's Secretary of State, John Forsyth, and his Secretary of War, Lewis Cass. Rumors came to Adams that Jackson was preparing to act. On March 3, Jackson's last day in office, the rumors were confirmed; Jackson announced, to the delight of Wharton and the despair of the Mexican minister, Gorostiza, that the United States recognized the government of Texas.

⇉ XI ⇇

UNTIL the Jackson period the White House had been a second home to John Quincy Adams—first as a young man whose mother, Abigail, had hung the family wash in the East Room, then for eight years in and out of it as Monroe's Secretary of State, and the next four years as President himself. During Jackson's eight years he had not once entered the gates. Now that Van Buren was in residence, he returned to pay a courtesy call.

The new President greeted him warmly in his upstairs sitting room, the room where Jackson, ailing but unbent, had spent most of his days these last years, smoking his long-stemmed old Powhatan pipe, the bowl resting on his crossed knees, while he consulted with Taney or Kendall or Van Buren and then firmly spoke his own mind.

Except for wear, the years had made little change in the mansion. The furniture was still the delicate Hepplewhite and Sheraton that Monroe had bought; now, with the trend to massive design, it was conspicuously old-fashioned. Spring had arrived, and although the windows were open and a breeze from the Potomac worried the curtains, the room still smelled of Jackson's Indian pipe and the cigars of his conferees.

Adams had heard that Van Buren was showing the strain he was under, but the President appeared buoyant and relaxed.

They talked of the oppressive climate. Adams reminded Van Buren that the Potamac was just down the back walk, and the old sycamore was still there on the bank, under which he, while President, had shed his clothes whenever he felt like it and gone for a refreshing swim upstream and back; nothing like it, he assured the President, to take the sludge out of your blood. They asked about one another's families. Van Buren, a widower, had his two sons with him, John, the eldest, serving as his secretary. Adams revealed his concern for Louisa. She drifted from one illness into another, worried unreasonably about trivial matters: that the new coachman, being an Irishman, might not live up to his respectable recommendations; that the grandchildren weren't eating properly. "The conversation," Adams said, "was . . . not at all upon the public affairs of the country," the one subject absorbing both of them.

The two men could never be intimate, but they respected one another's abilities—Van Buren, the alert statesman and politician, party man, devotee of Andrew Jackson, and Adams, the crusty Puritan and political iconoclast. Adams thought Van Buren had many of the qualities of James Madison, "his calmness, his gentleness of manner, his discretion, his easy and conciliatory temper." But the resemblance stopped there. "Madison," Adams remembered, "had none of his [Van Buren's] obsequiousness, his sycophancy, his profound dissimulation and duplicity. In the last of these he much more resembles Jefferson, though with very little of his genius. The most disgusting part of his character, his fawning servility, belonged neither to Jefferson nor to Madison."

Even as they talked, the country's economy was collapsing, the young nation falling into its worst depression. Along with the Whigs, Adams blamed Jackson's monetary policy: his feud with Biddle's Bank of the United States, his transferring the government's funds to selected state banks—"pet banks"—and finally the Specie Circular. The Democrats blamed the runaway speculation in government lands, and the state banks for overextending their loans and printing paper money beyond their capacity to redeem it.

The country had never been so prosperous as during the last

three years of Jackson's Administration. Everyone had been getting rich, at least on paper—everyone except the hard-pressed laboring class and members of the New England landed gentry like Adams. The population of New York, now the largest city, had escalated from 125,000 to more than 300,000 in the twelve years since the Erie Canal had opened a water route into the Northwest, to wilderness trading posts and stockades that had since mushroomed into cities: Chicago, Cleveland, Detroit, Buffalo. Other canal companies—the Chesapeake and Ohio, Louisville and Portland, Ohio and Erie—were mapping or digging water roads into the interior. And now the railroads were beginning to link the seaboard cities. Adams no longer had to sit cramped and frozen all day or night in a stagecoach between Boston and Providence. Now he could make the trip in a few hours, and the railway coaches were warmed by wood-burning stoves.

Land values had doubled and tripled in a few years, sometimes in a few months, as speculators moved into developing areas of the interior and syndicates mapped out "paper cities" on the new routes. Along with most of long-settled New England, Quincy did not share in the burgeoning prosperity. "Amidst the enormous rise in almost every other man's property," Adams wrote his son Charles, "mine seems to be everywhere declining. . . . I most earnestly wish that I could sell any part of my property to pay off all these debts."

Before he could leave Washington for the summer, Charles, as manager of Adams' 900-acre estate in Quincy and Weston, was asked to "contrive in some manner . . . to raise a sum of two or three thousand dollars to pay my current debts here and . . . my expenses in reaching home." His Washington income during the winter had barely met half his needs, he said. He listed it as "my pay [as a member of Congress] and one half year's dividends of the Franklin Insurance Company and a quarter's rent of the house in Sixteenth Street."

His most immediate need was for $1,000 to pay off a one-year loan from his former manservant, Antoine Giusta. The curious friendship between the statesman and his one-time valet dated back to 1814, when Adams was negotiating the

Treaty of Ghent in Belgium. Giusta, a native of Piedmont in northern Italy, had been conscripted into Napoleon's army and had deserted after the retreat from Moscow. Adams found him, a destitute wanderer in the Flemish countryside, and took him to London with him when he was subsequently appointed minister to the British. There the family hired a young English housemaid, and the two servants came with them when they returned to America. They were married in the White House and ran the staff there during Adams' Presidency.

In the informal Adams household Giusta was more companion than valet to the dour and solitary President. He accompanied Adams on his morning walks, swam with him in the Potomac. One day the two got into a leaking boat to row across the river and swim back. Adams' son, John, stayed on the bank, intending to swim across and bring the boat back. In midstream a squall upset the boat. Giusta was naked but the President had on his shirt, pantaloons and hat. His loose-fitting sleeves filled with water and almost dragged him down. He handed his hat to Giusta and struggled on, and with a final assist from Giusta, reached the shore. John swam across and, while the President and his son sat naked on the bank, Giusta put on Adams' wet pants and crossed the Long Bridge to bring the carriage and dry clothes.

When his term as President ended, Adams could no longer afford to keep the Giustas and persuaded Jackson's entourage to keep them on in the White House. But after two years they left, telling Adams they "could not stand his [Jackson's] slaves and his savage temper." With their savings they opened an oyster and coffee house in the capital, which was so successful that by the time they retired they were quite well-to-do. When, later on, Adams' debts became pressing, it was Giusta to whom he turned for help. Over the years his old servant had rescued him once with a loan of $3,000 and twice more with $1,000. Now the last note was four months overdue.

Charles managed to send him a draft for the necessary funds, although he wrote that it had not been easy; his father would have to watch his expenditures more carefully. Some of their tenants were falling behind in their rents. Business was slow;

171

prices were still high. Coal had gone up from $6 to $10 a ton in two years, flour from $5.62 a barrel to $12, pork from $10 a hundredweight to $19.25.

Although Charles had shared the concern of the New England conservatives over the soaring cost of living and the splurge of speculation, neither he nor they had fully realized the precariousness of the country's prosperity. The reversal had begun with a drought and crop failures in the middle states that had forced the farmers to renege on the improvement loans their banks had so willingly advanced. Simultaneously, a commercial house in London had failed, and the creditors had called in their American loans. Overproduction of cotton in the newly opened interior brought a sharp decline in its price. A few days after Van Buren became President, a large cotton firm in New Orleans folded, the first of a series of such failures. The state banks, including those which had been receiving the government deposits, could no longer collect on their loans. As demands for specie to meet commitments rose, the inflated paper currency got the well-deserved names "shin plasters" and "rag money."

On his way back to Quincy for the summer, Adams saw the depression panic in full flower. The day he was visiting Van Buren, a run had started on the big Dry Dock Savings Bank in New York, a crush of frightened depositers, mostly working people, drawing out their savings in specie. The run spread to the Bank for Savings, the Bowery and the Greenwich Savings Bank. Two days later the Dry Dock closed, its specie exhausted. The others soon followed.

Runs drained the inadequate hard money in the Banks of Baltimore, Philadelphia and Boston. In Philadelphia, Nicholas Biddle tried desperately to keep his Greek temple on Chestnut Street solvent, but succeeded only in holding out a few days longer than his smaller competitors. As Adams traveled up the seaboard, the cities wore a look of suspended animation. Business houses were locked. Groups of jobless men stood silently in the streets. In New York a hungry mob had sacked a flour warehouse. Militia with stacked arms occupied City Hall Park.

Except for the horse-drawn omnibuses on Broadway, there was little traffic.

For a while his reception at home took Adams' mind off the disaster Jackson's Democracy had met. A committee from the Massachusetts House of Representatives formally presented him with a gold-headed cane made, symbolically, from a timber of the frigate *Constitution,* the "Old Ironsides" of the War of 1812. Their spokesman read a proclamation praising his lonely struggle against the gag rule and the annexation of Texas to slave territory.

Subsequently, the villages of Quincy and Scituate honored him at mass meetings. For his surprising defense of their right to be heard, the women of South Weymouth feted him and Louisa at an elaborate picnic, the tables on the shaded green laden with spit-roasted beef and lamb, pit-baked beans, lobster salads, greens from their kitchen gardens, preserves and fruit pies.

Louisa, who for years had not shared her husband's public appearances, was polite but withdrawn. Among these stolid New Englanders, with their blunt ways, their spare talk and stern convictions, she would always be an outsider. She returned with relief to her needlework frame and John's widow, Mary, and to the two grandchildren for whom she had composed one of her little musical poems, "My Bluebell and My Rose":

> Geraniums rich in fragrancy
> With lilacs sweet combine.
> The morning glory's brilliancy,
> The creeking eglantine,
> The heartsease and the lily rare,
> The daisy blushing glows.
> Who could with flowers like this compare
> My bluebell and my rose?

But Adams thoroughly enjoyed the picnic. "I look to the women of the present age with the feelings of a father," he told his beaming hostesses from the pinnacle of his seventy years.

But he was not immune to the stimulation of a handsome figure or a piquant Puritan face. He heartily thanked the women for their approval. "The stake in question," he told them, "is your right of petition, your freedom of thought and action, and the freedom of speech in Congress of your representative."

While none of the speakers at these gatherings had mentioned emancipation, Adams believed the opposition to it in his district was shrinking. Morally, his Puritan constituents shared his abhorrence of "the sin of slavery." But socially and economically they were still not ready to share their freedom with Negroes. He was still "walking on the edge of a precipice." In time the United States must join Great Britain and the southern republics in ending slavery. In time. He hoped it would be by congressional amendment of the Constitution and not, as he feared, by civil war.

Meanwhile, the antislavery leaders' agitation for immediate abolition was unrealistic and, consequently, was inflaming public opinion in the North as well as the South. Adams urged his neighbors to stop petitioning Congress for abolition in the District of Columbia, since it was impractical under the Constitution. Far more important now, he told them, was the South's determination to annex Texas to the Union. If this great territory, ten times larger than Kentucky, were admitted as a slave state, the Southern economy and representation in Congress would be so strengthened that slavery might never be abolished.

Given its millions of acres of new cotton, sugar and tobacco land and its natural harbors on the Gulf of Mexico from which to ship to the English market, the South would become so self-sufficient that it could break away from the Union. The immediate peril, he warned again, was war with Mexico, since its government had not conceded the independence of Texas. Did they want to fight a war of aggression for the extension of slavery to a territory where a foreign power had already abolished it?

To Adams' family it was apparent that he was getting more deeply involved than ever in the conflict with the South and its supporters. Charles Francis and Mary joined Louisa in insisting that he respect his venerable years and stop his quixotic joustings against entrenched majorities. Failing, they called on influential friends for help. They tried—"some of the dearest friends that I have upon earth,"said Adams—with no more effective results. He was already being as restrained as his nature permitted.

If he needed moral support, it came at this time from the Quakers of neighboring Rhode Island. The Rhode Island State Anti-Slavery Society presented him with an embossed scroll proclaiming its "high approval of the conduct of John Q. Adams during the last session of Congress, . . . when other Northern representatives were recreant in . . . their high trust, and that he is . . . entitled to our thanks for . . . advocating the right *of the slave* to beg for mercy."

Adams was corresponding frequently now with Whittier. "My position," he told the poet of abolition, "makes it necessary for me to be more circumspect than belongs to my nature. . . . It [abolition] is the most dangerous of all subjects for public contention. In the South, it is a perpetual agony of conscious guilt and terror attempting to disguise itself under sophisticated argument and braggard menaces. In the North, the people favor the whites and fear the blacks. The politicians court the South because they want their votes. The abolitionists . . . kindle the opposition against themselves into a flame; and the passions of the populace are all engaged against them. . . . It behooves me well to consider my ways."

He asked Whittier not to doubt his motives in refusing publicly to support his cause, "for I had much rather you should impute to me great error of judgment than the smallest deviation from sincerity."

All the while, he was keeping a weather eye on the economy. In Boston 108 mercantile firms had gone bankrupt since the first of March. New York estimated the cost of its failures to date at more than $100,000,000, New Orleans at $27,000,000. An angry meeting of Boston businessmen in Faneuil Hall called on the government to repeal the Specie Circular. If it did not, they proclaimed, the hard-money law should be resisted, "peaceably if . . . possible, forcibly if . . . necessary. At any rate, it should be at all hazards resisted."

A Committee of Fifty representing the leading merchants of New York asked Van Buren to call the new Congress into special session to invoke relief measures; particularly, they wanted the Bank of the United States rechartered and the Specie Circular repealed. Adams read in the Whig newspapers of Boston that they returned dejected. Van Buren had listened to them, polite as always but noncommittal, and told them to put their demands in writing.

The delegation doubted that "the justice of our claims or the severity of our suffering will induce the Executive to abandon or relax the policy which has produced such desolating effects."

Little was being said about the working people whose jobs had vanished and whose suffering intensified daily. By now all the banks had stopped paying out specie. Since the paper currency they had issued and pledged redeemable in hard money was virtually worthless, so were the people's savings. The state legislatures of New York and Virginia supported the banks and their stockholders, absolving them for the time being from penalties prescribed for suspending specie payment.

Charles Francis was thinking of writing an article on the currency crisis for the *North American Review*. He tried to discuss it with his father, but all he got was evasions. The old statesman was having a struggle with his conscience. His supporters were the Whigs of his district, and the Whig party was making political capital of the panic, blaming it entirely on Jackson's "gold humbug" and denouncing "Little Van" as his sycophant. As Adams had written to Biddle, "I have received intimations that . . . we must be governed by parties and that . . . all political conduct must be accommodated to the main object of party pursuits. . . . I scarcely know what to reply. . . . I have made moral principles and not party or selfish purpose the standard of my conduct throughout my political life, and there is too little of the stake left that I can lose for me now to turn round and become a mere partisan."

And now this same old and trusted friend, Biddle, had reneged on his pledge to support his bank's paper money with specie.

Late in June, Adams received a challenging letter from William Foster, a philanthropic Boston merchant and leader in the young Workingmen's party—and a Democrat. Foster asked him, as "a person so sure of commanding attention," to state for publication his conclusions concerning the crisis, pointing out that "the public should be put in possession of your views." Adams took his time formulating a reply. In the meantime, he had received notification from Washington that Van Buren was calling the new Congress into special session on September 4. Reports were coming to him that the President was determined to retain the hard-money policy, and that he wanted to divorce the government from the banks and set up a separate depository for its funds.

Typically, he did not discuss the letter from Foster with his family, who, he knew, would have wanted him to ignore it. His reply appeared in the Democratic Washington *Globe* on August 1, and his Whig compatriots were furious.

First, Adams suggested "that Congress exercise its power to regulate the currency. But," he added, "they must do this (which they will not) without consulting banks, their presidents and directors. The legislatures of New York and Virginia have already shown what the presidents and directors of banks will advise."

His second suggestion sounded like a complete endorsement of Van Buren's reported plan. He would "detach the government from all banking and deal in nothing but the precious metals. If Van Buren is made of stuff to go through with this operation," he added, "I wish him well."

Then he turned on the bankers, and Nicholas Biddle was not excluded. "What is the suspension of specie payment," he wrote, "but setting the law of property at defiance? If the president and directors of a bank have issued a million bills promising to pay five dollars to the holder of each and every one of them, the suspension of specie payment is by one act the breach of one million promises.

"What is this but fraud upon every holder of the bills, and what difference is there between the president and directors of such a bank and the skillful artist who engraves a bank bill, a facsimile of the bill signed by the president and directors, and saves them the trouble of signing it by doing it for them?

"The only difference that I can see in the two operations is that the artist gives evidence of superior skill and superior modesty. It requires more talent to sign another man's name than one's own and the counterfeiter does at least his work in the dark, while the suspenders of specie payment brazen it in the face of day and laugh at the victims and dupes who have put faith in their promises."

He was roundly denounced by the Whig newspapers. In Washington, the *National Intelligencer* declared he was just not dependable. The Boston *Sentinel and Gazette* termed his letter "poor, base, slanderous," and accused him of puddling in the "dirty waters of *Locofocoism*," the radical wing of the Democratic party. It suggested he might rather, because of his years, be treated with pity than contempt.

Adams returned to Washington alone, leaving Louisa and the family to wait till the weather cooled there. Again a formidable stack of petitions had accumulated in his absence. A large proportion now, however, were directed against the annexation of Texas. Although the special session was supposed to be limited to solving the financial crisis, Adams maneuvered to present a good share of the petitions, to the outspoken annoyance of Virginia's Henry Wise who, the New York *Evening Post* observed, was never silent "except when forced to be so by an organic disease."

Van Buren's proposal that the government establish a sub-Treasury system—in essence, a federal bank—to receive and disburse its funds, passed the Senate but failed in the House by the narrow margin of 119 to 107. Adams approved the plan in principle, but he voted against it because the department would be operated by political appointees under the Secretary of the Treasury. The session was a failure, its only accomplishment the authorization of a $10,000,000 issue of Treasury notes to meet the immediate needs of the government. As for the depression, it was left to run its course into the early Forties.

In spite of the oppressive heat, the session had its moments. In the Senate, Daniel Webster and John Calhoun thundered at one another over Texas. By now, Webster declared, it was known "that annexation of Texas by the United States has become the subject of communication between the two governments. Freemen must make their voices heard." Calhoun retorted angrily that Northern agitation against the South's "peculiar institution" would, if persisted in, "destroy the Union."

And in the House John Quincy Adams made an extemporaneous speech on "Nouns, Pronouns, Verbs and Adverbs."

Churchill Camberleng, the corpulent Democratic whip and chairman of the powerful Ways and Means Committee, was presenting a bill to adjust the government's claims upon the delinquent deposit banks. Adams protested that the language was imprecise and asked Camberleng to explain it.

The perspiring New Yorker answered impatiently. At that late hour, he said—they were in evening session—"I cannot waste my time discussing nouns, pronouns, verbs and adverbs with the gentleman from Massachusetts."

"As language is composed of nouns, pronouns, verbs and adverbs," Adams retorted, "when they are put together to constitute the law of the land, the meaning of them may surely be demanded of the legislator, and those parts of speech may well be used for such a purpose. But if such explanation be impossible, it certainly should not be expected that this House will consent to pass a law composed of nouns, pronouns, verbs and adverbs, which the author himself does not understand."

The bill, which proposed that the deposit ("pet") banks be charged interest on balances due the Treasury, was so worded, Adams charged, that it provided no penalty for delinquency. "When that bill came from . . . the Treasury," he said, "it came with fraud upon its face!"

Camberleng's attempts to call him to order were stifled in shouts of "Go on!" And Adams proceeded to use the parts of speech to arraign the whole Jackson–Van Buren banking program as politically motivated to build up patronage in the Southern and Western states. Although the bill was adopted on a strictly party vote, the Whig press cashed in on Adams' speech.

In the fall election in Camberleng's New York State the Whigs won in all thirteen senatorial districts and the entire Whig ticket carried New York City.

The day after his speech, and the eve of adjournment, Adams had members of the Massachusetts delegation to dinner. For the past three years, he remarked, he had been unable to entertain—"one of the choicest enjoyments of this life to me"—because of Louisa's frequent illnesses and "embarrassments in my pecuniary concerns." Moreover, "the state of feeling between a large portion of the delegation [from Massachusetts] and me [had usually] deprived me of the . . . desire to associate with them at convivial meetings." But this rare moment couldn't be passed up: "I happen to be again upon terms of good understanding and good fellowship with them all. . . . It may be the last time."

Congress adjourned the next day, October 16, not to meet again until December, but Adams' time was now fully occupied with sorting and indexing the petitions that were "flowing in upon me in torrents." Whittier, who had originated the petition campaign, could hardly have foreseen its tremendous expansion this summer. The American Anti-Slavery Society, with Whittier, Weld and Henry Stanton in command, now had local units in nearly every county in the Northern states. Their volunteers, most of them women, stopped the farmer plowing his field, his wife and daughter at their chores, the woodsman and waggoner and tin peddler. They invaded the village barbershop, the hay-and-grain and general store; attended camp meetings, county fairs and log rollings, armed with not one petition but four or five, sent them from the New York headquarters: for abolition of slavery and the slave trade in the District of Columbia, against annexation of Texas, against the admission of Florida Territory as a slave state, to forbid slavery in all the territories, to abolish the interstate slave trade.

Often they were rebuffed by their men, but the women, whose social life, what there was of it, centered in the village church, its Friday-night prayer meetings, suppers, picnics and quilting bees, were ready converts. The petitioners were well indoctrinated. No less a personage than the former President of their

180

country, as God-fearing and devout as any of them, they pointed out, supported their cause in the Congress. For those who had not read of his warning that the slavemasters would go to war for Texas, they had the gist of his speech memorized. That it was only their right of petition and not emancipation of the slaves that Adams was fighting for was conveniently ignored by the doctrinaires in the New York headquarters.

The petitions were sent to the county centers, from where they were mailed to Washington, to the Congressman for the district or one of the state's Senators, or both, if they were sympathetic, which few of them were; and if not, they went to Adams.

Considering the deluge in his Senate office, Kentucky's Henry Clay wondered "whether the feeling of abolition is not becoming mixed up with other matters—such, for instance, as the belief that the sacred right of petition has been assailed."

No one knew that better than Adams. But now his attention was absorbed by an incident in the capital itself that poignantly demonstrated the whole tragedy of Negro bondage. The *National Intelligencer* for October 21 carried at the top of its front page an advertisement:

SALE OF SLAVES

I will sell at public auction, on Monday the 23rd of October the following slaves, purchased by me from Rezin Orme, and who were warranted sound in bodies and in mind, to wit, Dorcas Allen and her two surviving children, aged about seven and nine years (the other two having been killed by said Dorcas in a fit of insanity as found by the jury who later acquitted her). . . .

(signed)
JAMES H. BIRCH
EDWARD DYER

Nathaniel Frye, Adams' brother-in-law and manager of the family's little flour mill on Rock Creek, was sitting across the breakfast table. Adams asked if he knew anything about the case. Frye clearly did, but was reluctant to discuss it. A Washingtonian accustomed to slavery as a way of life, he preferred not to get involved in its unpleasant details. The notice, he said, had appeared once before on an inside page. Prodded by Adams, he said the woman had been given her freedom by her dying mistress some fifteen years before. She had married one of the waiters at Gadsby's Hotel, and they had raised four children.

The husband of her dead mistress had remarried and since died. His widow had married the Rezin Orme named in the notice. Orme had discovered that the former slave woman had failed to get a certificate proving her freedom, and he had taken her and her four children away from her husband and sold them to Birch and Dyer for shipment south.

Why had the court acquitted her of murdering her children? Adams asked. Frye didn't know. Probably because she was a healthy specimen, physically at least and, with the present high price of slaves, a valuable commodity. Frye hoped his brother-in-law would leave the matter alone. To present abolition petitions in Congress was one thing, but for a Northerner to interfere in a slave case here in the South was perilous, not only for himself but for his family.

"It is a case of conscience with me," Adams answered, "whether my duty requires or forbids me to . . . ascertain the facts and expose them in all their turpitude to the world."

He folded the newspaper under his arm and was off. As usual, it was to his diary that he confided his distress. This was a flagrant example of the slave trade callously going on in the very capital of the nation, and of its inhuman consequences. "The prohibition of the slave trade," he wrote, "is within the constitutional power of Congress. . . . Were there in the House one member capable of taking the lead in this cause of universal emancipation, I would withdraw from the contest, which will rage with increasing fury . . . to its crisis, but for the management of which my age, infirmities and approaching end totally disqualify me. There is no such man in the House."

At the office of the *National Intelligencer*, William Seaton, the editor, was also unwilling to say much about the case. It was an unfortunate situation, he said, but he thought nothing could be done about it. Since the Negro woman had no certificate to prove her freedom, she was legally still a slave, and her children were slaves. Orme had a perfect right to claim and sell them to the slave auctioneers.

Adams went to the courthouse and called on the judge in the case and the district attorney, Francis Scott Key. The woman was a sturdy animal, Key told him, but highly emotional. She had made a terrific scene, wailing and struggling, when Birch's men took her and the children away from her home. Birch had locked them in a cell in the slave prison until he could sell them. That night the attendant had heard the children cry out and had entered the cell to find she had already cut the throats of the two younger ones, a boy of four and a baby girl, and was about to kill the other two, both girls, nine and seven years old. As he struggled with her, she slashed savagely at her own throat. The judge said she had shown no remorse at her trial, only grief for the two who were still living. The younger ones, she believed, were safe in Heaven.

The matter-of-fact attitude of the judge—and to a lesser degree of Francis Scott Key, too, a man of gentle nature, an ardent churchman—was typical, Adams thought, of the Southerners toward the black race. The woman was a chattel. She had killed her children in a temporary fit of insanity. Otherwise, she was sound. So why execute or imprison her and deprive the auctioneer of his investment? Key added that the woman's plight was not completely hopeless. Her husband had the right to buy back his family. In fact, he said, a retired Army man, a General Walter Smith, of Georgetown, was trying to help the Negro waiter raise the money.

On succeeding days Adams visited the woman in her solitary cell, talked with her husband and, briefly, with the auctioneer, Birch. He consulted with General Smith and called on the mayor of Washington, Peter Force. He found the Negro woman beyond consoling, "weeping and wailing most piteously." The auctioneer was to Adams typical of his breed, a swarthy, bull-necked "man-robber." Since the case was arousing such prestigious concern, the slaver grudgingly agreed to forego any profit and return the woman and children to the husband for the amount he had in them—$475.

By then the Negro husband and father, Nathan Allen, was appearing almost daily at Adams' house, saying little, the brooding look in his eyes speaking eloquently for him. General Smith could not afford to underwrite the entire amount, which the Negro had pledged himself to pay back out of his waiter's salary, but Allen had the confidence of a child in Adams' ability to come to the rescue. The most General Smith could supply was $330. The $145 difference was more than Adams could afford to contribute. By stretching his resources he could come up with $50, which he promised. It was more than he earned in a week while Congress was sitting.

Adams searched into the background of the case with General Smith. He learned that Gideon Davis, the first husband of Orme's wife, had died insolvent and his estate had never been administered. So Orme had no right to sell the woman and her children; they had belonged to the creditors of Davis' estate. Who were those creditors? Francis Scott Key told him there was only one: the corporation of Washington. Then bring a habeas corpus action to make the slave auctioneers surrender the family, Adams demanded. Key said he doubted the city corporation would support such a move.

Adams said he would bring the action himself. What good would it do? Key asked. *They would still be slaves.* Besides, he warned, any such maneuver by Adams would be "stigmatized as mean and [Adams' italics] *dishonorable.*" He would bring down upon himself the full, and possibly violent, hostility of the slaveholders and slave traders in this Southern city. He reminded Adams of what had recently happened to the abolitionist editor, the Reverend Elijah Lovejoy, in Alton, Illinois. His attacks on slavery had so infuriated the local citizenry that they had smashed his presses three times and finally had murdered him.

"Such is the condition of things in these shambles of human flesh," Adams wrote in his diary that night, "that I cannot now expose this whole horrible transaction but at the hazard of my life." That alone would not have deterred the old crusader. But reflecting upon the greater issue, abolition, he knew he had gone "as far as the public opinion of the free portion of the country will bear, so far that scarcely a slaveholding member of the House dares to vote with me upon any question." Until now the people of his home district had supported him, "but one step further and I hazard my own standing and influence there, my own final overthrow, and the cause of liberty itself for indefinite time, certainly for more than my remnant of life." He could not "bereave the man-robber of his spoils."

But the next day Nathan Allen was back on Adams' doorstep, and with him was his wife! They were overjoyed. The promise Adams had made to help them had persuaded others to contribute, Allen announced, and he had already bought his wife's freedom. The two girls were still in the jailhouse, but with Adams' check he would have the whole amount and they, too, would come home. Adams immediately made out a draft on his Washington bank for $50 and told Allen he wanted to inspect the bill of sale from the auctioneers: there should be no slip-up this time. Watching them hurry away down the street, he felt greater satisfaction than he had in days.

⇒⇒⇒ XII ⇐⇐⇐

B Y the first regular session of the new Congress in December
of 1837 there was hardly a house in Washington that could
have accommodated the antislavery and anti-Texas petitions
inundating Adams; least of all, his modest home on F Street.
Many of his treasured books had to be packed off to Quincy.
Even so, he wrote his son Charles, his study was so crammed
that "I have no space to walk from the table to the fireplace and
from the fireplace to the door."

The country had never witnessed anything like the campaign
now under full headway; and it was no longer the strictly mas-
culine American Anti-Slavery Society that was the propelling
force, but the women of the North. The Society's dedication to
immediate emancipation had created friction with more tem-
perate abolitionists in its local units. The reluctance of the rural
chapters to take orders from and contribute to the expensive
upkeep of the headquarters, with its weekly newspaper, its
propaganda campaigns, its paid workers, was weakening the organization. At the propitious moment a pioneer feminist had
stepped in. Lucretia Mott, a dynamic middle-aged Quaker from
Adams' home state, had organized the Female Anti-Slavery Society and dispatched her followers to concentrate on the women
petitioners and swell their number. While they were not in
opposition to the American Society, the woman workers were

strictly independent of it; and they sent a resolution to Adams, thanking him for defending "so wisely and so well the right of women to be heard in the halls of legislation."

Adams had the petitions carted to the Capitol, where they soon filled to the ceiling an antechamber thirty by twenty feet and fourteen feet high. Since this Congress had not yet renewed the gag rule, he moved that the new petitions for abolition in the District be referred to the Committee on the District of Columbia, together with those of "upward of 50,000 signers" that had been tabled at the special session. This brought a quick and noisy protest from the Southerners. Wise demanded that they all be tabled again, and was supported, 135 to 73.

The anti-Texas petitions got identical treatment. In the Senate, meanwhile, Webster, who was as opposed as Adams to annexation, presented the duplicate petitions sent to him, and they, too, were tabled after an angry warning by Calhoun that refusal to take in Texas *as a slave territory* would violate the states' rights under the Constitution.

Now resolutions from state legislatures arrived in the House. Rhode Island prayed that Congress not degrade the United States in the eyes of the world by usurping a foreign territory for the restoration of slavery. Vermont and Ohio followed, and Michigan. At the same time, the legislature of Tennessee sent a strongly worded resolution demanding annexation, and so did Alabama, its preamble scolding "the well-meaning but misinformed females of some of our sister states."

Five days before Christmas the Southern delegation in the House withdrew to a committee room to organize their counteroffensive against Adams. The next day John Patton of Virginia presented the new gag resolution they had drawn up: "That no petitions relating to slavery or the trade in slaves in any state, district, or territory of the United States shall be read, printed, committed, or in any manner acted upon by the House." In the roll-call vote, Adams responded to his name by declaiming again that the resolution was "a violation of the Constitution, of the right of petition . . . and of my right to freedom of speech as a member of this House." The response, he said, was "a perfect war-whoop of 'Order!' "

The gag was reinstated, 122 to 74. By the same tally the House then quickly tabled the Texas resolutions of *both* the Northern and Southern states. This was perfunctory treatment for proposals from legislative bodies, but the anti-abolition majority was determined not to let Adams explore the issue further in debate.

Although he had no friends in the Administration, Adams did not miss much that was going on. He saw that Memucan Hunt, the new minister plenipotentiary from Texas, had ingratiated himself as successfully as his predecessor with members of Van Buren's Cabinet. Hunt appeared supremely confident. It was said that the Georgian slaveholder and Secretary of State, John Forsyth, had assured him the Administration favored annexation and was only waiting for Northern resistance to subside, and that Joel Poinsett of South Carolina, the Secretary of War, had observed that the Administration was merely moving with diplomatic caution. "There is," an informer wrote Adams, "a great deal of Texas influence about the President."

Adams was sleeping more poorly than usual these nights. Overshadowing his conviction that annexation meant war with Mexico was the growing fear that it would cause eventual dissolution of the confederation. Senator Calhoun was again warning that Northern agitation against both Texas and slavery, "the spirit of fanaticism which daily increases," would "by and by dissolve the Union."

While Van Buren gave every appearance of wanting to leave the question of annexation to Congress, both the information Adams had received from Lundy and his own instincts convinced him that the President was secretly maneuvering with the Southerners in his Cabinet to bring it about; Van Buren was "in conspiracy with the slavocrats." It went along with his pledge to them in his inaugural address that he was determined "to resist the slightest interference with it [slavery] in the states where it exists." Until now, Adams had been on friendly terms with Van Buren; he had called on the President a second time shortly before Congress reconvened and spent an amiable half hour discussing, among other safe subjects, England under her new queen, eighteen-year-old Victoria. "Youth at the prow," Adams said, "and pleasure at the helm." But on New Year's Day he pointedly stayed away from the reception at the White House. "I have found it necessary," he said, "to assume a position toward him and his Administration which forbids me from any public exhibition of personal courtesy which would import a friendly feeling."

That Van Buren was actually conspiring with the South is not supported by the history of the period, any more than Adams' belief in Jackson's duplicity. But a critical issue was at stake, and Adams was never for half measures. Surely, his forebodings were correct about war with Mexico and eventual Southern secession.

In the quiet of his study he worried about his progressive involvement in the slavery conflict. Without his lonely championship of the people's right of petition, he knew, the factional controversy would not have grown as it had by now; Texas would not have become so important; slavery would not have been seriously challenged, at least in his lifetime. Now the conflict appeared to be getting out of hand. Mob violence was growing, as demonstrated by the murder of the abolitionist minister, Lovejoy, for trying to publish his little newspaper on the Illinois border of slave territory: "the first American martyr to freedom of the press," Adams called him. Louisiana was determined now to drive all free Negroes out of the state—although no other Southern state would admit them—following an attempted insurrection for which ten slaves and three free blacks had been hung. Even in the House, the Southern leaders, particularly Wise and Dromgoole of Virginia and Waddy Thompson and Hugh Legaré of South Carolina, were noticeably more belligerent.

"I am under deep agitation of mind," Adams wrote, ". . . meditating upon the course proper for me to pursue hereafter; upon the moderation which reason and Christian charity and sound policy all concur to prescribe, and from which the unruliness of my temper so often urges me to depart; and upon the firm and daring spirit which a sacred sense of duty enjoins upon me as equally indispensable to the cause almost exclusively committed to my trust."

189

His intentions were always toward moderation but, like the ruthless business tycoon who is the soul of gentleness at home, his combative nature took over in the arena. When he next presented a large batch of anti-Texas petitions, Benjamin Chew Howard of Maryland, the chairman of the Committee on Foreign Affairs, moved that they be referred to his committee, which had a preponderance, six to three, of slaveholders. Adams instinctively attacked.

"In the face of this House and the face of Heaven," he shouted, "I avow . . . that the annexation of an independent foreign power [Texas] to this government would be *ipso facto* a dissolution of this Union. The question is whether a foreign nation, a nation damned to everlasting fame by the reinstitution of that detested system of slavery after it had once been abolished within its borders, should be admitted into union with a nation of freemen. For that name, thank God, is still ours!"

The Texas revolution, he declared, had been primarily a rebellion against Mexico's efforts to enforce abolition in the territory. The Southerners shouted to Speaker Polk to silence him. Polk ruled him out of order, but Adams defied him. "The time for this discussion must come," he went on against the uproar. "I do not think it will be forever smothered by the previous question to lay it on the table, and all the other means and arguments by which the institution of slavery is wont to be sustained from this floor—the same means and argument, in spirit, which in another place have produced murder and arson. This same spirit which led to the inhuman murder of Lovejoy in Alton, Illinois—"

A Democrat from that state now called him to order. Polk waved his gavel at Adams and shouted, "Sit down!" Wise of Virginia was never one to back away from a fight, but he stepped in quickly now; under his leadership the majority tabled both Howard's motion and all the anti-Texas petitions. The slaveholders, it was apparent, were not going to let Adams expose to the country the danger inherent in the Texas question. In the meantime Adams had had time to cool off; he took his defeat with surprising good grace, and waited. The Administration forces, he felt certain, would be able to muster enough votes in both the House and Senate in favor of annexation while the gag rule prevented him from using his petitions to turn the tide. But he thought he saw in Howard's move a solution for himself.

At this time the Southern code of honor provided a tragic interlude. During a speech in the House, Jonathan Cilley, a young Representative from Maine, charged that the editor of the New York *Courier and Enquirer,* James Watson Webb, had accepted a bribe for giving favorable publicity to the Bank of the United States. Webb, who had a reputation as a trouble-maker, was in Washington at the time and wrote to Cilley challenging him to a duel. The first two men he asked to deliver the message to Cilley guessed at its contents and refused. He then approached William Graves, a thirty-two-year-old Whig Congressman from New Castle, Kentucky. Graves asserted afterward that he had innocently agreed to deliver the letter and had been as surprised as Cilley when he discovered it contained a challenge. Although they were from different sections of the country and political opponents (Cilley was a Jackson Democrat), their relationship was friendly. Both were married and living with their children in the tight little boarding-house circle of the capital; both were scholarly and members of the bar in their home states; Cilley was serving his first term in the House, Graves his second.

Cilley rejected the challenge. His remarks on the House floor, he reminded Graves, were privileged. Moreover, he did not consider the editor Webb a gentleman, and so was not obliged to answer him. Graves took the word back to Webb. Although a Southerner, he knew little about the dueling code. Henry Wise and some of his other elders from the South sternly informed him that he had in turn been insulted by Cilley: in disparaging Webb, Cilley had implied that Graves would carry a challenge from someone not a gentleman. Graves went back to Cilley and asked him to issue a public statement saying this was not his intent. Cilley at first agreed, but on reflection apparently decided this was carrying the nonsense too far. He came from pioneer stock—his family had been prominent in

191

the Revolution, and Andrew Jackson was one of young Cilley's heroes—and it was not in his nature to yield meekly to any man. When Graves, prodded by Wise, sent him a challenge, he accepted and, since the choice of weapons was his, named rifles.

The two men met in a field beside the Marlboro Pike across the border in Maryland early on the morning of February 24. When a housemaid told Graves' wife that she had heard he had gone to fight a duel and that his opponent in rifle practice the day before had put eleven balls into a target the size of a man's hand, she grew hysterical. Curiously, although he had grown up in Kentucky, Graves had little experience with a rifle. Henry Clay, who lived in the same boarding house, heard Mrs. Graves' screams and tried to comfort her while they waited.

Out on the snow-crusted field, Henry Wise, Graves' second, and General Jones of Wisconsin, for Cilley, both experienced duelists, had paced off eighty yards and stepped back with cocked pistols to shoot either contestant if he flinched. On the first round, both Cilley and Graves missed. Cilley assumed that their personal courage had been demonstrated and that settled the matter, but Wise and General Jones insisted they try again. To the surprise of Cilley's second, who had witnessed his marksmanship the day before, he missed again, and so did Graves. Wise was still not satisfied. The flintlocks were loaded a third time. When they fired, Cilley staggered, clutched his stomach and dropped. He died in a few minutes.

Official Washington was shocked. From the Hermitage, the old duelist, Jackson, wrote deploring the "murderous death" of his young friend. The Supreme Court indicated its disapproval by refusing to attend Cilley's funeral. Petitions arrived in Congress demanding it outlaw dueling in the District. Northern members attempted to bring Graves and Wise to the bar of the House on criminal charges. Adams argued against it. Although he was bitterly opposed to dueling, he insisted that punishment for a capital crime belonged in the courts and not the House. But when Samuel Prentiss of Vermont introduced an anti-dueling bill in the Senate, Adams immediately became its co-sponsor in the House. As enacted, the Prentiss-Adams Law provided ten years' imprisonment for anyone giving, delivering or accepting a challenge in the District of Columbia if either party was killed, five years if no one was injured, and three years for assaulting a person who refused a challenge.

Wise lamented that now a gentleman could call another a liar and "there will be no fight."

"I maintain the contrary," Adams answered, ". . . for the independence of this House, for my own independence, for the independence of the members of the Northern section of this country, who not only abhor dueling in theory, but in practice; in consequence of which members from other sections are perpetually insulting them on this floor, under the impression that the insult will not be resented. . . . I am not willing to sit any longer here and see other members from my own section, or those who may be my successors here, made subject to the law of the duelist."

All this while, Adams had continued to present the petitions flooding his desk. On a single day, February 14, he had presented 350, containing some 35,000 signatures, against Texas and slavery. They were all tabled under the gag rule. At last a document arrived that promised the opening he had been waiting for: a resolution from the legislature of his home state opposing annexation of Texas. When George Briggs of the Massachusetts delegation presented it, Adams moved that it be referred for study and report to the Committee on Foreign Affairs, the same committee dominated by six slaveholders that had tried to get the other Texas petitions. The Southerners took the bait. Howard, the chairman, promptly had the other state resolutions, both for and against annexation, and all the petitions on Texas taken from the table and turned over to his committee for disposal.

The committee, Adams knew, would have to make a report, and it was his hope that he could get the floor then and circumvent the gag rule. He had to wait until the middle of June, only three weeks before adjournment. The majority report, presented by Dromgoole of Virginia, declared that, since no proposal for annexation of the territory of Texas was actually before the House, it would be inadvisable to prejudice future action by acting on either the state resolutions or the petitions. The committee should be discharged.

In the rambling debate that followed, and in which Adams for a change took no part, it became apparent to him that the committee had not even bothered to study the voluminous material turned over to it. Under his coaching, Caleb Cushing from Essex County, Massachusetts, presented a motion to recommit, with instructions that the committee report further on the resolutions of the state legislatures. This aroused Adams' old antagonist, Waddy Thompson. He amended Cushing's motion to read instead that the committee "report a joint resolution [with the Senate] directing President Van Buren to take the proper steps for annexation of Texas to the United States as soon as it can be done consistently with the treaty stipulations of this government."

Now Adams moved in. He offered an amendment to Thompson's amendment: "That annexing the people of any independent foreign state to this Union would be an usurpation of power, unlawful and void, and which it would be the right and duty of the free people of the Union to resist and annul." Under the House rules, an amendment to an amendment *could not be further amended*. Adams had the floor, and he kept it day after day after day throughout the morning hours devoted to committee work.

In the earlier debate, Chairman Howard had declared that most of the petitioners were "meddling females." To his mind, he said, the women of the North "have sufficient field for the exercise of their influence in the discharge of their duties to their fathers, their husbands and their children, . . . instead of rushing into the fierce struggles of political life."

Reading from his notes, Adams repeated Howard's words in measured cadences and then tore into them. For three days the aged son of Abigail Adams held forth on the virtues and responsibilities of womanhood, on women's God-given right to speak out against injustice, to help shape a better world for their sons and daughters. Howard had branded the petitions "discreditable not only to my own particular section of the country, but also to the national character."

"Discreditable?" Adams asked. "Was this from a son? Was it from a father? Was it from a husband that I heard these words? . . . It is to the wives and to the daughters of my constituents that he applies this language. . . . Are women to have no opinions or action on subjects relating to the general welfare?

"Why does it follow that women are fitted for nothing but the cares of domestic life, for bearing children and cooking the food of a family? . . . I say women exhibit the most exalted virtue when they depart from the domestic circle and enter on the concerns of their country, of humanity, and of their God!"

The majority members of the committee—Howard, Dromgoole, Thompson and his fellow South Carolinian, Legaré—were repeatedly on their feet demanding that the Speaker silence him. But Polk had to remind them that the motion to commit opened to discussion the entire merits of the main question.

Adams now turned on Legaré and provoked him into retorting that the petitions were a worthless nuisance. "I have no hesitation in admitting," the tight-lipped Charleston lawyer went on, "that I have not read the papers, or looked into them, nor was I bound to do so."

Adams looked surprised. "The gentleman from South Carolina formally admits that he has never looked into the documents referred to the committee on the subject of Texas?"

"Not one of them," Legaré retorted.

Adams took the *House Manual* off his desk and read the seventy-sixth standing rule: " 'It shall be the duty of the Committee on Foreign Affairs to take into consideration all matters which concern the relations of the United States with foreign nations, and which shall be referred to them by the House, and to report their opinions on the same.' There is the letter of the law." He read the rule again, very slowly, bearing down on each word, and fixed his watering eyes on Legaré.

"I fully considered the subject," Legaré protested. "It wasn't necessary to look into the argument."

Adams spoke again with slow emphasis. "The gentleman has taken into consideration the resolutions of *sovereign states,* and of a vast body of *memorials* and *petitions,* and *has never looked into one of them!"*

This brought a scatter of laughter from the floor, spontaneously echoed in the gallery. Polk rapped for order and looked hopefully up at the clock. It was near one, the hour set for taking up the orders of the day. Adams concluded: "When the meanest petition of the lowest and poorest individual in the country (I will not say slave) is presented in this House and referred, I hold it the duty of the committee, to the House, to the country, and to the petitioners, to look into the petitions before they make up their opinions."

The next morning Legaré was still his target. The galleries were now crowded, and, across the rotunda, there were empty seats in the visitors' section of the Senate, where an annexation resolution was also being debated, but sedately. Members of the Senate even came over to listen, having read the long account of the previous day's polemics in their morning copy of the *National Intelligencer.*

Adams now took up the state resolutions, one at a time, reading each with studied deliberation because, he explained ironically, neither Legaré nor the rest of the committee had seen them. And with each salient sentence came the repeated interposition: "But the gentleman from South Carolina does not know that. He knows nothing about it. He has not looked into the papers."

It was a good show, played almost daily to a packed gallery, Polk straining to keep order as the angry Southerners, Democrats and Whigs alike, probed for vulnerable openings to halt Adams. But Adams never let his temper trip him. He steered close to his course, a weather eye constantly on the rules of order. The gag rule got a thorough trouncing. He accused the Administration of withholding important documents on the Texas negotiations, of still plotting to annex the territory at the risk of war with Mexico. Repeatedly he dared the slaveholders to try to silence him with the previous question, knowing they could not get the necessary two-thirds vote.

196

This was no dull filibuster, but a vivid daily marshaling of the principal arguments against slavery and broadening the slave domain. The newspapers of the North were receiving daily accounts from their correspondents or reprinting them from the columns of the *National Intelligencer*. Alarmed readers were writing their Congressmen. Editorials echoed the *Intelligencer's* "Will the nation go to war for this?"

Turning to the petitions, Adams came to one from the women of Plymouth, "the principal town of the district I have the honor to represent," and read its preamble: " 'Thoroughly aware of the sinfulness of slavery, and the consequent impolicy and disastrous tendency of its extension in our country, we do most respectfully remonstrate, with all our souls, against the annexation of Texas to the United States.'

"Two hundred and thirty-eight mothers, wives and daughters of my constituents," he said, "the farmers, fishermen, tradesmen—freemen all—of the hallowed ground surrounding Plymouth Rock," had put their names to this prayer. And here was another, and another. Thousands of signers. Hundreds of thousands. And he was with them "from the depths of my heart."

"I do believe slavery to be a sin before the sight of God," he went on, "and that is the reason and the only unsurmountable reason why we should not annex Texas to this Union."

When Congress adjourned on July 9 Adams still held the floor. In the Senate, the Texas resolution had meanwhile been quietly tabled. Under the rules of the House, Adams could go on talking when the next session convened in December. But two months before that the Texas minister, Memucan Hunt, gave up and went home, and Texas withdrew her bid for annexation.

Angry Southerners now spiced Adams' mail with threats: to "cut your throat from ear to ear," "cut out your damn guts," "shoot you down in the street." The milder ones merely promised to "put you out of the way," "end your existence." Soon after the final session of the Twenty-fifth Congress convened, Adams, standing behind the petitions stacked on his

197

desk, asked the Speaker's permission to make a statement. The Southerners immediately objected on general principles, but it was to the abolitionists of the North that his words were directed.

"I have received a mass of letters threatening to assassinate me for my course," he said. "My real position has never been understood by the country. I wish distinctly to aver that, though I have earnestly advocated the right of persons to petition for the abolition of slavery in the District of Columbia, I myself am not prepared to grant their prayer."

The statement made headlines in the Democratic newspapers, both South and North. William Slade, the well-intentioned but erratic abolitionist Congressman from Vermont, had not yet returned to Washington. The statement shocked him. He wrote to Adams that the country was entitled to a fuller statement. Adams ignored him. To another Whig, Charles Kirkland of Utica, New York, he explained his position confidentially. He was wholeheartedly for the eventual emancipation of the Negro. He would vote for, and exert all his influence to bring about, the abolition of the slave traffic in the District of Columbia, which was "within the incumbent duties of the Congress." But the campaign of William Lloyd Garrison's group and the American Anti-Slavery Society to end slavery *immediately* in the District was impractical; its main achievement had been to increase the hostility of the South.

A few days later, on February 25, 1839, he presented three resolutions to the House embodying his own plan:

1. From and after the 4th of July, 1842, there shall be, throughout the United States, no hereditary slavery; but on and after that day every child born within the United States, their territories or jurisdiction, shall be born free.

2. With the exception of the territory of Florida, there shall henceforth never be admitted into this Union any state, the constitution of which shall tolerate within the same the existence of slavery.

3. From and after the 4th of July, 1845, there shall be neither slavery nor slave trade at the seat of the government of the United States.

The Southern bloc objected loudly. Adams' resolutions never came to a vote. But he had not expected they would. It was enough for the moment that he had put himself on record before the country. At home he began one of his long letters to his public. This one, however, was not addressed to his Plymouth constituents but "To the Citizens of the United States whose Petitions, Memorials and Remonstrances have been intrusted to me to be presented in the House of Representatives of the United States at the third session of the Twenty-fifth Congress." The writing went slowly. Night after night he labored at his work table until two in the morning. Finished, it ran 10,500 words, and he thought it was "long, dull and written in a hasty, slovenly manner, and requires a second letter."

He took it to the office of the *National Intelligencer*, where he found the Whig editor, William Seaton, reluctant to publish it. The Whig party was having enough trouble keeping the peace between its Northern and Southern factions. Seaton "regretted that this subject was to be agitated again."

"I expected as much," Adams answered. His temper rising, he went on: "If you decline to publish it, I will simply notify the petitioners of the fact and publish the letter in another newspaper. I shall use it as an illustration of the suppression of the freedom of the press, necessarily consequent of the suppression of the right of petition and freedom of speech in the House."

Seaton replied he had a different understanding of freedom of the press; it consisted of "editorial independence in refusing to publish what ought not to be published."

"I think there may be editorial independence in this," Adams retorted tartly, "but not much freedom of the press."

Adams won. Not only did the *Intelligencer* print the letter, but it printed the 14,000-word second letter which Adams immediately started on. Both were widely reprinted throughout the North, and the *Niles Register* gave them national distribution.

The zeal and perseverance with which he had fought for the right of petition, Adams wrote, had created the impression "not only that I was a confirmed abolitionist, but that I was affecting

199

to place myself at the head of the abolition movement throughout the land." He had "no such ambition." The immediate abolition of slavery in the District of Columbia was "utterly impractical." He went on:

"Public opinion throughout the Union is against it. No member of Congress from a slave state would dare vote for it, nor could he return [home] safely if he should. Nor is public opinion in the North, except possibly in Vermont, favorable to it. . . . The abolitionists are yet a small and, I lament to say, a most unjustly persecuted party in all the free states. It is their martyr age. A bill for abolition in the District would, if ever reported, be rejected four to one."

He was particularly harsh on the American Anti-Slavery Society for demanding *immediate* emancipation, a position "from which it cannot be dislodged."

The day would come when slavery would be extinguished not only in the District, but throughout the country. When it did, "it must be either by force, that is by civil war, or the consent of the owners of the slaves." Meanwhile, the unrealistic program of the abolitionists was inflaming hostility in the North as well as the South.

The leaders of the American Society read Adams' words with sinking spirits. Its funds reduced further by the depression (Lewis Tappan, the New York merchant who had been its heaviest contributor, was bankrupt) and with the refusal of the local chapters to support it, the society was floundering. Adams' attack was the lethal thrust.

Whether he wanted it or not, he had become—at the age of seventy-one—"the genius of the antislavery cause." No one before or since in the history of the country has been given such undisputed leadership of a cause as his battle for the abolitionists' right of petition had brought to him. Almost alone in a hostile House, with no title, no organization behind him, he was the one man to whom the hundreds of thousands of petitioners for emancipation looked to present their prayers. The canvassers, the women in their holy zeal, no longer needed a headquarters to direct them; and Adams' attack on immediacy had a softening effect on those who considered slavery a sin but feared the consequences of sudden emancipation. The petitions kept pouring in to him, and he kept presenting them. But now Adams had another mission, a *cause célèbre,* on which to focus.

⇛ XIII ⇚

"HOW bad it [slavery] is no one can imagine without understanding the details." So Adams had written a short while before. Now one of the "details" came ashore in his beloved New England. Not until the Supreme Court's Dred Scott decision, almost two decades later, was public interest so intensely aroused as it was by the case of the slave ship *Amistad.*

In June of 1839 an illicit slaver from Africa entered Havana harbor by night, her hold closely packed with Negro captives. The intercontinental slave trade had been outlawed for a generation by Spain, Portugal, Great Britain, the Netherlands and the United States. British and American warships patroled the long African coast, watching for the pirate ships, but few were intercepted; and in Spanish Cuba the authorities were easily bribed to admit the contraband cargoes.

During the two-month Middle Passage a number of the captives had died in the steaming, fetid hold. The survivors were marched in chains to the Havana slave market. Among them were fifty-three members of the Mendi tribe in the tropical jungle of Sierra Leone, flat-nosed, woolly-haired, the tallest five feet six but all strikingly erect from the custom of walking with baskets on their heads. Four were children, three girls and a boy, nine years and under. Two Cuban planters bought the lot for approximately $400 apiece, a bargain since prime slaves brought $1,000 in the Havana market and half again as much in New Orleans.

The two planters, Don José Ruiz, a young Spaniard with a copper-blond beard, and Don Pedro Montes, swarthy and middle-aged, obtained false papers from the Havana authorities, listing the fifty-three as lawful slaves (the going rate for this subterfuge, including Spanish names for the Africans, was $14 a head) and herded them aboard the 120-ton black-hulled schooner *Amistad* to take them to their sugar plantations in the Cuban province of Puerto Príncipe.

The *Amistad* cleared port the night of June 28, the Africans chained and padlocked together in the three-foot-high compartment below deck. Besides the owner-captain, the ship had a crew of two Spanish seamen and two Negro slaves, one of them the cook. In good weather the captives were briefly brought up for air while the excrement was shoveled out of their quarters. Not even the blacks in the crew knew the Mendi dialect, but one of the captives, who had been given the name Cinqué, contrived to ask the cook in sign language what was to become of them. The cook passed his finger across his throat and gobbled. While his little joke amused the cook, it confirmed for Cinqué what old men back in his village had reported: that the white men bought the blacks to eat them.

The fifth day out Cinqué found a nail during their respite on deck. That night he picked the lock on the chains that bound him to three companions. They broke open a box of the heavy knives used to chop sugarcane and crept out of the hold. A seaman on watch spotted them and gave the alarm. The captain and Negro cook rushed them and the captain killed one with his knife before Cinqué split his head with his machete. Another Mendi cut down the cook. They spared the Negro cabin boy and the two planters, Montes and Ruiz, who had come on deck in their nightshirts. The two Spanish seamen had meanwhile fled to the stern boat and escaped.

Cinqué had seen Montes occasionally lend a hand with the ship. At dawn he led him to the helm and, pointing his knife at the rising sun, told him in sign language that he would be killed unless he steered the ship back to their homeland beyond the horizon.

Under the attentive eyes of Cinqué, Montes obediently kept the ship on an outbound course during daylight, but at night he eased around, hoping to be rescued by coastal craft. Cinqué had unshackled the other prisoners. The son of a native chief, he was among the tallest, lithe and alert, powerful, with large, brooding eyes, a high forehead, broad nose—a nobleman of his tribe. His mates explored the ship's cargo. They found bright silks and gleefully decked themselves in them; they feasted on the wine, the raisins and *the medical supplies,* and ten of them died. But Cinqué ate sparingly and cautiously.

For two months the dark ship zigzagged up the American coast, its prow dutifully facing into each dawn but following the sunset in the night. Other craft sighted it but stayed clear of the strange ship with the gaudily dressed blacks on deck. The morning of August 26 Montes hove to off Montauk Point, on the eastern tip of Long Island. The Africans had no idea where they were, but their water casks were nearly empty. Cinqué sent a group ashore to refill them.

Coming out of Long Island Sound, the United States coastal survey brig *Washington* sighted the *Amistad.* Lieutenant Thomas Gedney studied her disheveled sails and outlandish crew through his glass and took an armed detail aboard. Montes and Ruiz rushed yelling to them. The Africans recognized firearms but, although they had found muskets in the hold, they did not know how to use them. They were quickly subdued, and Lieutenant Gedney took his prize into the nearest port, New London, Connecticut.

At the inquiry aboard the *Washington* by Judge Andrew Judson of the United States District Court of Connecticut, Montes and Ruiz told their story in voluble Spanish: the Negroes were their slaves. They had mutinied in Cuban waters and killed the captain and cook, and only the happy intervention of Lieutenant Gedney had saved Montes and Ruiz from eventual slaughter. The United States district attorney, William Holabird, charged Cinqué and the other adults with murder and piracy. Judge Judson bound them over to the United

States Circuit Court and held the four children and the ship captain's slave as witnesses. The men were carted to the jail in New Haven, their outlandish appearance in their silk raiments arousing wide-eyed interest along the road.

Overnight, the story became a newspaper sensation, appearing first in the New London *Gazette,* together with a letter from Montes and Ruiz thanking Lieutenant Gedney and his crew for saving their lives. The New Haven *Palladium* followed with a two-column detailed account of the *Amistad's* adventure and the court proceedings, which was promptly picked up by the Washington and New York newspapers, particularly by the New York *Emancipator.*

Puzzling facets developed which aroused intense interest among antislavery leaders. The two Spanish planters swore the Africans were slaves legitimately acquired in the Havana market; the *Amistad's* clearance papers listed them as "Ladinos," people not of pure Spanish blood but who spoke Spanish or one of its dialects with fair fluency. But the Negroes, it had by now been discovered, did not understand a word of Spanish. They spoke only their own jungle dialect, which no one who had seen them understood. Even African sailors brought from the waterfronts of New London and New Haven found them unintelligible.

If they were, as this indicated, natives fresh from Africa who had been carried to North America in violation of the laws of nations, they were not slaves. Moreover, it could be argued that they had not mutinied but had revolted against illegal captivity.

John Quincy Adams, puttering among his seedling beds and taking his daily long walks through the Quincy countryside, read the newspaper accounts with deliberately restrained interest. He was "slackening the strings of the bow," purposely wasting time to let his aging body recharge itself for the opening of the Twenty-sixth Congress in December. The kitchen of the old mansion had been remodeled under his direction and "modernized," including a new appliance called a cook stove, which particularly fascinated his daughter-in-law, Mary, and the grandchildren. Burning short lengths of wood, it cooked the food better and faster and was much cleaner than the yawning kitchen fireplace. Besides, it contained a tank which provided a ready supply of hot water! "Air-tights," cast-iron stoves for heating the house, were also on the market now, but there was controversy about their merit. One critic warned that they made the air too dry and consequently "the cells of the lungs become deprived of their necessary fluid." Another insisted they made the air "too moist." For the living quarters, Adams was content with the old fireplaces.

Then he read in the Administration newspaper, the Washington *Globe,* that the government felt it must surrender the Africans for trial in Havana if Spanish authorities demanded it. His interest mounted. A letter appeared in the *Emancipator,* signed by William Jay, the son of America's first Chief Justice. John Jay's son was a personage in his own right, an eminent jurist, a founder of the American Bible Society and a consecrated abolitionist. He wrote that the Africans of the *Amistad* were not murderers or pirates. They were heroes, who should be defended by the government. What they had done was fight for their freedom—every man's right. To turn them over to Spanish vengeance would be criminal.

In a confidential reply to Jay, Adams wrote that if the case could be kept in the American courts, he believed no grand jury would "be found capable of finding an indictment against them, far less any petit jury to convict them, nor any executive officer of this Union daring enough to lay his hands upon them to deliver them over to the mockery of a tribunal of slave smugglers in Cuba."

By now the two Cuban planters had arrived in Washington and the Spanish minister there was demanding that the federal government deliver their "property," the *Amistad* and its human cargo, to Havana. Holabird, the Connecticut district attorney, had already written to the Secretary of State, the Virginia slaveholder John Forsyth, for instructions. "Are there no treaty stipulations that would authorize our government to deliver them to the Spanish authorities?" he asked. Forsyth was sure there were—in the territorial boundary treaty signed in 1795 with Spain. He conferred with President Van Buren, now one of the most harried politicians in the country. While not in favor of slavery, Van Buren could not afford to antagonize its adherents. From Washington's day no President had been elected without the support of the Southerners in his party. Van Buren's bid for a second term was at hand. He accepted Forsyth's contention that the "mutineers" would have to be surrendered to Cuba, even though their leaders would be summarily executed and the rest delivered into slavery.

So it might be done simply by executive order, Forsyth instructed Holabird to "take care that no proceeding of your circuit court, or of any other judicial tribunal, places the vessel, cargo or slaves beyond the control of the federal executive." Unfortunately for Holabird, it was already too late. Not only had he been instrumental in having the Africans held for murder and piracy, but Lieutenant Gedney and his mates of the brig *Washington* had filed proceedings in admiralty for salvage of the *Amistad* and her Negro cargo.

Leaders of the antislavery crusade came immediately to the support of the *Amistad* captives. Here was a situation that not only demonstrated one of the worst evils of slavery but also involved the lives of innocent people. Now that the banks had reopened and resumed specie payment, the New York merchant-philanthropist, Lewis Tappan, was back in business and again able to help the cause—to a limited extent, since the depression was still on. He and his companions in the floundering American Anti-Slavery Society organized a defense committee and enlisted the best counsel they could find to appear for the Africans in the New Haven federal court.

In Quincy, a messenger brought a letter to Adams from an old friend and prominent abolitionist, the Boston lawyer Ellis Gray Loring, whose house was later a way station on the Underground Railroad. Loring, anxious to add the former President's prestige to the cause, asked Adams' opinion of "the knotty question involved in the case of the Spanish ship." Adams had already been told that Justice Smith Thompson of the Supreme Court, presiding in the Circuit Court of Connecticut, had decided that that court had no jurisdiction at present, since the *Amistad* was not an American ship and the alleged murder and piracy had not occurred in United States waters.

However, he ruled he could not dismiss the case as the ship and its "cargo" had been libeled for salvage by Lieutenant Gedney and, more recently, by the infuriated planters, Montes and Ruiz. This would have to be decided in district court. Justice Thompson and Adams had known and respected each other since they served together in Monroe's Cabinet, Thompson as Secretary of the Navy. His decision had not yet been published, and Adams sent word back to Loring that until it was he did not feel free to discuss the problem.

Actually, he was under pressure both from his inner voice and his son Charles to avoid getting involved. His age and infirmities, he reminded himself, prohibited it. He must relax more, coddle his failing energy for the work ahead in Congress. "Prudence would forbid my giving an opinion upon it at any time," he wrote in his diary, "and if I ever do, it must be with great consideration and self-control." The arguments of his only remaining son were also compelling. Charles, now thirty-two, was finally following his father and grandfather into politics; the Boston Whigs had nominated him for the Massachusetts House of Representatives. Among the Whig merchants the abolition crusaders were still looked upon as fanatics and irresponsible troublemakers. For his father publicly to lend his influence to the defense of the Negroes would "greatly embarrass the political party with which I have undertaken to act"—and consequently himself.

Strolling among the seedlings in the nursery at Quincy, father and son discussed the legal aspects of the case. Charles agreed that the problem was a complicated one for the defense and highly interesting. But since neither of the national parties was at all sectional, he insisted, an acquittal would be as disruptive to the Whigs, if they were involved, as it clearly would be to the Democrats. Furthermore, and he hoped this point would not be wasted on his father, the defense committee already had able counsel, headed by Roger Sherman Baldwin, a persuasive New Haven trial lawyer and grandson of Roger Sherman, the Revolutionary leader and signer of the Declaration of Independence.

The elder Adams, cropping the branches of a cherry sapling,

appeared in an acquiescent mood. But no sooner had Charles started back to Boston than his father let the seedlings shift for themselves and moved with the instinct of an old dog to the long-unopened law books on his study shelves. Blackstone's *Commentaries* came down, Bacon's *Abridgments*, Wheeler's *Law of Slavery*, and the works of two eighteenth-century French authorities on maritime law, René Josué Valin and Balthasard Marie Emerigon. From his files he drew reports on previous slave-ship cases: the sloop *Abby*, the *Antelope*. His interest, he told himself, was purely objective; he would not, absolutely would not, let himself get drawn into the *Amistad* case. But by now Justice Thompson's decision had been published, and he need no longer delay answering his friend Loring.

That Loring would not show his reply to the defense committee and to the abolitionist press was more than Adams could expect. While his earlier letter, to William Jay, had been confidential, the *Emancipator* had learned about it, since it had announced triumphantly that John Quincy Adams was taking an interest in the case.

He answered Loring's question by asking some of his own:

"By what authority did Lieutenant Gedney take possession of this vessel . . . and the persons in and belonging to her, and bring her and them into the port of New London? What law authorized him to make the capture?

"By what authority did the judge of the district court, Judson, hold the Negroes prisoners to be charged before the Circuit Court of the United States with the crimes of piracy and murder?

"By what authority did he hold the four African children, under the testifying age, to secure their presence as witnesses upon the said charges of murder and piracy?

"If he held these persons as prisoners upon the charge of piracy against the men, made by the two Spanish subjects on board, . . . by what authority did he hold the same Africans as prisoners upon a claim of the . . . two Spanish subjects to them as their slaves?

"If the Negroes were slaves, was not the property of their owners in them by the very laws of slavery forfeited by the commission by them of piracy and murder? And did not the white men, by charging them with these crimes, *ipso facto,* renounce and disclaim all right to them as property?

"If the children were slaves, were they competent to testify as slaves upon a charge of piracy and murder against the men? And if for this cause or for their age they were incompetent to testify, by what authority did the district court hold them as prisoners to make them testify?

"If the District Court judge had no authority to commit the Negroes to prison, may they not be liberated by habeas corpus?"

No sooner had Loring absorbed Adams' reply than the defense committee, now including prominent members from Boston, New Haven and Hartford as well as Tappan's New York group, filed a habeas corpus action in the district court for release of the four child witnesses. Judge Judson decided they could be freed on bail; but to do so their value would have to be established, and Roger Baldwin refused to consent to this, since the defense contended they were free Negroes and therefore not appraisable as property.

The case became progressively more involved. Van Buren consulted his Attorney General, Felix Grundy, slaveholder from Tennessee, who declared even more emphatically than Forsyth that its treaty obligations to Spain required the government to return the Negroes to Cuba. Van Buren obediently ordered the U.S.S. *Grampus* to stand by in New Haven to transport them. On representation of the Spanish minister, the government itself libeled the Negroes as property of the two Cuban planters. The district attorney for Connecticut, Holabird, asked a mandate to deliver them.

All this while a curious drama was being played out in the old county jail at New Haven. So far no one had been found who could communicate with the Africans. While this would seem to prove they were not "Ladinos," and therefore not slaves, it kept their story a dark mystery. Professors on the Yale faculty were trying to unravel it, together with prominent New England clergymen, among them the Puritan reformer and abolitionist, the Reverend Joshua Leavitt, and the idealistic young pastor of a New Haven church for Negroes, Simeon S. Jocelyn. Thomas Hopkins Gallaudet, a pioneer teacher of the deaf and dumb, attempted to pierce the communications barrier with sign language. Another regular visitor to the jail was Professor Joseph Willard Gibbs of the Yale Divinity School. By holding up one finger, then two, and so on, he obtained from the Africans their sounds for the first ten numerals. Thereafter the process bogged down. The simplest words were capable of a variety of interpretations. But an African seaman that Lewis Tappan found on the New York waterfront and brought to New Haven recognized the numeral sounds as those of a neighbor tribe in the Mendi jungle. With his help the scholars managed to work out an alphabet and tortuously extract fragments of their story from the captives.

Cinqué particularly interested the interpreters. Alert, quietly attentive, he displayed an inherent dignity and assurance, and the other tribesmen appeared to accept his leadership as a natural right. Simeon Jocelyn's artist brother, Nathaniel, set up his easel in the jail and painted Cinqué's portrait; now hanging in the New Haven Colony Historical Society, it shows a young man of noble countenance with a curiously brooding look in his dark, luminous eyes.

Adams had more visitors than usual that summer and autumn, and made more trips into Boston, all concerned with the *Amistad* affair. The leader of the defense committee, however, pointedly stayed away from Quincy: Lewis Tappan had not forgiven Adams for his corrosive denunciation of the American Anti-Slavery Society's policy of *"immediate* emancipation."

In Loring's Boston law office, Adams went over with him the progressive developments in the case, searched for additional precedents, reviewed the treaties with Spain and with Great Britain, which, since it had outlawed both the intercontinental slave traffic and slavery, was showing a lively interest in the proceedings.

Together with the visitors to Quincy, Loring kept pressing Adams to join the defense. They knew that the federal district attorney, Holabird, was a Van Buren appointee and working eagerly with the two slaveholding Cabinet members, Forsyth and Grundy. He was determined to turn the blacks over to Spanish authorities and let "slave-smuggling justice" take its course. And the district court judge, Judson, who had set the case for trial in November, was also an Administration appointee and an outspoken anti-abolitionist who had helped close a school for Negro girls in his home town of Canterbury, Connecticut. The defense committee desperately needed Adams' long diplomatic experience and national prestige.

Adams remained resolute. For once he was listening to his son—and his own sense of inadequacy. He learned with relief that Judge Judson in New Haven had postponed the hearing to January; by then he would have to be in his seat in the House of Representatives. But he had not seen the last of the *Amistad* case, or escaped involvement in it—not by a good deal.

⇥ XIV ⇤

NEVER before or since in the history of the United States Congress has one member's stature, and willingness to take on an irregular responsibility, projected him into the position of control that fell to Adams at the opening of the House that December of 1839. For a short time it even overshadowed national interest in the fate of the *Amistad* captives.

The House of Representatives was anything but a dignified body in Adams' time, with its assorted characters from the frontier West, the plantation South and the industrializing East. But Henry Wise did not exaggerate on the second day of the session, when he shouted, "Now we *are* a mob!"

Each new House elected its officers from the Speaker down. To organize, however, the clerk from the previous session was temporarily held over as chairman. At noon on Monday, December 2, the clerk, Hugh Garland, called the House to order and started the roll call. Commencing, according to custom then, at the top of New England, he named the members-elect from six states. Reaching New Jersey, he called off one name, that of Joseph Randolph, a returning Whig, and then announced that the election of the other five Representatives had been challenged. "Is it the pleasure of the House," he asked, "that I should pass over their names until the balance of the roll is complete?"

"Agreed!" "Agreed!" a scatter of voices responded, but Adams noted that they all came from Administration supporters. The Whigs recognized the clerk's motive. The New Jersey election returns had been contested. While the governor had certified six Whigs, the Democrats contended that their candidates had won in five of the districts. The House was so closely divided that the Whigs would be in the majority if the certified delegation from New Jersey were accredited, and the Democrats would keep control if they were excluded. Whichever dominated, that party could expect to elect the next Speaker and control the membership of the vitally important standing committeees.

Whig members demanded that the certificates of the five be accepted; the House would determine their standing after it had been organized. To Adams it was apparent that the clerk "had his lesson prepared for him" by his party bosses. A Democrat from Virginia, Garland firmly refused to continue the roll call unless the House, by general consent, permitted him to pass over New Jersey. At the same time, he would not recognize motions from the floor because a quorum had not been established. The stalemate lasted all day, and the next day he was no less adamant. He asked permission to read a statement. "Let him," the hot-headed Henry Wise shouted, "and then [let him] tell me as a native-born gentleman from my own mother state, and as a Christian, why he will not discharge his duties!" Other Whigs objected to that. The clerk's functions, they pointed out, did not include issuing statements from the chair. Resolutions that had been framed in late-hour huddles the night before were presented, heatedly debated and rephrased; but the clerk insisted he could not entertain them.

"The Furies broke loose," said Adams. Members yelled across the desks at each other, collected in the aisles arguing; Whigs denounced their Democratic colleagues for not stopping "this dastardly usurpation." Representative Luther Peck, a New York Whig, tangled with the "snarling and ranting" (Adams' description) South Carolina Democrat, Robert Barnwell Rhett, and was called "a liar, a scoundrel and a puppy!" Friends had to separate them.

As on the day before, the clerk even refused to "put the question" to adjourn, and it was then, as the members angrily headed for the dim lamplight of the corridors, that Henry Wise exclaimed, "Now we *are* a mob!"

During the next two days the stalemate became progressively more disorderly. Wise suggested that the clerk be permitted to pass over New Jersey and reach a quorum, but before electing a Speaker or organizing, the House should hear and rule upon the evidence for and against the challenged delegation. Aside from the fact that Garland appeared as reluctant to put the question on this resolution as he had on any of the others, the Whigs themselves took objection to it. Said William Johnson of Maryland, "But we would have no officers, no organization, *no means of ending debate.* It could go on for weeks."

It looked as though the stalemate *would* go on interminably, since the Whigs showed no intention of giving in to the clerk, and the clerk was standing his ground against all abuse. Repeatedly, when ordered under some new maneuver, he started the roll call again, but always stopped at New Jersey. Many of the Democrats were now as distraught as their opponents, but they could reach no meeting of minds. The capital's Whig organ, the *Intelligencer*, fumed daily against the "disgrace," the "outrage upon the people of the Union." Across the rotunda, the Senate sedately marked time under empty galleries waiting for the House to put itself in order for the President's State of the Union message; the House galleries filled early.

All this while, Adams had been at his desk but taking no part in the debate. Whig members came to him to consult, but he offered them no help. While the tumult roared around him, he was busy writing, evidently—in part, at least—bringing his diary up to date, because every salient detail of the proceedings was recorded in his shaky script, with characteristic interpolations.

Bynum and Vanderpoel: "Party speeches frothing with the rights of the people, technicalities and frauds."

Rhett: "Unstable as water."

Mercer of Virginia: "A towering passion."

Turney of Tennessee: "Pouring forth a volley of foulest-mouthed invective."

Hunt of New York: "When sober a worthy man, but his habits are intemperate and [this was on the third day] he has taken a double dose."

Duncan of Ohio: "Ranted and raved for two hours, till many seats were empty in the House and galleries for the first time since the session commenced."

At dark, Adams regularly sent out for a cup of coffee and two slices of buttered toast, then resumed writing. The afternoon of the fourth day, a correspondent at the press table saw him push away his papers and grasp the front edge of his desk, his usual manner of getting up. Garland the clerk, had started the roll again, stopping at New Jersey with, ". . . and the clerk has to repeat—"

Adams slid sideways out of his chair.

"I rise to interrupt the clerk!"

As the hall quieted, he turned his back on Garland. "Fellow citizens and members of the Twenty-sixth Congress: I address myself to you and *not* to the clerk in the chair.

"I have waited here four days," he went on, "with the fixed determination not to take any part in these extraordinary proceedings. I had hoped that this House would succeed in organizing itself, and that the business of legislation would be progressed in. But what a spectacle we here present! We do not and cannot organize; and why? Because [witheringly] the *clerk,* the *mere clerk,* whom we employ, and whose existence depends upon our will, usurps the *throne,* and sets us, the representatives of the whole people, at defiance. And what is this *clerk* of yours? Is he to control the destinies of sixteen millions of free men? . . . He refuses to call the roll! It is in your power to compel him to call it, if he will not do it voluntarily!"

A voice broke in harshly: "Compulsion cannot reach the clerk! He will resign rather than call the state of New Jersey!"

"Well, sir," Adams answered, "then let him resign, and we may discover some way by which we can get along without his all-powerful talent, learning and genius."

He paused to gather his thoughts.

216

"What is first? To organize! To organize in some form or other. Let us imitate what Mr. Jefferson says was done when Lord Dunmore dissolved the legislature of Virginia [on the eve of the Revolution]. . . . They adjourned to a tavern. They constituted themselves a convention, and they acted as the legislature of the colony. This was irregular. Well, I think on the fourth day of the session of the Twenty-sixth Congress that is to be, it is rather late to make objections on the score of irregularity."

He picked up one of the papers on his desk. "I call upon you in the name of the people to organize! You have not only duties to perform, but you are under a high responsibility to the people to perform those duties. Organize! I have no reference to the *clerk*. I propose that the House itself should act!"

Reading from the paper, he repeated a motion that had already been offered, requiring the clerk to proceed with the roll call. As the clerk stood his ground and began reiterating the phrases he had intoned for four days now—"since no quorum has been established," "solemn sense of duty"—other voices broke in upon him. "How shall the question be put?" "Who shall put the question?"

Adams answered, "I intend to put the question myself!"

So the old statesman and former President took upon himself an authority no other member of the House had the national prestige or, if it had occurred to any of them, the willingness to exercise. Irregular? Yes. But effective. His most persistent antagonist, Henry Wise, pushed through the members crowded around Adams and shook his hand. Robert Rhett of South Carolina, no less bitter an enemy, leaped onto a desk and waved his arms.

"I move that the Honorable John Quincy Adams take the chair of the Speaker of this House, and officiate as presiding officer, till the House be organized by the election of its constitutional officers! As many as are agreed to this will say aye!"

The response was loud.

"And nay?"

The ayes plainly had it. From the galleries now came such an uproar of applause mixed with hisses that Waddy Thompson of

South Carolina threatened to "call on the President for a military force to preserve order." Two members were appointed to escort Adams to the Speaker's chair. As they formed beside him, Henry Wise spoke again.

"Sir! I regard this as the proudest moment of your life; and if, when you shall be gathered to your fathers, I were asked to select the words which, in my judgment, are best calculated to give at once the character of the man, I would inscribe upon your tomb this sentence, 'I will put the question myself.' "

Adams occupied the chair for the next ten sessions, and it was an uncomfortable seat. His rulings, delivered with crisp certainty, were frequently and savagely challenged. "Nor even your gray hair," John White of Kentucky shouted, "should screen you from the odium due to the usurper and the despot." The sessions lasted long after dark. One night was so stormy outside and the meeting so late that Adams' coachman drove back to the house and stabled the horses, then returned afoot to escort his employer home. This was the same expatriate Irishman, Jeremy Leary, whose reliability Louisa had worried over a few years before.

Adams ruled that the five challenged New Jersey Representatives should be included in the roll call; their credentials had been legally certified, and to exclude them would deprive their state of its lawful representation. His decision was challenged, and the House overruled him by one vote.

On the first vote for Speaker, the Administration candidate, John W. Jones, was in the lead but short of a majority. Malcontents then began deserting the Democratic lineup, and on the eleventh ballot the opposition elected a Virginia Whig, Robert Hunter. However, the Democrats managed to reward Garland for his loyalty by keeping him in the clerk's chair. (An elections committee later rejected the credentials of the five New Jersey Whigs, and the House seated their Democratic opponents.)

"With an ejaculation of gratitude to God for my deliverance," Adams turned over the chair to the Speaker he had supported and "walked home with a lightened heart."

Waddy Thompson, still beaming good will, wanted to present a resolution of thanks for his services, but Adams entreated him not to, foreseeing that the Democrats, "exasperated in losing their Speaker," would have defeated it. Besides, any harmony with his Southern associates was bound to be brief. Already, the corridors were stacked again with antislavery petitions directed to Adams; the rural canvassers had reacted to his attack on immediacy simply by omitting mention of it from their prayers. And the anti-abolitionist bloc was preparing to impose the most stringent gag rule so far: that all slavery petitions be automatically tabled upon reception. The Rules Committee was considering another device: removing the desks from the chamber. Then Adams would have had to get down on the floor to sort through his petitions. Fortunately, the majority were not that willing to incommode themselves as well.

For the moment, much of the fervor both for and against the slavery issue was fixed upon the fate of the *Amistad* Negroes. The Administration and its district attorney in Connecticut, Holabird, fully expected that the federal district court would order the Africans sent back to Havana. In the South, politicians and editors pointed out that justice could take no other course if the slave communities were to be protected from further black insurrections. Northern propagandists as vigorously argued the other side: that free black men had as much right as whites to resist illegal captivity.

The trial began on January 7 before Judge Judson in New Haven and lasted a week. Adams, unsatisfied with the coverage in the Washington *Intelligencer* and *Globe,* subscribed to the New Haven *Palladium,* whose accounts were more factual and detailed. While the U.S.S. *Grampus* waited in New Haven harbor to take the Negroes back to Cuba, rumors came from New Haven that the artist who had painted Cinqué's portrait, Nathaniel Jocelyn, was plotting to free the Negroes by force if necessary; that Jocelyn and his friends had acquired a ship and would try to smuggle the captives out to sea. It sounded foolhardy to Adams, considering that the United States Navy was well represented in the area, but concern in New Haven had climaxed in emotional demonstrations on the Yale campus, where the students were protesting the enslavement of free Negroes, to spotty heckling by their Southern classmates.

Considering Judge Judson's known hostility to abolition, his decision surprised Adams. Interpreting the laws with studied concern, the court accepted the argument of the defense counsel, Roger Baldwin, that the *Amistad* captives were free Negroes who had been kidnapped in Africa, and ruled that, under the law of nations, including that of Spain itself, they should be released and shipped back to their homes. Lieutenant Gedney and his boarding party from the brig *Washington* were granted salvage rights on the *Amistad* and her material cargo, but not on the captives, who could not be considered property.

In Washington, President Van Buren was apparently as unhappy with the decision as his slaveholding Cabinet members, Forsyth and Grundy. Seth P. Staples, one of Baldwin's legal associates, recorded: "A gentleman . . . informed me that John Van Buren [the President's son and secretary] expressed great dissatisfaction at Judson's opinion, and said that the question had a great and important political bearing of which Judson had taken no notice. He [John Van Buren] spoke of the opinion in terms of great disapprobation."

The government had made no provision for returning the captives to Africa. Moreover, District Attorney Holabird, under orders from Washington, immediately appealed the ruling to the United States Circuit Court. So Cinqué and his tropical tribesmen spent the New England winter in their unheated cells.

The defense committee had not given up hope that they could persuade Adams to work with them. Baldwin sent a long anonymous letter to him and to the *National Intelligencer,* signed "One of the People," rehearsing the defense case against the government's appeal, in the hope that it would be used to bring the issue before Congress. Adams found nothing in it that he did not know, but he immediately presented a resolution calling on Van Buren to turn over to the House the government's correspondence with the Spanish minister and the Connecticut district attorney, "if not incompatible with the public interest." Despite opposition from what Adams called the "mobocracy"—the anti-abolition bloc—he managed to get the resolution adopted after a month of wrangling; and while the

Spanish documents were being translated and printed by the State Department the appeal came up in the United States Circuit Court.

At that time the circuit courts were presided over by circuit-riding members of the Supreme Court. Justice Smith Thompson, who sat in the case, upheld the district court decision, and District Attorney Holabird promptly appealed to the Supreme Court. So matters stood as Adams boarded the train to return to Quincy for the summer. He was more discouraged than usual. His abolition petitions had come up against a solid phalanx of opposition. On a single day, March 30, he had presented 511 and seen them all dispatched to the clerk's table without being entertained. John Greenleaf Whittier, in his soft-voiced optimism, had tried to console him. "This last outrage on the right of petition," Whittier told his old friend, "may be the best thing that could have been done to promote the cause of abolition. It is, at least, casting off all disguise." But did slavery feel any need for disguise? Once more, Adams' sympathy had compelled him to write a draft on his slender bank account, and he had been left to wonder what good it would do.

This time it was a Negro preacher who came to his home needing help to raise $450 to buy freedom for his three grandchildren, two girls and a boy, all under four years old. The old preacher had spent twenty years buying his own freedom and that of his sons. Then Henry Johnson, until lately a member of the House from Louisiana, had claimed the wife of one son and her three children. All the preacher's savings had been enough to buy back only the mother. Unless he could raise the additional $450, and promptly, Johnson would take the Negro children to his Louisiana plantation.

Meanwhile, the case of the *Amistad* captives kept intruding on Adams' peace of mind. On the surface, prospects looked fairly bright for the Negroes. But the defense committee was not optimistic, and neither was Adams. Fine points of international law were involved. The Spanish minister was now demanding surrender of the captives as assassins as well as slaves. While the Mendis were plainly not legitimate Cuban slaves, it was disputable whether the American courts had the right to do anything but accept the *Amistad*'s clearance papers on their face value. And now it was up to the Supreme Court, a court dominated by Jackson appointees, the majority of them slaveholders!

That summer Adams and his son Charles spent many evenings, lightened occasionally with a bottle of Madeira, discussing the intricacies of the case. Adams was more determined than ever not to let himself be drawn into the proceedings, and consequently Charles, who had built a summer home nearby, willingly shared his father's interest.

Louisa and Mary worried over Adams' persistent hoarseness and thought a sea voyage before returning to the damp cold of Washington might help him; sea voyages were the favorite treatment for all climatic ailments. So, in September, he boarded the little steamer *Acadia* with an armful of books and headed for Nova Scotia, a land he found wildly beautiful but touched, he thought, by a brooding sadness. Here, among the rocky inlets, lived the people who had once violently hated his father and everything he stood for. Back in his own childhood these expatriates—royalists to themselves, Tories to their opponents—had been as solidly entrenched in colonial America as the South's slave culture was at present. All that was left to them now was a wistful memory enshrined in nostalgic place names: Annapolis, New Brunswick, Dartmouth, Kingston, Newport, Weymouth.

Soon after his return, Adams learned from Loring that the *Amistad* defense committee was in deep trouble. Because of the lingering depression, contributions, which had never been large, had tapered off to almost nothing. The committee's inability to pay adequate fees had caused one leading New York counselor, Seth Staples, to withdraw, and the other, Theodore Sedgwick, Jr., also wanted out. This would leave only Roger Baldwin of New Haven, who alone appeared willing to accept whatever Lewis Tappan could raise among the abolitionists (his entire fees for almost three years' work came to $700). Now, more than ever, the Negro captives needed a prestigious champion to plead their case in the nation's highest court. The most persuasive man of the day, Daniel Webster, was not even considered; the committee knew he would not risk his standing in the Whig party; moreover, he never worked for a small fee. The only trial lawyer who approached Webster in courtroom eloquence was Rufus Choate of Boston. The committee pinned its hopes on him, but Choate, one of the organizers of the Whig party in Massachusetts and not in sympathy with the abolitionists, turned them down, pleading that his health—which held up for twenty more strenuous years—was not equal to it.

Lewis Tappan now put aside his resentment against Adams for having disparaged his Anti-Slavery Society's extremist program. With Loring, he drove out from Boston the morning of October 27. The Quincy countryside was blanketed with the season's first snow, the air biting crisp. Adams was at his study desk, his back to the lighted fireplace. He had listened unyieldingly to Loring many times, so it was Tappan, with his long white hair, sharp face and stern, drooping mouth, who made the appeal. The committee, he insisted, needed a lawyer with Adams' venerable and nationwide prestige to argue the *Amistad* captives' case in the Supreme Court. The district and circuit courts had merely passed along their fate to the Supreme Court, with its preponderance of proslavery justices. The Whig and Democratic parties, the Administration, all were equally dependent on Southern support, and willing, even eager, to rid themselves of this unpleasantness. The Spanish minister had the entire royal court at Madrid behind him, as well as the American Secretary of State and Attorney General.

Charles Francis had been closing his Quincy house for the winter; he came into the study now with books he had borrowed, and returned them to their places on the shelves. Sitting there with his back to the fire, his father appeared even older than usual this morning. The light on his head and fringe of white hair emphasized the webbing of fine lines etched on his face. As Tappan talked on, Adams kept making little coughing sounds and mopping his wet eyes with the kerchief crushed in his hand. Now he answered, politely but firmly.

"I will cheerfully do what I have hitherto offered; that is, to give any assistance of counsel and advice to Mr. Baldwin. But I am too old to do more, too inefficient, too inexperienced, after a lapse of more than thirty years, to assume the defense of the Africans before the Supreme Court."

That was final to Charles. Obviously, Tappan did not understand his father. When the old man made up his mind, mountains of oratory, of persuasion, could not move him. But Tappan did not know he was beaten.

"It is a matter of life or death to these poor Negroes," he went on. Roger Baldwin was a good man, and nobly doing all he could for the Africans; but he lacked the commanding presence, the nationwide respect—and no one realized it better than he himself did—to stand up against the organized determination of the anti-abolitionists to sacrifice these unfortunate black pawns to international and national expediency.

"Life or death!" "Life or death!" Tappan rang the phrase until Charles almost knew in advance when he was going to repeat it. "These unfortunates!" "So critical."

Now Adams was interrupting him, and Charles, with the election barely two weeks away and his Whig candidacy, he thought, at stake, heard him, stunned, his spirit sinking.

"If, by the blessing of God, my health and strength shall permit, I will argue the case before the Supreme Court!"

Lewis Tappan did not mention a fee, nor did Adams expect, or receive, one. But he had Tappan's assurance that Roger Baldwin was anxious to work with him, and Tappan left with him a scrapbook of newspaper clippings concerning the case.

The next week he put Louisa and Mary and the children on the Providence train to return to Washington. The weather remained cold and, since the Quincy house could not be kept comfortable in winter, he moved in temporarily with Charles on Beacon Hill. Charles was resigned to his father's helping the *Amistad* captives. He had not sought the nomination to the state legislature, he pointed out. "Therefore, I will be disappointed at nothing. The whole matter is in the hands of a higher power."

November 9 Adams walked the nine miles out to Quincy to vote, then finished packing. His district stood solidly by him again, and in Boston Charles wrote triumphantly, "I am this day elected to the first place I ever held in my life." Across the country, the Whigs saw brighter days ahead. Van Buren was out and William Henry Harrison, gentle, dull old "Log Cabin and Hard Cider Harrison," was in. "Tippecanoe and Tyler too!"

⇶ XV ⇷

ROGER Baldwin had responded to Tappan's announcement that Adams would head the defense by sending
Adams a fifty-two-page outline, "Narrative of the Case of the
Amistad," and inviting him to stop in New Haven on his way
back to Washington.

His new responsibility weighed heavily on Adams. "I implore the mercy of God," he said, "so to control my temper, to
enlighten my soul, and to give me utterance, that I may prove
myself in every respect equal to the task."

Despite all the help Providence might give him, he doubted
that he was equipped, either by nature or training, for the ordeal. He had had little trial experience, none since his youth.
But mainly it was his impulsive irascibility—which seemed to
him to worsen with age—that worried him. To flare out at his
opponents in the heat of debate was one thing, but to let his
temper get the upper hand, even for a moment, before the nine
black-robed justices of the Supreme Court could be disastrous.
Yet such was his measured opinion of his contemporaries that
there was no one among them, no one equally committed to the
cause, to whom he would have turned over the responsibility.

"My eyes are threatening to fail me [but he still would not
wear glasses]. My hands tremble like an aspen leaf. My memory daily deserts me. My imagination is fallen into the sear and
yellow leaf and my judgment sinking into dotage."

And the lives of the innocent black men had been committed to his trust!

The new railroad sped him to Hartford, where he changed coaches to ride through the bleak winter farmlands into New Haven, and went to bed in the Tontine Hotel.

Roger Baldwin, who had been alerted to Adams' early rising, arrived with the first light, bringing a bundle of documents and a brisk sense of urgency. Over the breakfast table in the hotel ordinary, they rehearsed the case so far, and Baldwin outlined the strategy he had in mind. Adams was a patient listener. He took an immediate liking to the grandson of his father's colleague in the Continental Congress, taller by a head than himself, clean-shaven, spectacled, groomed in black from his stock to his oiled boots. At thirty-seven, Baldwin was already rated the best trial lawyer in Connecticut; a nominal Whig, he was active in politics as well as in the abolitionist cause and was being mentioned for governor. A point of early agreement between them was that the "slavocracy"—a word that Baldwin would hear often and with biting emphasis from Adams—was solidly resolved that the *Amistad* Negroes must be sacrificed to Cuban revenge and Southern security.

As the day brightened, members of the Yale faculty, who had been working painstakingly with the captives, arrived in their carriages, and Adams rode with them to Westville, a half hour out from the campus, where the Negroes were now confined under the guardianship of the United States marshal. The four children had been taken into her home by the marshal's wife. The men were confined in a barracks thirty feet by twenty with eighteen cots along the two sides. They were thirty-five now. Two had died of natural causes in the year and three months since they had been taken into federal custody. The third had grown moody toward the end of the summer, and one day, while swimming with his companions in a nearby pond, had been heard talking with his ancestors. He was a strong swimmer, and the others knew that when he waved to them from the middle of the pond and disappeared, he had deliberately left them.

Tappan's defense committee, in its persistent watch along the waterfronts, had finally come upon a Sierra Leone sailor who could speak the Mendi dialect. With his help the New Haven scholars now had learned their detailed story from the captives, and George Day, a young instructor in the divinity school, was teaching them English and making them into Christians. He showed Adams the Mendi alphabet he had made up, and had several of the captives read passages out of the New Testament in their groping English. None of them was over thirty; Cinqué, who moved among them with the natural assurance of a chieftain, appeared to be about twenty-five. Adams agreed with the New Haven artist, Jocelyn, that he had a "very remarkable countenance." The little people, Adams thought, should have warmer clothes and more bedding. Even though they were allowed out for exercise whenever the weather permitted, he could see from the veiled bewilderment in their eyes that the long confinement was straining their primitive natures.

The college outdid itself to make the day a memorable one for its distinguished visitor. After an early dinner with the Baldwins, Yale's president, Jeremiah Day, came in with prominent members of the faculty, and a delegation escorted Adams to the Reverend Henry Ludlow's meeting house, where the faculty and student body listened attentively to his lecture on "Society and Civilization."

Next morning Adams put in three hours at his writing desk before going down to breakfast. There a Yale senior presented himself, asked for his autograph and announced he had been delegated to attend him until he boarded the steamer for New York. The young man was "over-officious in his attentions." Adams could complain to his diary about his infirmities, but he resented being reminded of them; he was glad to get out of the young man's persistent clutches.

New York, now a city of 312,000, its East River skyline dark with the furled masts and spars of sailing ships, had another busy schedule waiting for him. Tappan and the Reverend Joshua Leavitt, now editor of the *Emancipator,* met him at the Astor House next morning and spent most of the day with him, going over details brought out at the hearings on the *Amistad* and suggestions for the final appeal contributed by William Jay and other attorneys among the abolitionists. Jay had passed along a curious distortion in the government's translation of the *Amistad*'s papers. Adams would look into *that* when he got to Washington.

That evening he was taken to Brooklyn to lecture on "Faith" before the Hamilton Literary Association; a hansom cab brought him back to his hotel "after midnight." What had been intended as a short stopover extended to three crowded days. A painter named Marchant persuaded him to sit for his portrait. He attended the Log Cabin and Tippecanoe Ball, celebrating Harrison and Tyler's victory, and was guest of honor at levees and banquets, until he complained that "the life I lead is trying to my constitution and cannot be long continued with impunity. . . . I live in continual bustle." Nevertheless, among congenial associates, he was an entertaining guest. Philip Hone, New York's former mayor and man-about-town, commented after one of these gatherings that Adams "was the fiddle of the party; gay, witty, instructive, and entertaining." He added, "It is a privilege, and an era in one's life, to see him as he was on this occasion."

Hone belonged to a club of prominent New York Whigs who met irregularly at each other's homes for dinner. Daniel Webster, Washington Irving and James Fenimore Cooper had been among their guests. Thurlow Weed, an original backer of President-elect Harrison, recalled years later that it was about this time that he attended one of the gatherings and found Adams the honor guest. The dinner was at the Park Place home of the merchant, Roswell Colt, who had the finest wine cellar in the city—no small distinction considering that Hone himself counted 2,023 quart bottles and 237 gallons of vintage Madeira and sherry in his bins that year. After the cloth had been removed, Colt opened fourteen bottles of fine old Madeira, "crusted," said Weed, "with dust and cobwebs," and asked his guests to try to identify them. Adams topped them all by naming eleven. Weed remarked that he must have had a lot of practice.

Back in Washington, Adams happily discarded the celebrity image. Here, in the streets that had known his father and Jefferson, Madison, Monroe, Jackson; where a common sight was Van

Buren or Clay jogging by on horseback, or Webster in his carriage, here he was still just another elder citizen. His concern at the moment was how to keep public interest in the *Amistad* case alive, so it would not be an almost forgotten issue when it reached the Supreme Court. The abolitionist press would do its best, but it could not go on endlessly rehashing the story.

The answer came, hand-tailored, from Van Buren's State Department. William Jay's charge that the documents filed by the Spanish minister had been deliberately falsified in translation brought an indignant protest from the State Department's official translator, Robert Greenhow. Since it was Adams' resolution that had brought the papers to light, Greenhow came to him in the House to deny that he was involved. The important word in the Negroes' passport, issued by the governor-general at Havana to the *Amistad* before it cleared port, was "Ladinos." Greenhow swore he had left it unchanged, since it was apparently the crux of the dispute whether or not the captives were legitimate slaves.

Adams called for the original documents and the State Department's printed translations. He found that "Ladinos" appeared nowhere in the English version. Instead, the *Amistad* captives were listed as "sound" Negroes. He called on the House for appointment of a select committee to investigate who in the State Department had apparently collaborated with the Spanish minister to disguise the fact that the Negroes had been recently brought from Africa in violation of the laws against slave smuggling.

Speaker Robert Hunter appointed Adams chairman of the committee of five, and for three weeks they held hearings which the press, sensing a scandal, assiduously covered. The translator, Greenhow, took the witness stand and stuck by his story that he had realized the peculiar significance of the Spanish word and therefore had let it stand. The compositor who had set the translated version insisted he had faithfully followed copy. A galley proof was eventually produced from the composing room of the House printers, Blair and Rives, who also published the Administration newspaper, the Washington *Globe*. On it "Ladinos" was found to have been marked out and "sound Negroes" substituted. Now a proofreader took the stand and swore that he had made the change in good faith and on his own responsibility. Adams was not convinced, but the hearings had served a purpose: they had renewed and stimulated interest in the case, and had dramatized the defense contention that the Africans were not Cuban slaves.

Adams chafed because his House duties and the abolition petitions flooding in on him for the new session absorbed much of the precious time he needed to prepare his argument before the Supreme Court, which had the case on its docket for January 20. He was corresponding frequently now with Baldwin, and while they both assumed the legalities of the case were in their favor, Adams had little hope that the nine justices would be judiciously impartial. Five of them were Southerners and, of the four Northerners, two had outspokenly defended slavery in the past. Five had been appointed by President Jackson: Roger Taney of Maryland, the Chief Justice; Philip Barbour of Virginia, whom Adams had termed "a shallow-pated wildcat" when it appeared he might succeed John Marshall; Henry Baldwin of Pennsylvania, who had occasional spells of insanity; James Moore Wayne of Georgia, and John McLean of Ohio. Two were Van Buren appointees: John McKinley of Alabama and John Catron of Tennessee.

The only two that Adams felt he could count on for a sympathetic hearing were his old Salem, Massachusetts, friend and fellow lecturer at Harvard, Joseph Story, and Smith Thompson of New York, the oldest justice at seventy-two, who had presided at the *Amistad* hearing in the circuit court.

And now, together with the letters from Baldwin and the mounting correspondence from Simeon Jocelyn in New Haven, Loring in Boston and Tappan, Leavitt and Jay in New York, came two packets that, while they pleased Adams, made him feel more inadequate than ever for the task he had undertaken. One was signed "Ka-le" and the other "Kinna," and they came from Westville, where young Mr. Day was teaching the Mendis the language of the country that was trying its best to deliver them back to their slavemasters. The young African who signed himself "Ka-le" wrote, in surprisingly legible penmanship:

Dear Friend Mr. Adams,

I want to write a letter to you because you love Mendi people & you talk to the great court We want to tell you one
thing José Ruiz say we born in Havanna he tell lie we all
born in Mendi we no understand Spanish language Mendi
people been in American 17 moons We talk American language a little not very good we want you to ask the court
what we have done wrong what for Americans keep us in
prison. Some people say Mendi people crazy dolts because we
no talk American language Americans no talk Mendi American people crazy dolts? . . . Mendi feel bad O we can not
tell how bad Every day and night we think about our country . . . Give us free we glad—if no give us free we sorry—
we sorry for Mendi people little—we sorry for American people
great because God punish liars. We want you tell court that
Mendi people no want to go back to Havanna we no want to
be killed. Dear friend we want you to know how we feel. . . .
Cook say he kill he eat Mendi people We afraid we kill cook
we never kill captain if he no kill us. . . . All we want is make
us free . . . send us home and we bless you and all Mendi
people will be your dear friend Mr. Adams.

The letter from Kinna was less legible:

I want to write you open letter my dear friend because you
love us because you talk to the Great Court and tell American
people to make us free We want to go home to Mendi country
and see our fathers and mothers and brothers and sisters Judge
Judson say you be free but government say no. . . . If man
have knife and come to American people and say I kill I eat
what American people do? . . . Dear friend Mr. Adams we
love you very much we ask we beg you to tell court Mendi
people go free.

"Be assured," Baldwin wrote Adams, "that these letters were
wholly composed by the Africans." Adams answered, "Let them
know that I think of them, hope for them and pray for them
night and day."

A week before the hearing date, Baldwin arrived, greatly concerned: his own argument was still not complete; there were documents, citations he needed to look into in the Supreme Court Library at the Capitol; worse, his busy trial practice required him to be back in New Haven on the twentieth. Justice Taney obligingly postponed the case for a month. Meanwhile, Adams had found another error in the records supplied to the House: the printed version of a letter from the Connecticut district attorney, Holabird, read that the United States Circuit Court had decided that "it *had* jurisdiction of any offense committed by the blacks on board the *Amistad.*" The word *no* after *had* had been omitted. Infuriated, Adams called on the chief clerk of the State Department to order a correction; he received such evasive answers that he doubted, and correctly, that the clerk intended to comply. In the same letter a sentence appeared that the State Department possibly considered irrelevant; Holabird wrote, "I should regret extremely that the rascally blacks should fall into the hands of the abolitionists, with whom Hartford is filled."

Francis Scott Key now came to Adams. "I am afraid there is not a chance for the poor creatures," he said, and recalled that as United States attorney for the District he had handled the case of another slave ship, the *Antelope,* which had been libeled by Spain and Portugal. "I argued for the freedom of the Negroes," he said, "but was overruled. I suggest the defense committee make up a purse and pay for them [the *Amistad* captives], and then send them back to Africa."

Where, Adams wondered, would the defense committee get that kind of money, when it was having trouble meeting the routine expenses of the appeal?

At the same time, the British minister in Washington, Henry S. Fox, told Adams, "I have heard with great surprise that the decision of the Supreme Court will be to deliver up these unfortunate men."

As the hearing date neared Adams' left eye suddenly became so inflamed that "it threatens me with complete disability to perform my final duty before the Supreme Court." The inflammation cleared up, but a worse "visitation of Providence" immediately occurred. His coachman, the devoted Irishman,

Jeremy Leary, drove Adams to the House two days before the court was to take up the *Amistad* case. Adams left the carriage to watch a demonstration on the Capitol slope of Samuel Colt's new repeating firearm, a musket that discharged twelve cartridges in twelve seconds. At the first round, the team bolted and threw both Leary and the footman, John Causten. The footman was merely bruised, but Leary was so badly injured that Adams sent to his parish church, St. Matthew's, for the priest to administer the last rites. He was at Leary's bedside next day when he died.

Monday, February 20, Adams arrived early in the Supreme Court chamber, then directly below the Senate hall. The courtroom was soon filled, a rare occurrence except when it was known that Webster would speak. Unlike the Webster audiences, Adams noticed, "there were not many ladies." The eight members of the court (McKinley was absent) filed in and put on their black robes. Below the walnut bench sat the new Attorney General, Henry D. Gilpin; a Jackson Democrat from Philadelphia, he had been appointed by Van Buren when Grundy resigned a few months before. He was brisk, conspicuously self-confident. Roger Baldwin, tall and immaculate in black broadcloth, wore the constrained, urbane demeanor of the seasoned trial lawyer. Adams sat stiffly beside him, his band of white hair curling over the rolled collar of his double-breasted gray frock coat, hands clasped and fidgeting, his wrinkled face and high forehead the color of old chamois.

Justice Taney announced that the government would present the opening and closing arguments. Adams asked the court's indulgence once more: would it recess at two o'clock so he might attend the funeral of his servant? Taney agreed.

Gilpin spoke for two hours and resumed the next day. The *Amistad*, he argued, was a regularly documented Spanish schooner employed in the coastal trade of Cuba; the passports of the Africans had been properly signed by the governor-general at Havana and proved "beyond all controversy" that the Negro passengers were the property of Ruiz and Montes. By the comity of nations, he went on, the American courts could not "go behind or enquire into the validity of these documents."

234

The captives should be restored to their owners, and the circuit court had erred in pronouncing them free men.

Baldwin followed with a four-hour presentation, disputing each of Gilpin's premises; Adams thought it "sound and eloquent, but exceedingly mild." With great caution—since he and Adams had agreed they "must avoid exciting Southern passions and prejudices"—Baldwin argued that, as kidnapped free men, the Negroes had "the right of self-emancipation."

Gilpin's rebuttal took up the rest of the day, and now Adams' turn had come. He rode to the Capitol the next morning "with increasing agitation of mind, now little short of agony." He had slept hardly at all. "The very skeleton of my argument is not yet put together."

When he heard Justice Taney announce that the court was "ready to hear Mr. Adams," he raised himself uncertainly out of his chair. But the moment he was up he was completely self-possessed. He looked long and deliberately at the eight men staring down at him over the burnished railing of the bench.

"In rising to address this court as one of its attorneys and counselors, admitted at a great distance of time," he began, "I shall perhaps be more likely to exhibit the infirmities of age and the inexperience of youth than render the services I desire to the individuals whose lives and liberties are at the disposal of this court. But I derive consolation from the thought that *this* is a court of *justice*. Justice, 'the constant and perpetual will to secure to every one his own right.' "

He was off, marshaling facts, arguments, citations, drawing them out of his prodigious memory and deftly fitting them into their places as he had not been able to do night after night at his study table.

"It is painful to me to arraign before this court, and before the civilized world, the position of the existing Administration in this case. But I must do it." The Administration had shown itself deliberately "sympathetic to the Spaniards." Without looking at his notes, he quoted verbatim extracts from Secretary of State Forsyth's correspondence with the Spanish minister, from the communications of Forsyth and Grundy to and from Holabird and Lieutenant Gedney.

"All the proceedings in this matter, on the part both of the executive and judicial branches of the government, have had their foundation in the *assumption* that these persons *alone* [Ruiz and Montes] were the parties aggrieved, and that their claims . . . were founded in fact and justice. . . . The sympathies of the executive government, and as it were of the nation, [have all been] in favor of the slave traders and against these poor, unfortunate, helpless, tongueless, defenseless Africans."

He was pleading for human lives, and he had never been more earnest, more anxious to persuade. As he went on, hour after hour, charging that Lieutenant Gedney and his crew of the survey brig *Washington* had no right to seize the *Amistad* in the first place, that there was no legal authority, no statute, precedent, treaty, empowering the government to hold the Africans or deliver them back to Cuba, his rheumy eyes remained fixed on the bench: and he "witnessed little flagging of attention by the judges."

Now it was four and a half hours since he had begun, and he still had far to go, but the time to adjourn for the day was at hand.

"I know of no law," he concluded, "except"—he raised his arm to the copy of the Declaration of Independence hanging on a pillar across the room—"except that law. I know of no other law that reaches the case of my clients but the Law of Nature and of Nature's God on which our fathers placed our own national existence."

"Extraordinary!" Justice Story wrote to his wife from his boarding house that evening. "Extraordinary, I say, for its power and its bitter sarcasm, and its dealing with topics far beyond the record and point of discussion. . . . The old man is full of his accustomed virility and belligerency."

Justice Philip Barbour, sixty years old and to all appearances in excellent health, died in his sleep that night. His funeral was held in the Capitol chamber where he had listened with somber attention to the man who had once called him a "shallow-pate." Adams was one of the distinguished mourners, seated with the remaining justices in the front row of the courtroom, and he rode with the cortege to the cemetery.

When the court reconvened the following Monday, March 1, he briefly recapitulated the salient points of his argument, then went on to ridicule the contention of Grundy and his successor, Gilpin, that the government had no authority to "go behind or enquire into the validity of the *Amistad*'s papers." Suppose, he said, Van Buren had acted on Grundy's contention that the Africans were Spanish property and had delivered them to their Cuban slavemasters. "What would have been the tenure by which every human being in this Union, man, woman, or child, would have held the blessing of freedom? Would it not have been by the tenure of executive discretion, caprice, or tyranny, at the dictate of a foreign minister?"

For three hours he continued his castigation of Van Buren and his Southern Cabinet members, of District Attorney Holabird, of Lieutenant Gedney. Much of the material stored in his mind had not yet been touched. But it would be unwise, he realized, to tire his so far attentive audience. He stopped abruptly, and looked in turn at each of the faces above him. Every one of these men he was appealing to was younger than himself, Thompson by only a year, but the others by ten- to twenty-odd years, and yet by contemporary standards they were all old men, too. He went on:

"May it please your honors: On the seventh of February, 1804, now more than thirty-seven years past, my name was entered and yet stands recorded on the rolls as one of the attorneys and counselors of this court. Five years later, in February and March of 1809, I appeared for the last time before this court in defense of the cause of justice. Very shortly afterward, I was called to the discharge of other duties—first in distant lands, and in later years within our own country. Little did I imagine that I should ever again be required to claim the right of appearing in the capacity of an officer of this court. Yet such has been the dictate of destiny, and I appear again to plead the cause of justice, and now of liberty and life.

"I stand before the same court, but not before the same

judges. As I cast my eyes along those seats of honor and of public trust, now occupied by you, they seek in vain for one of those honored and honorable persons whose indulgence listened then to my voice. Marshall, Cushing, Chase, [Bushrod] Washington, Johnson, Livingston, Todd. Where are they? Alas! Where is one of the very judges of the court, arbiter of life and death, before whom I commenced this anxious argument? Where are they all? Gone! Gone! All gone! Gone from the services which in their day and generation they faithfully rendered to their country. I humbly hope, and fondly trust, that they have gone to receive the reward of blessings on high. In taking this, my final leave of this bar, and of this honorable court, I can only ejaculate a fervent petition to Heaven, that every member of it may go to his final account with as little of earthly frailty to answer for as those illustrious dead, and that you may, every one, after the close of a long and virtuous career in this world, be received at the portals of the next with the approving sentence, 'Well done, good and faithful servant; enter thou into the joy of thy Lord.' "

The next day Gilpin spoke in rebuttal, sticking closely to the legal points at issue and ignoring most of Adams' polemic accusations. Adams walked home in the raw winter afternoon filled with uncertainty. "My anxiety over the decision," he said, "is intense and deeply distrustful."

He "waited upon tenterhooks" for the justices to hand down their ruling. In the meanwhile the Twenty-sixth Congress adjourned and William Henry Harrison, the sixty-eight-year-old hero of the Battle of Tippecanoe, was inaugurated the first Whig President of the United States. Although Adams had little respect for Harrison's intellect or administrative ability, he considered him "amiable and benevolent," and hoped for the best. One of Harrison's first errands upon arriving in Washington had been to call on his former President. Adams had been away on one of his long walks, but he had promptly returned the visit, spending an agreeable hour with the old general in his rooms at Gadsby's Hotel. He watched the inaugural parade from an upstairs window of his home in the company of Joshua Leavitt. The day was bleak, and a sharp wind rippled the rusty puddles along F Street. The two men at the window had difficulty distinguishing the new President in the cavalcade of Whig dignitaries as the two-mile-long parade passed with its log-cabin floats and "Tippecanoe" bands. Harrison wore a plain frock coat—hardly adequate for the weather—and was mounted, Adams said, "on a mean-looking white horse."

On March 8 Adams was informed that the Supreme Court would present its decisions the next day. He spent another wakeful night and was in his chair in the chamber a half hour before the court convened. Taney then announced that the court's majority opinion would be read by Adams' old friend, Justice Story, and Adams' spirits rebounded. But he had to sit for what seemed an eternity while Story reviewed with grave deliberation and measured pauses each detail of the involved case and its legal aspects. Would he never reach the decision? At last it came.

"There does not seem to us to be any ground for doubt that these Negroes ought to be deemed free; and that the Spanish treaty interposes no obstacle to the just assertion of their rights."

The opinion reversed a finding of the district court, that the captives should be "turned over to the President of the United States to be sent back to Africa," since no such provision had been included in the government's action. It directed the circuit court to order them discharged from the custody of the United States marshal in New Haven.

The only dissenting voice was that of the eccentric Henry Baldwin of Ohio. Adams did not wait to hear him finish his rambling opinion. His cane whipping in brisk beat with his legs, he hurried home and wrote to Tappan. The Negroes were free! "Thanks! Thanks, in the name of humanity and justice!"

Congratulations flooded back: from Roger Baldwin, who had returned to New Haven; from Joshua Leavitt, Simeon Jocelyn, William Jay, Ellis Loring. The abolitionist press forgot its resentment over Adams' attack on immediacy and hailed him as the hero of their cause. The outraged South spiced his mail with threats. "Nothing but a good horsewhip will serve you and you must and shall have it," wrote a Virginian. "The Devil will have his own when he gets your rascally soul!"

The immediate question was how to get the Mendi men and children back to Africa. Daniel Webster was now Secretary of State, and Adams called on him. "Since the Negroes have been declared by the court not slaves, not pirates, not robbers, yet were taken from a vessel in their possession, indispensable to them for their voyage home," he said, the government should turn the *Amistad* over to them for that purpose.

Webster, he said, "was startled at the idea." But the new Secretary did concede that the government should provide a vessel for their passage. Before any action could be instigated, however, President Harrison died of pneumonia, his frail health worn down by the campaign and the even worse ordeal of coping with the rush of office seekers demanding their rewards. The cold ride without an overcoat in the inaugural parade had not helped, nor the bleeding and blistering, the opium, brandy and Indian remedies—snakeweed and petroleum—administered by his frantic doctors. He lived in the White House only thirty-one days, and his wife learned of his death as her carriage was on the road from Ohio to join him.

John Tyler was the first Vice President to step into the Presidency. A Virginia gentleman and slaveholder, he had been put on the ticket to draw in the Southern vote; he was as hostile to abolition as he was antipathetic to the Whig platform on which he had been elected. Webster quietly pigeonholed Adams' appeal for the *Amistad* victims. Tappan and his defense committee took the Mendis on a New England tour, admission one shilling, and exhibited them at the Broadway Tabernacle in New York City, tickets fifty cents, and eventually bought their passage back home.

One of the anonymous letters from the South urged Adams to retire while he still had "some dignity left." Curiously, he took it seriously. His seventy-fourth birthday was approaching and the years had left him "with a shaking hand, a darkening eye, a drowsing brain, and with my faculties dropping from me one by one, as the teeth are dropping from my head." Again his constituency had overwhelmingly reelected him. Was not now the time to step down, with his crowning achievement the rescue of the innocent Africans? In the cluttered study of his house in F Street he mulled over his decision long and painstakingly that evening.

His first thought was, "I cannot afford it." His economic condition was no better than the country's: the rents from his New England farmlands were hardly meeting the taxes and upkeep, and he was not yet out of debt to his old manservant, Antoine Giusta. But Charles Francis, he knew, would dispute that argument; and so would Louisa. No. The compelling reason was rooted deep in his nature: the "vacuity of occupation in which I could take an interest."

"More than sixty years of active intercourse with the world has made political movement to me as much a necessity of life as the atmospheric air," he wrote in the diary that would be his legacy—and apology—to future generations of Adamses. "This is the weakness of my nature which I have intelligence enough to perceive but not energy to control. And thus, while a remnant of physical power is left me to write and speak, the world will retire from me before I shall retire from the world."

Even if he had decided to retire, he soon would have changed his mind. Already another spectacular contest was in the making, one that would pit his "dropping faculties" not only against the anti-abolitionist majority in the House but the top strategists of the Whig party as well. And the Democrats had not heard the final words from him on the *Amistad* case.

XVI

I N the House, the Southern wall against Adams' petition crusade was now tighter than ever, but its underpinning was weakening. Session after session, the proslavery coalition had strengthened their gag rule until, in the past Congress, they had made it a standing rule, the twenty-first, for all sessions thereafter: "No petitions, memorials, resolutions or other papers, praying for abolition of slavery in the District of Columbia, or any state or territory, or the slave trade between the states and territories of the United States in which it now exists, shall be received by this House, or entertained in any way whatsoever."

To achieve this the South had depended on support from Representatives of the Northern states obedient to party harmony, both Whig and Democrat. But the support had been steadily shrinking. In 1836 eighty-two Congressmen from the free states had voted with the South. In 1839 the number had been forty-nine, and in 1840 it had fallen to twenty-six.

The expanding petition campaign, with its emphasis on the right of citizens to assert themselves—"If Congress can bury 10,000 names this year, let them have 20,000 next year, and 40,000 the next"—had increased the nucleus of antislavery Congressmen from the solitary veteran, William Slade of Vermont, to a dozen. For the 1840 election the abolitionists had even created their own Liberty party, but their candidate, James G. Birney of Ohio, had polled only 7,059 votes.

Now that the American Anti-Slavery Society had finally collapsed altogether, its leaders turned to establishing an abolition lobby in Washington to work with the antislavery Congressmen and help handle the petition flood. Joshua Leavitt moved to the capital for the *Emancipator*, and he took Theodore Weld with him to coordinate the work and do the research. Three members of the congressional group were disciples of Weld, converted to abolition in his platform days. They were Joshua Giddings of Ohio, an enrolled Whig, a Quaker and already one of Adams' closest friends; Sherlock Andrews, also of Ohio; and Seth Gates of New York. They had rooms in Mrs. Sprigg's boarding house on First Street at the foot of Capitol Hill, and Leavitt and Weld moved in with them. Soon Slade and several others joined them there, and it became known, sardonically at first, as Abolition House. Mrs. Sprigg worried "that the character of her house would be hurt and members of Congress would shun it," Weld wrote his wife, Angelina Grimké. But, instead, it had become "the only boarding house in Washington which has *all* its rooms and beds occupied, and she has not, as most of the other boarding houses have done, *lowered her prices* at all." Mrs. Sprigg, a Virginian, did decide, however, that the atmosphere was not healthy for her slave help; she farmed them out to friends and hired free Negroes. *"Stick a pin there!"* said Weld.

That New Year's Day, in 1842, Weld and Leavitt strolled up Pennsylvania Avenue to look in on President Tyler's levee. The fashionable crush inside the White House had become so great, with hundreds more visitors still collecting on the lawn, that the porter had locked the doors "to avert the danger of suffocation." Weld and his companion went away, "saddened at the pomp and tinsel and display of magnificence." On their walk back to their lodgings Leavitt turned into F Street, and they fell in with the line entering the red-brick house of John Quincy Adams.

Adams wrote that night that "this was the thirtieth New Year's Day in the course of my life I have passed in Washington," and he and Louisa had had 500 callers, more than twice as many as ever before, diplomats, clergymen, members of Tyler's Cabinet, but mostly Whig politicians with their wives and children, among them "some slaveholders." When Leavitt introduced his shaggy companion, Adams said, "Is this Mr. Theodore Weld? Yes, I know you well by your writings." He took the author of *American Slavery as It Is* by the hand and led him across the crowded room to Louisa.

"Found him and his wife living in a plain house," Weld wrote Angelina, "plainly furnished, and themselves plainly dressed— the old gentleman *very plainly*." Louisa was wan and remote, quietly grieving the recent death of her twelve-year-old grandchild, Mary's youngest daughter, Georgiana Frances, of fever. When Adams introduced him, Weld wrote his wife, "I was glad to hear him call her 'my dear,' as I think you told me they lived unhappily together." (Angelina had visited Adams in Quincy four years before to enlist his open support for abolition; the practical reasons he had given her for refusing had made her "sick at heart over political morality.")

Despite the procession of visitors now, Adams kept Weld beside him, his face going stonily vacant one moment for a passing handshake, then brightening again as they resumed their colloquy: old friends immediately.

A week later the Adamses had Weld to dinner, along with two other boarders from Mrs. Sprigg's establishment, Leavitt and Gates. "All teetotalers," Adams discovered; "recharbites who drink no wine." Weld also turned down the roast, explaining in his husky voice—a casualty of the crusader platform— that as a Grahamite he did not touch animal food. But dull the dinner was not. "It was a genuine abolition gathering," Weld said. "The old patriarch talked with as much energy and zeal as a Methodist at a camp meeting. Remarkable man!"

The abolitionists were organizing their little bloc of House colleagues into a select committee on slavery. Weld, with his talent for persistent research—he would spend hours in the libraries of Congress and the Supreme Court tracking down obscure bits of record—was to pass the ammunition. The topic absorbing him at the moment, and his fellow guests as well, was another slave-ship insurrection. Two months before, the coastal schooner *Creole* had set out from Hampton Roads to deliver 135 young Virginia-bred slaves to the New Orleans market. The Negroes had mutinied, killed one of their owners and sailed the ship into the emancipated British colony of Nassau. There the authorities had executed the ringleaders and freed the rest. Southern Congressmen were demanding that the British government pay for the liberated slaves and calling for an ultimatum to Britain that, if she did not, America would consider it an act of aggression. Secretary of State Webster was worried; he was having enough trouble getting along with Tyler and preparing to work out a treaty with the British commissioner, Lord Ashburton, on the northeastern border between the United States and Canada.

Weld argued at the dinner that the South did not have "a leg to stand on" in the *Creole* case. He expanded with trenchant eloquence on his municipal theory: that the Constitution made slavery the responsibility of the states where it existed; therefore, the federal government was not required to enforce it outside their territories. His Supreme Court victory, Weld reminded Adams, had done more to publicize the evil of slavery than all the petitions flung against the South's "wall of silence." Here was an equally flagrant issue. Adams appeared to agree, but he declined to get involved in another slave-ship case; besides, these Negroes were already freed. At the same time he showed such a keen interest in the select House committee that Weld and his fellow guests got the impression he was inviting himself onto it. Actually, it developed, Adams wanted it for himself but modified to his rigid requirements, for it appeared under his tutelage as the Friends of the Right of Petition.

On January 15, having discussed his plan with Giddings, he called the abolitionist Congressmen together in a committee room at the Capitol. Besides Giddings and Andrews from Ohio, there were, from New York State, Gates, Daniel Barnard, Francis Granger, Thomas Chittenden and Archibald Linn; from Vermont, Slade; from Massachusetts, William B. Calhoun; from Maine, David Bronson; and from Pennsylvania, Joseph Lawrence. They listened politely to Adams' explanation that the imperative need was still to break down the barrier against discussion of slavery in the House of Representatives, "the people's forum." His awareness that the group was not wholeheartedly in agreement was confirmed when only a few showed up at the next meeting to hear his resolution condemning the gag rule as unconstitutional. But he was not disheartened.

Neither was there any change in his friendship with the Abolition House coterie, particularly Weld and Giddings; they were just not as Constitution-minded as he. Visiting with Weld on the eve of the twenty-first, he revealed he was about to resume his own war on the slavocrats, this time with some provocative petitions dodging the gag rule that would "set them ablaze." Weld should be at the House early to get a good seat.

Members were still allowed to bring guests onto the floor, and Adams found an empty desk for Weld near his own. He started off by presenting a petition from Massachusetts asking amendment of the naturalization laws to permit "free colored foreigners" to become citizens and hold real estate. Henry Wise indignantly had it tabled. Adams' next petition, also from Massachusetts, prayed that Congress "secure to each of the states representative government," pointing out that in thirteen states —and it listed the slave states—the government was "absolutely despotic, onerous and oppressive in its exactions on a great number of its citizens." That, too, was peremptorily laid on the table. The third was a resolution from the Quakers of Pennsylvania alarmed over the *Creole* case: "Whereas it is proposed that this country go to war with England to oblige the British government to assist in holding natives of the United States in slavery . . . resolved, that such a war would be as unrighteous as that which was waged against this country in 1766 [*sic*], as the wrongs inflicted on the slaves in some of the states exceed in magnitude the wrongs which led to the Declaration of Independence."

By now the Southern members had again left their desks and thronged around Adams. As soon as the substance of the petition became apparent, they started interrupting him, shouting he was out of order, demanding that the Speaker cut him off.

"But," Weld wrote his wife, "he contrived to get through the whole." The petition was sent to the table with the rest.

Now that Adams had his audience properly conditioned, he took up the petition that he had been leading up to. In reshuffling the committee assignments at the beginning of the session, the Whig Speaker, John White of Kentucky, had finally made him chairman of the Committee on Foreign Affairs, the position that every Democratic Speaker had denied him in spite of his experience and interest in that field. Because of his hostility to taking Texas into the Union, the appointment had not pleased the Southern Whigs, but they had accepted it.

"I have another petition to present which, unfortunately, is somewhat personal," Adams said. "It comes from Georgia and complains as a great grievance that I have been appointed chairman of the Committee on Foreign Affairs. The petition is couched in the most respectable language, and I ask, nay demand it as a right, that the House hear me in defense against the charge."

He read from the preamble: " '. . . We believe he is possessed of a species of monomania on all subjects connected with people as dark as a Mexican, and therefore is not fit to be entrusted with the business of our relations with Mexico.' "

The petition was no surprise to some of the Southern leaders, but they were surprised that Adams was presenting it. He had shown it to several of them, and they had dismissed it as a hoax concocted by some irresponsible Georgians to annoy him. They forgot that Adams had a talent for turning hoaxes against their perpetrators. Wise asked Adams to yield for a brief statement. The petition was "purely mischievous" and not worth discussing, he said; Adams should withdraw it. Richard Habersham, of Savannah, Georgia, said the paper was postmarked from his own district, where he knew everybody, and he had told Adams there was not a name on it that he recognized. Thomas Marshall, a junior member from Kentucky, tall, handsome, the personable young nephew of the late Supreme Court justice and already a Southern favorite, proposed that, since Adams had brought up the subject himself, it should be considered: "For one, I am more than halfway of the opinion of these petitioners,

247

that the gentleman from Massachusetts—I intend no disrespect to him—is a monomaniac, . . . and I am anxious to hear how he will defend himself."

Exactly what he intended to do, said Adams, and demanded that, as a personal privilege, he be permitted to proceed.

Would it not be better, asked James Spriggs of Kentucky, to bring Adams to trial "before a court of lunacy"? The roar of applause from the Southern seats was gaveled down by Speaker White; he put the question of privilege to the House, and it was tabled by the close vote of 94 to 92.

Adams had not surrendered the floor, and the next day he explained, with apparent humbleness, that his intention had been to present his defense and then move that the matter be referred to the Committee on Foreign Affairs with the recommendation that, if it were so inclined, it elect a new chairman. On that ground the House obligingly reversed itself—and Adams had what he had been maneuvering for: a devious path around the gag rule. Habersham tried to forestall him by announcing he had further proof that the petition was a hoax. "Whether it is genuine or whether it is a forgery," Adams retorted, "it is equally an outrage on me and the House."

Wise was his first target. "The gentleman from Virginia" had protested to the Speaker, Adams said, when his chairmanship of the committee was announced, and he had complained further that the committee had been "loaded with a majority of non-slaveholders." Wise had persuaded his colleagues on the committee to block recognition of the black government of Haiti, playing into the hands of Britain and France, which had done so much to their economic profit.

Habersham came next. He had said "he would have put it [the petition] in his pocket. I know the gentleman's course with petitions. He puts all such petitions in his pocket. . . . The great right of petition of the people of the United States is trampled on."

Another legislator had proclaimed that for slavery "to assure permanent ascendancy it is only necessary to understand the prophetic truth of Mr. Jefferson that 'the democracy of the North is the natural ally of the South.'"

"There!" said Adams. "The democracy of the North is the natural ally of the slave traders! Is it?"

W. Cost Johnson, together with Wise and Habersham, was now shouting to the Speaker to rule Adams out of order and make him take his seat.

"I see where the shoe pinches," Adams yelled back ("with much acrimony," wrote the reporter for the *Congressional Globe*). "There is an alliance between the Southern slave traders and Northern Democrats. . . . This charge is not a trifling one. I give warning to the slave-trading Representatives, and their Northern auxiliaries, *Whig and Democrat*, that I am willing to abide by their vote, and let the question go to the Committee on Foreign Affairs."

"The gentleman from Massachusetts is out of order," Speaker White broke in. "The gentleman—" But Adams would not be stopped. The *Congressional Globe* was then the official journal of the proceedings of Congress, but by now its reporter had given up trying to winnow Adams' voice from the "perfect uproar" in the hall. "The noise and confusion that prevailed," he complained, was so great that he could not hear much of what went on. Weld, however, was again in his seat.

"Old Nestor lifted up his voice like a trumpet," he said, "till slaveholding, slave trading, and slave breeding absolutely quailed and howled under his dissecting knife. . . . Wise of Virginia, Rayner of North Carolina, W. Cost Johnson of Maryland, and scores more of slaveholders, strove constantly to stop him by starting questions of order and by every now and then screaming at the top of their voices: 'That is false!' 'I demand, Mr. Speaker, that you put him down!' 'I demand that you shut the mouth of that old harlequin!' 'Are we to sit here and endure such insults?'

"A perfect uproar like Babel would burst forth every two or three minutes as Mr. A., with his bold surgery, would smite his cleaver into the very bones. At least half of the slaveholding members of the House left their seats and gathered in the quarter of the hall where Mr. Adams stood. Whenever any of them broke out upon him, Mr. Adams would say, 'I see where the shoe pinches, Mr. Speaker. It will pinch *more* yet. I'll deal out to the gentlemen a diet that they will find it hard to digest. If before I get through every slaveholder, slave trader and slave breeder on this floor does not get material for better reflection, it shall be no fault of mine!' "

The Speaker was now gaveling so violently that Adams could no longer disregard him. "The gentleman from Massachusetts is *clearly out of order,*" White shouted. "He *must* take his seat!"

Adams slid sideways into his chair—smiling.

"I am in my seat."

The Foreign Affairs Committee subsequently voted not to remove him from the chairmanship, but five Southern members resigned, declaring they would not serve with Adams; and White was hard-pressed to find willing replacements. More important, the Southern Whigs met in secret caucus and decided it was finally time to rid the House of Adams. Their Northern supporters agreed. He was endangering party harmony. To pacify the Southern wing, he had to be punished, and severely. Moreover, anything less would encourage others to disruptive tactics.

The Democrats remained aloof, except to vote. "This was entirely a family affair, in which Whig met Whig," wrote Edward G. Black of Georgia, a Whig at the time and later a Democrat. "The Democrats stood by, . . . without taking part in the conflict."

Adams did not keep the Whig party waiting. His next petition caused such a stir around him that members up the aisles damned the peculiar acoustics of the hall and asked each other what the "old reprobate," "curmudgeon," "harlequin," "miscreant," "rapscallion," "obstructionist," "scalawag," "knave" could be up to now. Across the desks the answer came back: He was presenting a paper for *dissolution of the Union!*

" 'To the Congress of the United States . . . pray that you will immediately adopt measures peaceably to dissolve the Union of these States.' "

The wintry voice went on, for once with no interruption:

" 'First, because no Union can be agreeable or permanent which does not present the prospect of reciprocal benefits.

" 'Second, because a vast proportion of the resources of one section of the Union is annually drained to sustain the views and course of another section, without any adequate return.

" 'Third, because, judging from the history of past nations, that Union, if persisted in, in the present course of things, will certainly overwhelm the whole nation in utter destruction.' "

The petition was from Haverhill, in Massachusetts, the home village of the abolitionist poet Whittier, but his name was not among the forty-six signatures (and no one ever *proved* that he fostered it).

"I move its reference to a select committee," Adams went on, "with instructions to report an answer to the petitioners showing why their prayer should not be granted."

Henry Wise was out of his chair.

"Mr. Speaker! *Mr. Speaker!* Is it in order to move to censure any member presenting such a petition?"

"Good!" said Adams, settling into his seat.

"You may judge what followed," wrote Dr. D. F. Bacon, the correspondent for the New York *American*. "Amid a furious uproar, Mr. Gilmer [Thomas Gilmer of Virginia] moved that the gentleman from Massachusetts had subjected himself to censure of the House."

Gilmer's resolution brought a prompt response from Adams: "I hope it will be received and debated, so I may have the privilege of addressing the House in my own defense." He added slyly, "Especially as the gentleman from Albemarle [Gilmer] has thought proper to play second fiddle to his colleague from Accomac [Wise]."

"I play second fiddle to no man," Gilmer retorted, "but I have been endeavoring to prevent the music of one

Who in the course of one revolving moon
Is statesman, poet, babbler and buffoon.

That ended the day's session, except for a not uncommon rumpus up one of the aisles. Thomas Arnold, a Whig from Tennessee, a Westerner who admired Adams, and John Dawson, a Louisiana Democrat, were calling each other "blackguard" and "damned coward." Dawson, who habitually wore a

251

Bowie knife, leaned over Arnold's desk, his hand on the knife. "Stand up and I'll cut your throat from ear to ear!" Arnold, who was not armed, sensibly stayed in his chair.

The next day Thomas Marshall, the aggressive Congressman from Kentucky, amended Gilmer's resolution to accuse Adams of treasonable conduct. Although Marshall was serving his first term, the Southern Whigs had assigned him a prominent role, partly for his prestige as the Chief Justice's nephew and also because he was not recognized in the North as one of the "angry slavocrats." Adams "might well be held to merit expulsion," Marshall said, "but in grace and mercy they [would] only inflict upon him their severest censure for conduct so utterly unworthy of his past relations to the state. . . . For the rest, they turn him over to his own conscience and the indignation of all true American citizens."

In presenting the "so monstrous" Haverhill petition, he said, Adams had not only committed a high breach of privilege; he had "offered to this House, and each member of it, . . . a direct proposition to commit perjury, . . . its consequences the destruction of our country and *the crime of high treason!* . . . His action strikes me with horror, it stupefies me. I had not thought it possible that there could be men wild enough in the country, and mad enough, to propose that the government of the United States should terminate its own existence, and then to submit it to this House."

The charge of high treason astonished him, Adams answered. "What is high treason? The Constitution of the United States says what high treason is, and it is not for him, or his puny mind, to define high treason or confound it with what I have done. I desire the clerk to read the first paragraph of the Declaration of Independence." Shrilly: "The first paragraph of the Declaration of Independence!" At the top of his voice: *"The first paragraph of the Declaration of Independence!"*

The clerk read: " 'When in the course of human events, it becomes necessary for one people to dissolve the political bands which have connected them with another, and to assume among the powers of the earth, the separate and equal station to which the Laws of Nature and of Nature's God entitle them, a decent respect to the opinions of mankind requires that they should declare the causes which impel them to the separation.' "

Proceed!" Adams demanded. "*Proceed! Proceed!* Down to 'the right and duty'!"

" 'We hold these truths to be self evident, . . . Life, Liberty . . . pursuit of Happiness. That to secure these rights, Governments are instituted among Men, deriving their just powers from the consent of the governed. That whenever any Form of Government becomes destructive of these ends, it is the Right of the People to alter or to abolish it. . . . When a long train of abuses and usurpations, . . . evinces a design to reduce them under absolute Despotism, it is their right, it is their duty, to throw off such Government—' "

Adams slapped his hand down on the desk. "Right and duty to *alter* or *abolish* it! If there is a principle sacred on earth, and established by the instrument just read [which he did not have to remind them his father had helped write], it is the right of the people to alter, to change, to destroy the government if it becomes oppressive to them. There would be no such right existing if the people had not the power, in pursuance of that right, to petition for it."

The people of the North, he went on, had been oppressed "for eight or ten years" by the petition gags, "by this coalition of Southern slaveholders and Northern Democrats. . . . It is time for the Northern people to see if they can't shake it off, and it is time to present such petitions as this. I can say *it is not yet time to do this;* the other means have not been tried. I say that if the petition is referred and answered, it will satisfy the petitioners. They will see that there are other measures to be pursued; and, first of all, to restore the right of petition."

His opponents wanted the resolution voted on immediately; that would have prevented Adams from defending himself further. He demanded time to prepare. "Was it ever known," he asked, "that, to a man on whom charges of this kind were started of a sudden, and totally unexpectedly, no time was to be allowed for his defense?"

Speaker White was unsympathetic. "You can submit a motion for further time, by yourself or by a friend," he answered. Horace Everett of Vermont tried, but was shouted down.

"Now!" "Now!"

Fortunately for Adams, Henry Wise got the floor and talked till adjournment. He spoke, said the *Congressional Globe,* "with great vehemence but with a voice so fitful and unsteady that the closing part of many sentences was inaudible." Wise explained he had a bad cold, "in the lungs and head." Apparently his medication had been bourbon. He had the clerk read a paragraph from Washington's Farewell Address as President, warning against "small, artful, enterprising minorities." That much his audience heard. The rest was a long ramble, punctuated with coughs and heaves.

The next day Wise's cold was better. Washington had read in its morning newspapers that Adams was on trial and might—"should," said the Democratic *Globe*—be expelled from the House; the gallery was packed. So many journalists were on hand that there was not room at the press table, and an indignant Congressman protested that some of them had taken seats "within the bar of the House."

Wise held the floor all day, a compelling figure: the Virginia cavalier, country squire, rider to the hounds, tall, dark, spare-limbed, his cravat and long-tailed frock coat wearing the careless look of the plantation gentleman. If the walnut butt of a pistol showed at his waist no one mentioned it, nor would they have been expected to; it was commonly part of his attire (Bowie knives were for the men from the new South and the West) .

With a hard look across the desks at Adams, Wise assured his audience that he had admired "this venerable man who has come to this House from the Presidential chair, one of the greatest and most profound diplomats of the age, one of the highest authorities now living on international law. But now"—his voice boomed—"now words cannot express the personal loathing, dread and contempt I feel for the man!"

Wise went on to explore, point by point, virtually every current grievance of the plantation South against the abolitionists and "their protagonist here, this gentleman from Massachusetts." The case of the slave ship *Creole* came in for detailed examination, and the North's unwillingness to force Britain to pay for the slaves she had liberated; the opposition to annexing Texas; the "petition nuisance"; the campaign to abolish the slave trade in the District of Columbia. He read long extracts from the *Emancipator*, whose editor, Leavitt, was busily taking notes, from Garrison's *Liberator* and the *Anti-Slavery Reporter*.

Adams, he said, was a member of the "pro-British party" in New England, the descendants of the old Federalist hierarchy, now toadying to the English abolitionists. He elaborated on Senator Calhoun's assertion that slavery was a positive good: "Wherever black slavery exists, there is found an equality among the white population," he told the House, "but where it has no place such equality is not found. Look at England! The principle of slavery is a leveling principle; it is friendly to equality. Break down slavery, and you will with the same blow destroy the great democratic principle of equality among men."

Leavitt was watching Adams. The old man was restraining himself, his face taut, fingers gripping the edge of his desk. Wise took a moment to stare silently at "this fiend, the inspirer and leader of all abolition," and went on: "That one should so have outlived his fame! To think of the veneration, the honor, the reverence that would have been attached to every word he uttered, so that the moment he rose to speak every breath should be hushed! To think how he would have been looked upon with awe, . . . as the last link that bound this age to the Revolutionary Fathers! . . . I thank God that the gentleman, great as he was, neither has, nor is likely to have, sufficient influence to excite a spirit of disunion throughout the land. . . . The gentleman is politically dead! Dead as Burr! Dead as Arnold! The people will look upon him with wonder, will shudder, and retire!"

With a sweeping gesture of disdain, he dropped exhausted into his chair. Millard Fillmore, a leading Whig from abolitionist upstate New York, tried to come to Adams' assistance, but his motion to table the censure resolution was loudly defeated, and the House adjourned. Adams walked home, a lonely figure in the January dusk, but there was no weariness in his gait. As usual, the debilities he complained of in introspective moods were forgotten. He was in for a rough fight, possibly the roughest in his life. The arithmetic of the situation alone was defeatist. A hundred members of the House were committed to slavery, "four-fifths of whom would crucify me if their votes could erect the cross; forty members, representatives of the free, in the league of slavery, . . . would break me on the wheel; and four-fifths of the other hundred and twenty are either so cold or so lukewarm that they are ready to desert me at the first scintillation of indiscretion on my part."

He had not realized the effect these last days' turmoil was having on his household. The downstairs was dark. He found Louisa in bed, with Mary and their house guest, his cousin Louisa Smith, hovering over her. She had become so agitated that she had fainted. Later in the evening Theodore Weld appeared at the door. He had been among the standees against the back wall of the House gallery all day, he said. What a distinguished audience there had been in front of him, and even inside the bar, among them members of the Senate and the foreign embassies. All Washington was engrossed in the spectacle. Judging by the crowded press table, it was certain the country soon would be, too. He had come to offer Adams his help. Were there not matters he could research: references, citations, documents? Arguments to compile? He and his fellow boarders at Abolition House were "highly excited by these motions of censure on you."

"I thank you," Adams answered. "I accept your offer gratefully."

Weld entirely put aside his other work. The association that began that evening, between the frosty old New Englander and the shaggy evangelist in "John the Baptist garb," was one of the most intimate in Adams' long career. Since neither ate supper, they were at the table in Adams' study soon after each day's session, working long into the night. Adams laid out a detailed program of research, and Weld pursued it tirelessly in the nook Giddings had provided for him in the Library of Congress, breaking off only to squeeze into the packed gallery at intervals to watch Adams fling his invective-tipped shafts and parry those of the phalanx of Southern and Northern Whigs determined to punish him.

To recount the day-by-day progress of Adams' battle would bury it in a mountain of verbosity. The record filled ninety-odd columns of fine print in the *Congressional Globe,* and the *Globe*'s reporters complained frequently that they could not catch even the sense of some of the speakers for the brawling, the shouting and general turmoil around Adams. A Northern correspondent wrote, "It is little better than a house of rowdies. Nine times out of ten, when a member yells, 'I rise to a point of order,' he means, 'I rise to kick up a row.' "

Marshall's "perjury and high treason" amendment had made the censure resolution essentially his. "Where did he get his law?" Adams asked. "Assuredly not from his uncle. . . . Let him go home, let him go to some law school and learn a little of the rights of the citizens of these states and of the members of this House. . . . I will show that they [the Haverhill petitioners] have a right to petition for dissolution and that the House has no power to suppress that right."

Behind his personable façade Marshall had a closely guarded weakness: he had trouble staying sober. "I hear he has taken the pledge," Adams said. "I hope he will succeed in that reform." Meanwhile, "let him learn that if there is a disgrace in this House it is the presentation of such a resolution as he has offered against me. For these crimes [perjury and treason] I could only be tried by a regular circuit court, by an *impartial jury*. I deny the right of at least one hundred members of the House to sit in judgment upon me, their personal and pecuniary interest in the question carrying such a bias."

He cited the Sixth Amendment to the Constitution: "In all criminal prosecutions, the accused shall enjoy the right to a speedy and public trial, by an impartial jury . . .'" and went on, "These slaveholders are not by whom I ought to be judged. Their bias would make them challengeable as jurors in any court."

As for the House punishing him "for presenting a petition— *a petition*—if they say they will, they must. If they say that in *grace and mercy* they will spare me expulsion, I disdain and cast their mercy away. . . . I defy them. . . . I shall require the benefits which the Constitution secures to persons tried in judicial courts. I shall claim to be heard in my defense, *fully!*"

To which Henry Wise replied, " 'Come on Macduff,/ And damn'd be he who first cries, hold, enough!' "

The next day Adams accommodated him. He recalled the duel four years before between the two Congressmen, Jonathan Cilley, from Maine, and William Graves of Kentucky. Henry Wise, Adams reminded the House, had been instrumental in forcing the duel, and as Graves' second had insisted on a third round after the contestants had twice missed one another, and young Cilley had been killed. The infuriated Democrats had demanded that the House try Wise, along with Graves, for murder.

"There came into this House then a man with his hands and face dripping with the blood of murder," Adams said, waving a finger at Wise, "the blotches of which were still hanging upon him. . . . The man who pulled the trigger was but an instrument in his hands."

"That is as base and black a lie," Wise yelled, "as the traitor is black and base who utters it!"

Adams went on, "The question was put, should he be tried by this House for that crime—the crime of murder. I opposed the trial of that man by this House because it was, like at the present, a case in which the charges were of a higher nature. I thought they should be tried where they would have the advantages which this instrument"—he held up his copy of the Constitution—"secures, a public trial by an impartial jury of the state and district wherein the crime was committed. It is very probable that *I* saved this blood-stained man from the censure of the House at that time."

"Mr. Speaker! Mr. Speaker!" Wise protested. "Is it my conduct that is on trial here?"

He was merely citing a precedent, Adams explained. "If I am to be tried by the slaveholders I shall not have an impartial trial. I come from a part of the country where slavery is known only by name. I represent here the descendants of Bradford and

Winslow and Carver, and John Alden—the first who alighted on the rock of Plymouth. And am I, the representative of the descendants of these men, of the free people of the state of Massachusetts, am I to come here and be tried for high treason for presenting a petition—*a petition*—to this House, because the gentleman from Kentucky supposes there was anti-slavery or the abolition of slavery in it?"

That evening Adams opened his door before Weld could lift the knocker; he ascended the stairs to the study "as fresh and elastic as a boy," said his guest. Weld's admiration by now bordered on worship.

"The energy with which Mr. A. speaks is astonishing," he wrote his wife. "Though seventy-five years old, his voice is one of the clearest and loudest in the House, and his gestures . . . are most vigorous and commanding. . . . He had been in the House from twelve o'clock till six, and for nearly half that time engaged in speaking with great energy against his ferocious assailants. . . . I told him I was afraid he had tired himself out. 'No, not at all,' said he. 'I am all ready for another heat.' He then began and went through with the main points which he designed to push in his speech the next day, and with as much rapidity and energy of utterance and gesture as though he had been addressing the House. I tried to stop him, telling him he would need all his strength for the next day; but it was all in vain. He went on for an hour, . . . in a voice loud enough to be heard by a large audience. Wonderful man!"

Weld's prediction that interest in the case would expand far beyond the House gallery was already confirmed. From the press table the new railroads, trailing their black plumes of wood smoke over the countryside, carried the daily reports to the seaboard cities and villages; by turnpike and river steamer they filtered inland. Baltimore and Philadelphia were only a day behind the Washington newspapers, New York was two, Boston, three. Around whale-oil lamps and fireplaces, families read to each other, skimming the items about President Tyler's break with the Whig leaders, the Senate's debate of the Bankruptcy Act, the "Boz Ball" for Charles Dickens' heralded visit to America, to follow the day-to-day polemics. Hot arguments raged on around the stoves in the feed and general stores and barbershops, the harness makers', the blacksmiths', wheelwrights', coopers'.

At first the general reaction, even in the North, was against Adams. *Dissolution of the Union!* Treason, indeed! Adams' former host at dinner parties, New York's conservative former mayor, Philip Hone, spoke for his fellow Whigs: "The former President's insane movement . . . *for a repeal of the Union* because the petitioners are deprived of the privilege of agitating the terrible question of slavery . . . disgusts his friends."

But as Adams' defense developed, the Northern mood changed. Dr. Bacon, Washington correspondent for the New York *American,* defined his position, and other Whig correspondents agreed with him. "The merits of the abolition cause have nothing to do with the present question," said Dr. Bacon. "The real issue is free speech and Northern rights. If Mr. Adams had not been gagged, he would have remained innocuous, and abolition petitions might have run through the House almost unnoticed."

Adams was not done with Marshall. That gentleman had first called him a monomaniac, he said, and now "he has converted the monomaniac into an incendiary and traitor. Is it customary to charge an insane man with the commission of a crime?" That brought laughter from the gallery. To Marshall's discomfiture, Adams produced a letter he had written to a Kentucky journal before joining the Southern contingent in the House. The letter denounced slavery and called for "immediate remedy!"

Although the Democrats were letting the Whigs lead the attack, some among them could not keep out of the melee. One of the most bitter was the South Carolina "fire eater," Robert Barnwell Rhett. After a castigation by Rhett, Adams sorted through his papers and produced a letter the South Carolinian had written to constituents three years before in response to an attack on slavery by Slade of Vermont. Had Rhett forgotten the resolution he had included in that letter? Adams asked. " '*Resolved,*' " he read, " 'that the Constitution of the United States having proved inadequate to protect the Southern states in peaceable enjoyment of their rights and property, it is expedient that the said Constitution should be amended, *or the Union of the states be dissolved.'* "

"I did not present it," Rhett shouted.

"No. Your friends dissuaded you."

Weld was carefully monitoring the out-of-town newspapers and getting reports from his agents in the North. Even the Whig editors who knew the party leaders' purpose were beginning to show a grudging admiration for Adams, standing up alone and tirelessly against the battering of his opponents. More important, Northern constituents were writing to their Congressmen and petitions were pouring in, the signatures collected so hurriedly that the ink was smudged. Now New York's Philip Hone was calling Adams "that indomitable, pugnacious, wonderful man of knowledge." And, a few days later, "the old hero." The New York *American*'s Dr. Bacon hailed him as the torchbearer of independence and reported he was being called "Old '76."

When, in the second week of the contest, Adams announced he would need "another three weeks" to complete his defense, the response was "an uproar." He reminded the House that a half century before, the retired governor-general of India, Warren Hastings, had taken seven years to defend himself on charges of high crime against the British Empire. To all appearances, Adams was ready to go on that long, but by now his opponents, frankly worried by the support Adams was getting from the North, wished they had never started the contest. Even Washington's *National Intelligencer,* which had at first loyally supported the Whig leaders, so loyally that Adams had denounced the party organ for distorting its reports, had come to his defense. "We would not in his place have presented the petition which has produced such a sensation in Congress," it declared. "[But] let no reader of ours fall into the error of supposing that Mr. Adams has proposed or countenanced a dissolution of the Union. On the contrary, he absolutely discountenanced and repudiated the proposition. . . . We cannot but think that adoption of it [the censure resolution] is to be deprecated."

Thomas Gilmer, who had presented the original censure, offered to withdraw the entire resolution if Adams would take back his petition.

"No! No! I cannot do that," Adams answered. "That proposition comes to the point and issue of this whole question; that is to say, to the total suppression of the right of petition to the whole people of this Union. If I withdrew the petition, I would consider myself as having sacrificed the right of petition, as having sacrificed the right of habeas corpus, as having sacrificed the right of trial by jury, as having sacrificed the sacred confidence of the post office, as having sacrificed the freedom of the press, as having sacrificed the freedom of speech, as having sacrificed every element of liberty that was enjoyed by my fellow citizens, because if I should prove craven to my trust under intimidation of the charges of the gentleman from Albemarle and the gentleman from Kentucky, never more would the House see a petition presented from the people of the Union, expressing their grievances in a manner that might not be pleasing to the members of the 'peculiar institution,' until at length the people should teach them the lesson that, however their representatives might be intimidated from the discharge of their duty, they the people would be their own champions and the defenders of their own rights. There is the deadly character of the attempt to put me down."

There was only one thing left to do. John Minor Botts, a Virginia Whig, moved to table the resolution. This time the vote was 106 to 93 in favor!

"Right is vindicated and victorious!" wrote the Whig correspondent, Dr. Bacon. "The House of Representatives have done justice to themselves at last, to the 'Old Man Eloquent,' and to the Constitution!"

In the Cradle of Liberty, Boston's Faneuil Hall, an abolition mass meeting presided over by William Lloyd Garrison broke up in cheers on hearing the news. Adams' mail was flooded with congratulations—and dark warnings from the South. One letter, from Norfolk, Virginia, contained his caricature with a bullet hole in the forehead. Another, from North Carolina, warned,

"Unless you very soon change your course, death will be your portion. Prepare! Prepare!"

Adams filed them under "letters received" and continued his unprotected daily walks in the dawn-empty streets of Washington. He had given the gag rule a good mauling, but it was still in force, and for all he knew would outlive him. In the customary anticlimax after a triumph, he was feeling his age again.

XVII

THE change in Adams' public image was now complete He who had been the least popular President so far had become the most venerated—and hated—man in the country. Every day the mail brought "letters from the North, and sometimes from the West, asking for my autograph and a scrap of poetry or prose." A Vermonter wrote: "The voice of the Green Mountain Boys is with you in your late manful defense of the right of petition." A Pittsburgher: "Old man, there is a reverence round thy name." Church groups wanted copies of his defense. Invitations poured in to address public meetings, so many of them that he had to have a formal refusal printed. When Charles Dickens visited the House of Representatives, fresh from tumultuous receptions in New York and Boston, the person he asked to shake hands with was Adams; and four days later Adams was an honored guest at the Washington dinner party for the lionized British novelist.

The day's mail was delivered to his house between nine and ten at night, and by the time he had finished his replies it was often midnight. Interfering further with his customary bedtime—ten o'clock these later years—were the dinners protocol required him to attend, given by President Tyler and Secretary of State Webster and by the new British border commissioner, Lord Ashburton; all of which "necessarily delays for two hours my rising time." Getting up at six killed half the day. Yet, *Sex horas Somno*; he needed his six hours' sleep.

On the surface, his relations with the new President were compatible, but to his associates he confided a growing dislike. As the first Vice President to be elevated to the Presidency by the death of the Executive, Tyler had set a precedent that Adams disapproved: "Mr. Tyler . . . styles himself President of the United States, and not Vice President acting as President, which would be the correct style," he said. "It is a construction in direct violation both of the grammar and context of the Constitution, which confers upon the Vice President, on the decease of the President, not the office, but the powers and duties of the said office. . . ." He doubted "whether the Vice President has the right to occupy the President's House, or to claim his salary, without an act of Congress." But the issue was "not worth contesting," he decided. Of greater concern was the fact that Tyler was a states' rights Southerner and a "slave-monger." His misgivings increased as it became obvious that Tyler was more a Democrat than a Whig, that he opposed internal improvements and a new national bank, both dear to Adams, and, worse still, clearly favored annexation of Texas.

But despite his gloomy forebodings, Adams saw some dreams near realization. Now, in 1842, when he moved that the House rescind the standing gag rule, he was defeated by only four votes! And he was finally making headway in a project that he more than anyone else, and often alone, had fought for since 1835: establishment of the Smithsonian Institution.

James Smithson, an English scientist of distinction, the illegitimate son of the Duke of Northumberland, had left his estate to a nephew with the stipulation that if he should die without issue the residue was to go to the United States "to found at Washington, under the name of the Smithsonian Institution, an Establishment for the increase and diffusion of knowledge among men."

When the nephew, Henry James Hungerford, died in 1835 without an heir, President Jackson was notified of the strange bequest. The sum amounted to slightly over £100,000, which in American exchange came to $508,318. Smithson's motive was never revealed. He had never been to the United States, had no close friends here.

Jackson doubted the propriety of the nation's accepting the bequest. In a special message he left it up to Congress. Adams was enthralled. America lagged behind other nations of the world in scientific research and interest, particularly astronomy. In his first State of the Union message as President he had deplored that the country had no astronomical observatory to study the riddles of the stars. Unfortunately, he called it a "lighthouse of the sky." His opponents had changed "of" to "in," and laughed it off.

Since then, the project had languished, but Adams' concern had not. During his ministries abroad he had become deeply interested in the work being done at the Greenwich Observatory in London and at France's Bureau des Longitudes. He had brought home with him the writings of Isaac Newton and Joseph Lalande and their successors. Attemping to persuade his alma mater, Harvard, to set up the first American observatory, he had contributed $1,000—a lavish gift considering his circumstances—to start an endowment fund, but the enterprise had fallen through. And now, as if Heaven-sent, had come this gift of $500,000 for the "increase of knowledge among men." What better use could be made of it than to explore the mysteries of the universe?

To his disgust, the unusual bequest did not interest the Congress; scientific research was far removed from the pressing regional problems of the day. Since Adams was showing such fervent concern, he was made chairman of the House committee named to examine the bequest. The Senate put Asher Robbins of Rhode Island, a Greek and Latin scholar, at the head of its committee, and went on about its more material business, except that Calhoun and his South Carolina colleague, William Preston, protested it was beneath the nation's dignity to accept the gift of an illegitimate foreigner. Besides, Calhoun argued, Congress had no authority to establish an institution to promote knowledge, whether a university or a "lighthouse in the sky." That right was reserved to the states.

Through successive sessions of Congress, the discussion went on. Adams appealed to President Van Buren to get the project moving, but Van Buren did nothing. Harrison showed no more interest; neither did Tyler. As continuing chairman of the House committee, sitting in occasional joint sessions with the Senate group, Adams finally succeeded in having the fund accepted, but how it would be used could not be settled. Robbins, now getting ready to retire from the Senate, came up with a solution that his states' rights friend, Preston, supported: a District of Columbia, as distinguished from a national, university, *with Robbins as its chancellor.* Adams moved in fast to scotch that. He would stand for no sinecures, "jobbing for parasites, . . . sops for hungry incapacity." Moreover, he argued, another university would not fulfill the purpose of the bequest. In a report to his committee, later published, he wrote:

> The "increase and diffusion of knowledge among men," presents neither the idea of knowledge already acquired to be taught, nor of . . . youth to be instructed; but of new discovery, of progress in the march of the human mind.

The best solution, he declared, was to use the income from the fund (the principal, he insisted, must not be touched) to establish first a national observatory.

> The express object of an observatory is the increase of knowledge by new discovery. The physical relations between the firmament of heaven and the globe alloted by the Creator of all to be the abode of man, are discoverable only by the organ of the eye. Many of these relations are indispensable to the existence of human life, and, perhaps, of the earth itself. Who can conceive the idea of a world without a sun, but must connect it with the extinction of light and heat, of all animal life, of all vegetation and production? The influence of the moon, of the planets, . . . of the fixed stars, scattered over the blue expanse in multitudes exceeding the power of human computation; the influence of these upon the globe which we inhabit, and upon the condition of man, . . . is great and mysterious. . . . The extent to which they are discoverable is and must remain unknown; but to the vigilance of a thinking, combining

and analyzing mind, secrets are successively revealed, not only of the deepest import to the welfare of man in his earthly career, but which seem to lift him from the earth to the threshold of his eternal abode; to lead him blindfold up to the council chamber of Omnipotence; and there stripping the bandage from his eyes, bid him look undazzled at the throne of God.

The observatory, he went on, need not be the only project, merely the first. After it was established, the income from the fund (some $30,000 a year at six percent; a sizable amount then) could be used to expand research in other sciences: a museum of natural history, geology, minerology; a botanical garden; a library.

Adams' eloquence failed to persuade the lawmakers, but it had a material side effect: it stimulated academic interest in astronomy. Harvard's trustees resurrected his observatory proposal, and this time it became a reality, with Adams on the governing committee. And in Washington the Navy Department installed a modest telescope at its Depot of Charts and Instruments. So did Williams College and Western Reserve.

So the matter stood as Adams returned north after the March adjournment of the Twenty-seventh Congress, expecting to resume the comfortable routine of Quincy: "to see the sunrise and to visit and study my seedling plants and listen to the matinal minstrelsy of the bobolink, the spring bird and the robin, with the chirp of the sparrow and the new whistle of the quail, . . . all the aerial music of the time and place."

But the old house was no longer a rural haven. The National American Lyceum, the "march of the intellect," was now in full stride in Boston and the towns and villages of eastern Massachusetts. Founded by a New England educator and lecturer, Josiah Holbrook, "for the dissemination of knowledge on the arts, sciences, history and public affairs," the lyceums provided top-quality speakers on everything from Greek antiquities to chemistry and political economy. For a $2 season ticket—ten to fifteen lectures—audiences were treated to the eloquence of Ralph Waldo Emerson, William Ellery Channing, Oliver Wendell Holmes, Edward Everett, Horace Mann. Directors of the local bureaus immediately descended on the last of the scholar-Presidents so far—and for generations to come—besieging Adams "to such a degree that I have neither leisure or quiet and am kept in constant agitation to escape from them." Cambridge wanted him; so did Salem, Springfield, Bedford, Dedham, Haverhill, Framingham. A chaise overtook him on one of his sunrise walks with "a letter from seventeen citizens of New Bedford." Adams accepted the invitation from Dedham, asking him to speak on the tyranny of the gag rule, and stalled off the others, pleading his age and infirmities.

Fortuitously, an escape was at hand. Charles Francis' wife, Abigail, was not feeling well, and the family physician, Dr. John Bigelow, decided she needed a change of scenery. Her father, Peter Chardon Brooks, arranged to take her on a leisurely journey to Niagara Falls, then the country's leading natural wonder. Adams had never been there; in fact, he had seen more of the European continent than he had of America. When Brooks invited him to go along, he readily accepted. They started the afternoon of July 6 in "the cars" of the Western Railroad, together with Abigail's ten-year-old son, the second John Quincy Adams. Also in the party were Mr. and Mrs. Joseph Grinnell of New Bedford and their daughter and niece. Grinnell was president of the Boston and Providence Railroad and a handy friend to have along in these early days of rail travel.

Sitting at his car window, Adams thought "the face of the country like the Garden of Eden." It was haying time, and the Massachusetts farmers were in their meadows, swinging their long-handled scythes, their wives and children gathering the hay into cocks. Between the meadows and pastures lay "fields of corn, rye, potatoes, oats," and snug farmhouses with their kitchen gardens and weathered barns, and well-poles slanting against the sky. At nine o'clock they arrived in Springfield for the night, having covered the ninety miles in five and a half hours by Adams' watch. The next day he visited the government's Springfield arsenal and was shown a new development in firearms-making, the first since before the Revolution: rifles for the Army were being fitted for percussion caps instead of powder and flint.

Beyond Springfield the country changed dramatically, became "a wild region of dark forests and stupendous rocks." This was the beginning of the West; far reaches without a sign of a homestead, now and then the thin scar of a roadway twisting down a valley. They stopped at Pittsfield and took a carriage over one of the "heavy mountainous roads" to Lebanon Springs for the therapeutic baths. Their hotel stood high up the slope of a mountain, a frame structure with porches three quarters around each floor. Adams was up next morning at four, as usual, writing until breakfast time. Looking across the porch rail from his bedroom window, he saw a horseman come up the road and dismount at the hitching rail. After a few minutes the man appeared on the porch outside Adams' window. He approached shyly and held out his hand.

"Sir, my name is Spellman. I come from Pittsfield. I heard you were here and came to ask if I could shake your hand."

Adams held out his hand. They shook silently, and the man turned and walked away, to ride the ten-mile road back to Pittsfield. Adams guessed someone at the station must have recognized him. He had hoped to remain inconspicuous, simply an old man in a company of tourists.

From the springs the party rode in easy stages by rail and steamer to Saratoga, Lake George, Ticonderoga, up Lake Champlain to Fort St. John, Montreal, Quebec, and back down the St. Lawrence to Niagara Falls. There Adams found Millard Fillmore of nearby Buffalo waiting for him. Fillmore (the future President) was then chairman of the House Ways and Means Committee and a leading New York State Whig. A Boston colleague had alerted him to Adams' coming, and he had prepared "a little reception," he said.

After a tour of the falls, a steamer chartered by Fillmore took them down the Niagara River to Buffalo. To Adams' surprise, the harbor banks were filled with people. As the little steamer nudged up to its pier the crowd began shouting; men waved their hats, women their parasols and handkerchiefs.

Fillmore led Adams to an open barouche and they rode through the crowd to the bandstand in a nearby park, which was soon packed to its edges, the more agile perched in the trees. Fillmore formally welcomed the Old Man Eloquent to Buffalo, "the venerable champion of the rights of man, of freedom of speech, freedom of petition, . . . the glorious leader in the battle against human bondage." All of it was completely unexpected, and Adams had difficulty finding words to answer. But the audience applauded long and heartily, then queued up before the bandstand, "some hundreds men and women," to shake his hand. After dark, the volunteer firemen of the town marched past his hotel in a torchlight parade.

Visitors crowded Adams' room, among them representatives of Rochester and Syracuse, who wrung from him a reluctant promise to stop in their towns on his way homeward. Another visitor stood patiently aside until he could be alone with Adams. He was Professor Ormsby M. Mitchel, a prominent scientist from Cincinnati, Ohio, and he brought with him a formal invitation to Adams from the newly created Cincinnati Astronomical Society to deliver the main address at the cornerstone-laying ceremony for the society's observatory "some day in the month of November."

The observatory, Mitchel explained, was a sizable one, and the people of his town had contributed generously to equip it with a telescope better than any in the East. Adams was fascinated. Here was what could be a Heaven-sent opportunity to lecture the country on the importance of astronomy, arouse popular interest and consequently persuade Congress that the income from the Smithson bequest should be used to build even a finer national observatory. But he did not want to promise hastily. A journey deep into the West at that time of the year, he realized, would be "arduous and hazardous," and, since the professor did not offer to pay the fare, it would also be expensive.

"I must have time," he told Mitchel, "to make up my mind upon a proposal so strange to me and so flattering that I scarcely dare to think of it with composure."

His worry was whether he had sufficient vitality left for so strenuous an undertaking. But it was worth the risk. Already, his mind was busy planning how he would relate this provincial start at penetrating the heavens to the advancement of science in America. "My task," he wrote in his diary, "is to turn this transient gust of enthusiasm for the science of astronomy at Cincinnati into a permanent and persevering national pursuit, which may extend the bounds of human knowledge and make my country instrumental in elevating the character and improving the condition of man upon earth. The hand of God Himself has furnished me this opportunity to do good."

Mitchel had his acceptance the next morning. When Brooks and Grinnell heard about it they were appalled. Did Adams realize, Grinnell asked, what winter travel out there could be like? Trains marooned in snowstorms with no food for the passengers or dry wood to heat the cars. Engines frequently derailed, cars overturned. As a pioneer railroad man, he could tell Adams it was enough to discourage a young man. And only two weeks ago they had toasted Adams' seventy-sixth birthday. He did not have to be reminded of his age, Adams said; his body was doing that to his increasing annoyance. But what did age have to do with it? The importance of the project was what mattered.

Next day they started for home. Word had gone on ahead, and when the train stopped at Batavia to take on firewood and water, the station was so crowded that it collapsed. At Rochester "an immense crowd of people shouting" greeted the Adams party. The local militia fired a salute. The church bells rang. Francis Granger, the retired Postmaster General, came aboard and rode with them to Canandaigua, where Adams was met by a military cavalcade, a band and a procession of carriages "a mile long" which escorted him to a park where, after the cannon salute and to the accompaniment of church bells, Granger delivered a glowing welcome "which left me in an amazement to enquire of myself what all this was for." His response, he realized, was "shamefaced and awkward—unprepared."

Darkness overtook them at Auburn, where the former governor of New York, William H. Seward, led Adams to his home for the night through a hand-shaking crowd lighted by the torches of the volunteer firemen. Syracuse was more of the same. At Utica a delegation of colored citizens stepped out of the crowd and their spokesman thanked him with moving simplicity "for your efforts in protecting the right of petition and promoting the abolition of slavery." Herkimer next. Little Falls. Schenectady. Albany. Even at remote crossings where the locomotive took on more water and firewood people were patiently waiting to shake hands with him "till the bell called me back to my seat." By then Adams understood the reason for the turnouts. These were the people—the town merchants, the craftsmen, farmers, woodsmen—who since the beginning of the antislavery crusade had been directing their petitions year after year to him in Congress, who believed as fervently as he did that human bondage was a sin against God. This northern section of New York was the country of Charles Grandison Finney, the seedbed of the abolition movement, along with antifundamentalism, temperance, women's rights.

He arrived home exhausted. Charles Francis thought the trip had improved his wife's health, but he was concerned about his father. He did his best to make him call off the unseasonable journey to Ohio. So did Louisa. They were no more successful than Brooks and Grinnell had been. Single-minded as always, Adams brushed off their protests and started gathering notes for his speech. The deeper he got into his research, the more convinced he became that he had been given the opportunity of a lifetime to stimulate an American interest in the most challenging of the sciences. Here was a subject that had fascinated ancient Egypt, Babylon, China, Arabia, Greece, that had absorbed men from Ptolemy to Copernicus, Galileo, Descartes, Newton. European astronomers had charted some 47,000 stars, traced the pathways of the sun and moon, measured their influence on the seasons and the tides, their changing distances from the earth. And America, under the same brilliant, everchanging canopy, walked with its eyes on the ground.

The difficulty of his task, he soon discovered, was "to compress a history of astronomy into a discourse of three hours." He worked on it all through September and into late October.

The three days before his departure, October 25, he sat up nearly all night condensing and revising the final draft. He left Quincy "so worn down with weariness and anxiety that my faculties seemed benumbed." These last three nights, he estimated, he had had only "two hours of refreshing sleep." Accompanying him again was Joseph Grinnell, and another family friend, Benjamin Andrews. W. C. Johnson, a relative by marriage, would join them along the route. Grinnell, besides being an insatiable traveler, was entering the next Congress with Adams, having been chosen by the Massachusetts Whigs to replace Barker Burnell, who had died in June.

Winter came early that year. The train left Boston under a gloomy sky, and in western Massachusetts they ran into the season's first snowfall. Ferrying across the Hudson River to Albany, Adams "felt as if I was encrusted in a bed of snow." The rattle of hail against his hotel window kept him awake most of the night. He was up, nevertheless, at four, to light his lamp and transfer to his diary his notes on the distances covered the day before and the varying speeds of the train as he had measured them by checking the passing mileposts against his pocket watch. At half past six he went down to the barbershop to be shaved.

After breakfast Adams took his seat in the railroad car, but the locomotive's wheels were frozen to the rails. A team of horses strained for an hour and a half before they broke them loose. Then it took another half hour to get up steam. Sitting at his window watching the white landscape slide past, Adams decided that "there is no uniformity in human life more monotonous than traveling in railroad cars." The countryside was "dreary and desolate," and, unlike two months before along this same route, "my passage now is silent and unnoticed."

But at Buffalo the next day a reception committee braved the drifts and cold to welcome him, and a delegation from Erie, Pennsylvania, 100 miles up the lake, asked him to stop off there. The little steamer *General Wayne,* bound for Erie, cleared the harbor next morning through a curtain of snow and ran immediately into a northwestern gale and turbulent sea. After "an hour of pitching as if the boat would come to pieces," the captain made for the Canadian shore and anchored in a cover behind Point Abino. It was "cold as Nova Zembla," Adams said, and most of the passengers were violently seasick. Adams was not. His "predominating sentiment was vexation—uneasy at the imbecility of being wind-bound and nothing to do." The wind howled and snow filled the sky for two days, "lost days." He found a Bible in the lounge and a volume of the *Memoirs of the Life of Aaron Burr* by Matthew Davis. But the Bible was a "stereotype" distributed by a men's Christian organization and did not include the Apocrypha. He sternly disapproved "the omission." After a few pages of the *Memoirs* he gave that up in disgust; it confirmed his opinion that Burr was a profligate.

The gale ended the second night as suddenly as it had blown up, and next morning the steamer made for Erie, arriving after dark. The town was waiting, a military escort hurrying to the dock, a band, and the firemen lighting the night with their torches. Adams went through the City Hall ceremony with an effort. He had developed a deep cough and a sore throat, and he felt feverish.

At Cleveland, which he reached the next day, he felt no better. Again there was a torchlight parade, through the Public Square. The newspapers quoted him at length on the importance of advancing interest in the sciences. The Cleveland *Whig* and the *Herald* hailed him in glowing prose. "No two men have ever lived and filled so large a space in our public life, whose names will be transmitted to future ages with more true greatness and patriotism, than John Adams and his illustrious son," said the *Herald*. "Blessings on thee, patriot, statesman and sage!"

Like Buffalo, Cleveland was in the snow belt and in the grip of an early winter. No railroad linked the town with southern Ohio. By stage, the journey to Columbus, halfway to Cincinnati, would take a night and day over dangerously bad roads. The alternate route, twice as slow but less hazardous, was by packet 232 miles down the Ohio Canal. Joseph Grinnell decided they should go by boat. Stagecoach accidents were common here at this season. The winter before, he reminded Adams, five members of the House on their way East from Ohio had been badly hurt when their coach overturned.

After a midday reception on November 1, Adams and his party were driven down the steep road into the Flats, the valley of the Cuyahoga River, which the canal paralleled part way. The packet *Rob Roy* was already burdened with twenty-odd passengers when they came aboard. She was a squat vessel, eighty-three feet long and fifteen wide. The interior was divided into six compartments: in the bow the ladies' parlor with a long settee on each side, separated by a curtain from a similar chamber for the men, also equipped with two settees, each of which slept two men foot to foot. An iron stove stood in the center of this compartment, its fat belly a rosy glow. Next door was the stable, with stalls for the four horses which pulled the boat, two and two. Beyond that was the dining hall, then a long dormitory with wall bunks, and in the stern the kitchen and crew's quarters.

Snow was falling heavily again, and the packet's departure was delayed two hours. The windows had to be kept shut and the wood stove had the men's parlor oppressively hot. "So much humanity crowded into such a compass" was to Adams "a trial such as I had never before experienced and my heart sunk within me when, squeezed into this pillory, I reflected that I was to pass three nights and four days in it." His cough and sore throat were worse, and he knew definitely now that he had a fever.

The horses, plodding along the tow path, dragged the packet at two and a half miles an hour. Adams got little sleep on the narrow settee, with his feet touching his bed-mate's and his *"tussis senilis* [old man's cough] in full force." Every mile or so they entered a lock—he counted 200 in all—and each time he was almost jolted out of his bed, the packet crunching against the walls and jarring to a stop against the lock gate, "staggering like a stumbling nag." He got up once and went on deck. The crewman leaning on the tiller eyed him silently. On the path the team plodded with their heads down against the snow, the driver walking in front of them with his lantern.

By the next afternoon he was in better spirits. He thought his fever was down, and his throat felt no worse. But, mainly, he had found congenial companions among the other occupants of the parlor-bedroom compartments, particularly two young ladies. Charlotte Macy was surprisingly pretty and effervescent, and a Miss Langdon of Buffalo, while not as good-looking, made up for it with captivating manners. They and their parents played whist with Adams and then taught him euchre, a card game he had not encountered in the East.

By the time they reached Hebron, from where a private coach took Adams and his party overland to Columbus, the packet had passed through forty-five villages. In the coach were a three-man reception committee from Cincinnati, much embarrassed. They had gone to Cleveland to meet him, but had arrived a few hours after he left. So they had rushed back to Columbus, engaged the coach and come down to the landing to await the lumbering packet.

Governor Shannon of Ohio headed the capital's reception committee, and, since it was Congress that he hoped to influence, Adams was pleased to find several members of the state's congressional delegation in the group. The turnout was even larger than the one at Cleveland had been. Strangely, "these proceedings [seemed to] increase like a ball of snow. I cannot realize," he said, "that the demonstrations are made for me; and the only comfort I have is that they are intended to manifest respect and not hatred."

At dawn the next day a mulatto, David Jenkins, knocked on his door. This was the only time, he explained, that he could expect to get within speaking distance of Adams. He had been delegated by the Negroes of the town to thank him "for my exertions in defense of their rights."

At Lebanon, then twenty-two miles from Cincinnati, an open barouche with four horses in sparkling harness was waiting with a delegation from the Astronomical Society, including Mayor Spencer of Cincinnati and Professor Mitchel. Adams was escorted to the Henry House, where the mayor stepped out on the balcony with him and delivered a glowing welcome. His reply, Adams thought, was "confused, incoherent and muddy; yet it was received with shouts" from the crowd.

To his dismay, he learned that the cornerstone ceremony was to include only a short speech, and his main address was to be delivered the following day in the Methodist chapel. He sat up till one o'clock composing and was up again at four to finish. The snow had been left behind, but the sky was overcast, and as he stepped into the open barouche for the ride to the hilltop observatory site heavy rain began to fall. The horses slipped on the muddy slope of the hill.

Looking out from the platform, Adams faced a field of umbrellas. "I supplicate the throne of Heaven," he said, "that the erection of this building may be conducive to the improvement of the condition of man upon earth." America could link its towns with canals and toll roads, build railroads so that a week's journey of a generation before now took less than a day, yet it had been deplorably indifferent to the exploration of "God's firmament." Fortunately, "the Astronomical Society of the city of Cincinnati have determined to wipe the reproach from the fair fame of our beloved country." Most of his audience probably did not hear a word he said, but they stood patiently in the rain till he finished, and applauded and cheered.

The chapel was the only sizable auditorium in the town, but too small for the crowd. Adams' sore throat made speaking a torturous effort, but he went on for two hours, reviewing the history of astronomy from its beginnings in mythology to modern explorations in England and France. Some there were, he said, who believed God did not want His people to tamper with the mysteries of the sky—an argument raised by the fundamentalists and some members of Congress. They were wrong. The Founding Fathers had intended the Union to grow strong in knowledge and achievement as well as power.

"The God in whose name they spoke had taught them, in the revelation of His Gospel, that the only way in which man can discharge his duty to Him is, by loving his neighbor as himself, and doing with him as he would be done by—respecting his rights, while enjoying his own, and applying all his emancipated powers of body, and of mind, to self-improvement, and improvement of the race."

His audience, he noted, listened throughout "without a symptom of impatience or inattention." At the close a resolution was read, and thunderously adopted, that the hilltop observatory be named Mount Adams. Outside, as Adams was escorted back to his carriage, the crowd respectfully opened a path for him and cheered. Hands reached out to touch him. A group of fifteen Negroes briefly blocked his way while their spokesman said, "Thank you, Honorable Mr. Adams, for what you are doing for our people."

Through the medium of the country's newspapers, many of them one-man operations which assiduously clipped and reprinted each other's articles, his trip and the ceremonies at Cincinnati were widely publicized. During the four days he stayed on in Cincinnati he received invitations to go to St Louis and Indianapolis. Louisville, Kentucky, wanted him; so did Lexington, Frankfort and Covington. Adams was too ill and tired to extend his journey, but he could not resist making an appearance at least in Kentucky, remembering an exchange with its ebullient Congressman, Marshall, at his censure trial. Marshall had suggested that Adams should go to Kentucky to acquaint himself with the "true condition of the slaves."

"To be lynched?" Adams had asked.

"Very likely," Marshall had answered.

With a delegation headed by Kentucky's former governor, Charles Morehead, he crossed the Ohio River to Covington and was warmly received; so was his speech praising Henry Clay, Kentucky's most illustrious citizen and the leading Whig candidate to succeed Tyler (he made no mention of abolition). Again at Maysville, homeward-bound on a river steamer, he stopped off to eulogize Clay, whom he had not always agreed with, particularly on slavery, but would rather see in the White House than any other contender. And now, for the first and only time, he replied to the charge that he had won the Presidency nineteen years ago through a deal: the promise to make Clay his Secretary of State in exchange for his support. It was not a public denial, only a sentence written that day in the diary he was leaving strictly for his descendants: "And here I solemnly declare that the charge of corrupt bargaining which had been trumped up against him and me was utterly without foundation."

He was terribly weary by now; his cough was no better, and he was sleeping fitfully. At the dock in Pittsburgh another delegation, headed by the mayor and the town dignitaries, met him, and again there were crowds and a day-long reception. He stood up to it grimly. But now that he had completed his task he thought "the pageant of this day of no earthly importance." His appearance at Cincinnati had had "a moral purpose, an important end, . . . the improvement of the condition of man upon earth." After that it was "all vanity, . . . ostensibly all honorable to me," and painfully unwelcome.

Still ahead of him were receptions at Cumberland and Harpers Ferry as the stagecoach brought him across the twisting Allegheny Mountain roads with their frequent hairpin turns for the horses to rest. On November 24, a month after he had left Quincy, he reached his house in Washington, with the Twenty-eighth Congress convening in less than two weeks. Looking back on his mission, he thought, "It is not much in itself. It is nothing in the estimate of the world. [But] in my motives and my hopes it is considerable. The people . . . do not sufficiently estimate the importance of patronizing and promoting science. . . . I indulge dreams of future improvement to result from this popular homage. For whatever of vainglory there may be in this I pray to be forgiven."

He was more certain than ever that he had "little life left in me," and this time with good reason. He awoke at four, still weary but unable to go back to sleep. His strength was "prostrated beyond anything that I ever experienced before." Rest no longer replenished it.

Years later, his son Charles, looking back to this time, said, "There can be little doubt that . . . Mr. Adams had much overtaxed his physical powers on this trip."

⇒⇒ XVIII ⇐⇐

THIS was no time to be weary. President Tyler, Adams knew now, was determined to annex Texas to the slavery domain. From Webster he learned that the President was conducting secret negotiations with Sam Houston's agents in Washington. Now that the treaty with Lord Ashburton, fixing the northeastern boundary of the United States and Canada, had passed the Senate, Webster had followed the rest of the original Cabinet into retirement, announcing he would no longer work with Tyler and his Southern Administration. Although Adams had no intention of retreating on Texas, he saw that the forces against him had become formidable.

But these days before Congress convened he had little time to think about Texas. His study was stacked higher than ever with petitions from the North, all to be read, classified and indexed before they could be carted off to the corridors of the Capitol. The petition campaign was finally in full swing, under the guidance now of Abolition House. The members of the anti-slavery bloc in the House of Representatives, who boarded at Mrs. Sprigg's, had been formed into a tight, smoothly functioning organization by Theodore Weld. They had issued a proclamation, distributed by the abolition leaders and their press, calling on the petition canvassers to redouble their efforts. To assure that none of the petitions was quietly ignored, they asked that they be told to which Congressman they were sent, so those who "truckle to Southern power" could no longer remain anonymous.

Adams had a big share in swelling the petition flood. The appeal was signed by all the Congressmen living at Abolition House: Giddings and Andrews of Ohio, Slade and General Mattocks from Vermont, Gates of New York, Borden of Massachusetts, James of Pennsylvania and several others. But the signature that headed the list was that of John Quincy Adams.

He still refused to join the abolition cause. But instead of counseling against petitions, as he had until a few years before, he was now asking for them. Two things had changed his mind: the warm evidence of popular support he had received on his trips across upstate New York and into the West, and the dwindling majority the gag rule was mustering in the House.

An episode that influenced him further was the censure of his good friend Giddings, whom he considered the most dedicated opponent of slavery in Congress. Adams loved the upright Giddings as a kindred soul, a feeling he put to verse:

> And here, from regions wide apart,
> We came, one purpose to pursue,
> Each with a warm and honest heart,
> Each with a spirit firm and true.

After Adams' victory in his censure trial, Giddings had defied the Whig leadership by proclaiming that the government had no legal right to demand England surrender the slaves involved in the *Creole* mutiny. He was a rough and ready fighter for abolition, but he lacked Adams' prestige and punishing savagery in the clinches. The Whig majority decided to censure him as an example to other insurgents. Giddings resigned and went home to ask his district to reelect him. Party stump speakers and the local Whig newspapers mounted a vigorous campaign against him, but his Ohio constituents, the same people that had flocked to see Adams, sent him back to Congress with a heavy majority. He resumed his attacks on the slaveholders, and when Whig members wanted to chastise him again their

282

leaders called them off; Giddings' supporters would only continue to reelect him. The Whig ranks had been breached.

On December 4, the day after the Twenty-eighth Congress convened, Adams offered his regular motion to repeal the gag rule, which had now become the twenty-fifth standing rule of the House. As the vote proceeded alphabetically down the list, he kept careful score at his desk. Adams, loud and clear, "Yes." Anderson, "Yes." Arrington, "No." Atkinson, "No." Barnard, "Yes." Barringer, "No." The tally was so close that Adams' hopes were now up, now down. At the end, it stood 94 to 91 against repeal; the closest vote yet. Twenty-seven members from New York, his tally showed, had voted for his motion, and only 5 against it. From Pennsylvania, 12 were for and 8 against; from Ohio, 13 for and 5 against.

The next day he was back on the offensive, his desk stacked high with petitions that he intended to argue did not come within the restrictions of the gag. The first promptly embroiled him with the new Speaker, John W. Jones, a Virginia Democrat, and with W. Cost Johnson, Jesse Bynum of North Carolina, and Henry Wise, Tyler's good friend and now the Administration's spokesman in the House.

This memorial, from 586 citizens of upstate New York, started out by calling for abolition in the District of Columbia. That part, Adams explained, was not admissible. But their second prayer was. It proposed that "Congress pass such laws or propose such amendments to the Constitution of the United States as would separate forever the people of New York from domestic slavery." The mercurial Johnson yelled that this amounted to "dissolution of the Union." Not at all, Adams argued. It merely meant that New York wanted no part in slavery, from the return of fugitive slaves to sharing responsibility for "the sin of bondage." The Speaker ruled the petition was not receivable. Adams, citing precedent, insisted that it was, since it did not advocate abolition or interference with slavery in any state where it existed. Bynum forced adjournment, and the Southerners went into a huddle with their Speaker, but after four days of consultation Jones had to reverse himself; the petition was referred to the Committee on the

Judiciary, which eventually rejected it. But Adams had got it into the record.

He presented a stack of anti-Texas petitions; those that mentioned the slavery issue the Chair ruled not admissible; one from Ohio simply protesting against taking Texas into the Union was referred, after a heated wrangle, to the Committee on Foreign Affairs, safely weighted with Democrats.

"I have plenty more of the same description," Adams told Wise, "with hundreds of thousands of signatures."

"The gentleman knows it is out of order," the Speaker warned, "to debate the subject of these petitions."

Adams looked aggrieved. "I do not debate it, sir. I submit with lamb-like patience."

He unrolled his next petition. It prayed "that Congress pass some law confessing our national sins." That brought loud laughs. It was no laughing matter, said Adams. "This petition comes from 226 respectable citizens of Illinois, and deserves to be treated with respect." The petition went on to pray that Congress pass a law "acknowledging the domination of Jesus Christ"; that it define "what the law of God is"; and last that the Constitution be amended "to secure to *all the people* in the United States the self-evident truth contained in the Declaration of Independence—the right to life, liberty and the pursuit of happiness."

Out of the uproar the Speaker recognized Wise. The petition was tabled. But the vote was surprisingly close: 98 to 80.

Adams walked home, tired but moderately content. Christmas was five days away, and here and there a brown brick house had green wreaths and candles in its windows. New York, he had heard, was adopting the custom, too, under the persuasion of its continental traveler, Washington Irving. He wondered how long it would be before Puritan New England came around to observing the day: "To the church of which I am a member there are no religious holidays save the Christian Sabbath; but personally I sympathize with those who solemnize the two anniversaries, Christmas and Easter—the birth and resurrection of Jesus." He was reminded that he had not heard from the family in Boston for some time. They were all well, he hoped.

So few were left, he thought, feeling suddenly lonely, where once there had been so many. Of his own generation he alone was still here; his brothers, Thomas and Charles, his sister Abigail, all were in the graveyard at Quincy now, together with their parents.

The mail came soon after nine, bringing a packet from Boston. It was a resolution adopted by the Massachusetts legislature, demanding amendment of the federal Constitution to abolish the clause permitting the slaveholding states to include slaves in their apportionment for representation in the House, counting three votes for every five slaves. If the provision could be abolished the South's domination of the House would be broken. The proposal was not new; Adams had advocated it himself time and again. Yet by the time he had read the document to its end he was so agitated that he "could do nothing but pace my chamber." The author of the resolution and chairman of the committee that had guided it through the Massachusetts House of Representatives was his son, Charles Francis!

Until this moment Adams had had no indication that Charles would take an active part in the contest with slavery. In their many intimate talks during the past summer his son had never once hinted that he was receding from his position of stern detachment, even occasional annoyance at his father's deep and persistent involvement. The decision had been entirely his own, arrived at, as was his nature, after deep consideration. Years later, Charles himself wrote that "there had not been the smallest previous understanding on the subject between father and son."

Pacing his study, Adams was both elated and torn with anxiety; elated that, now with his own end so near, a strong hand would be waiting to carry the banner he had raised; worried over the trials and heartbreaks that would accompany it. "May the God of Justice be his guide and guard," he said, "and the God of Mercy protect him."

Next day he presented the resolution to the House. His comment that it "caused a memorable debate" was an understatement. Wise, Johnson, Gilmer, Bynum and Rhett denounced it furiously. Adams heard them out, praying meanwhile for "coolness, firmness, prudence and fortitude beyond all former examples," and he answered with unusual restraint. Had not the Southerners said time and again that the slaves were their machines? Well, the New England cotton mills did not ask extra representation for their looms, the New York tanners for their vats, the iron works for their forges. Henry Wise, fuming that it was time "this House renounce for all and forever this war against Southern rights," moved that the resolution be peremptorily tabled. The vote was taken, and his motion lost, 104 to 64, a majority that surprised Adams as much as it did Wise. Clearly, the slaveholders' Northern colleagues saw no profit to themselves in keeping the South disproportionately strong. (To Charles Francis in Boston the vote was "obviously the effect of the popular ovations given to Mr. Adams during the previous summer.")

Adams now moved successfully that the resolution be referred to a select committee of nine to give it the consideration an act of a state legislature deserved. Speaker Jones named Adams chairman but weighted the committee solidly with Democrats.

That New Year's Day was a greater hardship for Adams than any in the past had been. Both his energy and patience were exhausted by the procession of visitors from ten o'clock till three in the afternoon. Among them this time were "some of the bitterest enemies, North and South, that I have in the world." The most conspicuous was Charles Jared Ingersoll, the Philadelphia political pundit, now chairman of the Committee on Foreign Affairs and a leading supporter of Texas annexation. Adams gave him a civil though cold handshake. To his mind Ingersoll was "the cunningest and most treacherous cat of them all."

He went to bed thinking, "Tomorrow recommences the struggle which . . . can terminate only with my life." One of his principal opponents was now out of the House; Thomas Gilmer, Tyler's close friend and fellow Virginian, was the new Secretary of the Navy. And Tyler apparently intended to reward Wise, too, by naming him minister to France. But the very fact that these Southerners were willing to give up their seats showed they had no fear that slavery was in serious danger.

If he could only get to sleep. But his weary mind kept drifting from one subject to another. Now it was the old Negro who had come to his door one morning to implore him to save his wife from being sold away. He naïvely asked Adams to buy her, for $400. When Adams said he could not, the old man went away "in a state almost of distraction." Now it was Tyler's refusal to approve a national bank; now his transparent plotting to annex Texas; now the continuing stalemate in Congress over the Smithsonian bequest.

Of late his morning walks had been taking him more frequently around Capitol Hill, past the little round-domed frame building that housed the government's new forty-two-inch refracting telescope. Since the Smithsonian gift had started Adams on his campaign for a national astronomical observatory, the Depot of Charts and Instruments had been renamed the United States Naval Observatory, and two scholarly naval officers had been commissioned to equip and organize it. The observatory was a start, as were those in Cincinnati and Cambridge, but America still had a long way to go before it could catch up with the work being done in London and Paris. And meanwhile the Smithsonian fund had been loaned to the depressed Western states, and they were defaulting on the interest; he hoped they would not default on the principal.

The day after Congress resumed he put through a resolution calling on the Treasury for a detailed report on the current status of the fund. Colleagues seated around him noticed that his hands appeared to tremble more than usual and his voice was unsteady. Still, he had been among the first to arrive and was one of the last to leave. When an invitation came to join a select Presidential party for a cruise down the Potomac on the warship *Princeton,* he turned it down; it would require his absence from the House for the day.

The cruise was to demonstrate a new gun, the "Peacemaker." On the second round it exploded and killed five members of the party, including the Secretary of the Navy, Gilmer, and the Secretary of State, Abel P. Upshur. Tyler's choice for his new Secretary of State pleased Adams no better than it did the old Unionist-Democrat, Andrew Jackson. He named the nullificationist John Calhoun, and Calhoun promptly negotiated a treaty of annexation with the republic of Texas. The Senate rejected it, but Tyler and Calhoun were not discouraged. They had another method in reserve.

A pleasant interlude for Adams occurred one evening in March. A delegation of his supporters from the North presented him with an ivory cane made from a single elephant's tusk. The cane was tipped with silver, with a gold-inlaid eagle for a handle. Inscribed under his name were the words, "Right of Petition Triumphant," and beneath that was a space for the date to be inscribed when—and if—the gag was finally abolished. Adams was deeply moved, but he would not deviate from his policy of refusing gifts. The Commissioner of Patents, H. L. Ellsworth, was one of the group, and he took the cane in trust to the Patent Office.

Writing his son about the gift, Adams also told him the House had disposed of the Massachusetts resolution to abolish the three-five ratio for slaves. "A porcupine of objections bristled up against me," he said, when the select committee presented its reports, and the resolution was tabled. While the letter was on the way, Adams read in the Boston *Courier* that Charles Francis had made a strong speech in the Massachusetts House against annexation of Texas. "My heart aches," he wrote in his diary, "at the prospect of the dangers and trials that await him."

⇶ XIX ⇇

WASHINGTON had now become the refuge that the homestead in Quincy could no longer provide. Here Adams could still walk almost unnoticed. Back home his life was no longer his own, to pass in the privacy of his study and garden. He had become a symbol for public adulation, the venerable defender of individual freedom, champion of antislavery, of progress in the sciences, the last stalwart link with the Founding Fathers: his opinions asked on questions of the day, his presence sought at public ceremonies, casual acquaintances constantly bringing strangers to meet him.

When Congress adjourned in mid-June he stayed on, although the heat was already oppressive. Louisa, now a frail sixty-eight, would have been content to remain all summer. With her relatives around her, dropping in for tea, staying occasionally for family dinner with the Madame and the President, Washington was more of a home to her than any other place on either continent had ever been. The old brick house drowsed behind its shutters, closed with the dawn to keep in the coolness of the night. Adams took his morning bath in a tub of cold water from the back-yard well and gave himself a vigorous rubdown with a horsehair strap and mitten.

One sultry day, after finishing his morning stint with his correspondence and diary, he had the coachman drive him to the spot behind the White House where he had so often gone swimming in the Potomac. His favorite rock was occupied by naked youngsters, their clothes in little mounds under the old sycamore. He strolled past them unrecognized. Upstream he waded to a rock partly submerged by the tide. By the time he had taken off his clothes the tide was ebbing, and he had to walk out some distance to deep water. He swam around for five minutes and came out "washed and refreshed." Two mornings later he was back again. He was now seventy-seven, but "from the exercise of swimming," he said, "I cannot totally abstain." It had, he believed, "promoted my health and prolonged my life many years."

Late in the summer of 1844 the family returned to Quincy. While Adams would take no part in the Presidential campaign, he was deeply apprehensive. Clay had weakened himself with the Whigs in the North, particularly in New York, by equivocating on Texas, announcing he would agree to annexation if it could be accomplished "without dishonor, without war, . . . and upon just and fair terms." Polk had the solid support of the Democrats and the added prestige of old Andrew Jackson's friendship. Adams knew Polk well enough to expect that, as a Tennessee slaveholder and confirmed expansionist, he would stop at nothing to bring Texas into the slavery domain, if Tyler did not beat him to it.

By November 7 the election returns were in except for pivotal New York. That night Adams heard the cannon boom twice across the bay in Boston and knew what it meant. Polk had carried New York and would be the next President. It was the signal, he wrote, "for my retirement from public life; the victory of the slavery element in the Constitution of the United States. From the sphere of public action I must, at all events, very soon be removed. My removal now is but a few days in advance of the doom of nature, and gives me time, if I have energy to improve it, which will not be lost."

Firm as his intention was at that moment, he could not bring himself to retire. On December 2 he was back in his seat in the House. The next day Romulus Saunders of North Carolina presented the usual resolution that the standing rules of the House be reinstated. Adams had already announced that he would present his own resolution. Now he read it, "That the twenty-fifth standing rule [the gag rule] . . . be and the same is hereby rescinded."

Jacob Thompson of Mississippi moved that it be tabled. Adams and his Ohio friend Giddings were on their feet at the same time, calling for the yeas and nays. At that moment young John Tyler, Jr., entered the house with his father's State of the Union message. Thompson demanded that it be read immediately. Adams insisted that the vote proceed, and the Speaker sustained him. The motion to table the resolution was defeated, 104 to 81. Now the roll was called on the resolution itself. Three more members had meanwhile taken their seats, all of them, Adams observed, from the North. With rising hopes, he tabulated the vote as it went along. And now he had the total, and so did the House: 108 for rescinding the gag rule, 80 against.

For a moment an electric stillness hung over the hall. Then Adams' friends were standing up, applauding, cheering, and Speaker Jones was rapping for order. They gathered around Adams' desk—Giddings, Slade, Gates, Andrews, Borden and their colleagues—shaking his hand, slapping his frail shoulders. His eight-year battle was won. The South's stranglehold on the House, progressively weakened by the loss of Northern support, was finally broken. The constitutional "right of the people peaceably to petition the government for a redress of grievances" had been restored. The abolitionist Congressmen, all of whom except Slade had been elected after Adams, could expose the evils of slavery, and no one could silence them.

"Blessed," Adams said, "forever blessed, be the name of God!" He left the House that evening feeling his old self again. He might have had a small regret: his volatile adversary, Henry Wise, had not been there to hear the vote. Wise was now minister to Brazil, Tyler's second choice after the Senate had rejected his appointment to the legation in Paris. The reaction over the country was no better or worse than Adams had expected. The upper house of the South Carolina legislature denounced the rescinding as "a flagrant outrage" on the rights of the South. The Democratic Washington *Globe* and the Southern press, he noted, were "much envenomed." The abolitionists and their journals were jubilant. And in Boston Charles Francis thought it would be "the last triumph of Mr. Adams in his difficult career in the House of Representatives."

The succeeding days Adams unloaded his backlog of petitions and saw them all respectfully referred to their proper committees. He visited the Patent Office and had the date, "December 3, 1844," engraved on the gold-handled ivory cane, which he left to "the people of the United States." But his elation was brief. While the Senate had failed to advise and consent to the treaty with Texas by the required two-thirds majority, Tyler now, in the last days of his Administration, proposed to Congress that it take Texas into the Union by joint resolution, which would require only a majority vote in both houses. The Democrats now had a working majority and regarded Polk's victory as a mandate for annexation. Adams had fought against it as long as it was practical; to argue any longer, he realized wearily, was useless. He contented himself with a loud "No!" and saw the resolution passed by 132 to 76 in the House. The Senate barely approved it, 27 to 25. "A signal triumph of the slave representation," Adams said. "I regard it as the apoplexy of the Constitution."

And now Polk was in the White House, challenging Mexico to carry out her threat to fight for Texas, whose independence she had still not conceded. "Manifest destiny" was the new catchphrase. The nation's "manifest destiny" was to expand to its natural boundaries, to the Rio Grande, to the Pacific. Polk would buy California from Mexico, or take it if her unstable government refused to sell. And in the north there was the Oregon Territory, jointly controlled by Great Britain and the United States by treaty since 1818, a treaty indefinitely extended by President John Quincy Adams in 1827, with the proviso that either country could terminate it by giving a year's notice.

The new Administration was determined to extend the nation's northwestern boundary to the fifty-fourth parallel; "fifty-four forty or fight" was the slogan. The British ministry let it be known it *would* fight rather than agree to a line that far north. The Columbia River (the present southern border of

Oregon) was what it wanted to settle for. Until two years before, neither country had shown much interest in coming to terms on the northwestern wilderness, a remote land of fur traders and wandering Indian tribes. Then the Oregon Trail had been opened, and the Great Emigration had begun, caravans of pioneers from the Middle West adventuring over the horizon to stake out new farms for themselves in the primeval country; the first trains in 1842; by the next year 900 wagons with 1,000 head of stock. And with them had gone missionaries to the Indians. The pioneer settlements were clamoring for government protection against the hostile natives, and "manifest destiny" demanded that they be heard.

The Southern wing of the Democratic party was opposed to bringing the Oregon Territory into the Union. It expected to carve four or five states out of the Texas acquisition and increase its representation that much in the Senate and House. Oregon would be free territory and would serve only to cut back the South's strength. For once the slaveholders felt confident that Adams would be on their side. He opposed war with Mexico over Texas. So he would oppose war with Britain over Oregon. While Secretary of State and then President, he had arranged the dual control of the territory with Britain. And, clearly, he was hostile to both the new President and his proslavery Administration. As the debate developed in the House, he showed no inclination to get involved. Day after day he sat silently at his desk, doodling occasionally on one of the papers in front of him, more often letting his eyelids fall as the wordy argument went on. Robert Barnwell Rhett, the states' rights South Carolina Democrat, was carrying the load for the opposition in the House as Calhoun was carrying it in the Senate. England, Rhett warned, would never agree to a line as far north as the fifty-fourth parallel, far beyond the upper tip of Vancouver Island. She would go to war instead. In fact, she was already preparing her people for war and building up her fleet. He did not want another war with England, any more than "that gentleman [pointing to Adams] had wanted the War of 1812, which the gentleman voted against."

Adams raised himself out of his chair. Rhett had his history distorted, he told the Speaker. "I was at that time the American minister to Russia, and not a member of the Congress." Furthermore, he went on, "I apprehend no war, because I believe the present Administration *will finally back down from their own ground.*" Although he did not say so, he still believed, as he had back in his own Administration, that the logical line was the forty-ninth parallel, and he expected that the two nations would eventually compromise on it. But his reflection on President Polk did not go unchallenged. William Yancey, an Alabama planter, protested, and the new Speaker, John W. Davis, Polk's friend from Indiana, told him to sit down; he was out of order.

Adams sank obediently into his chair. The old fire seemed extinguished. Thomas Butler King, a Whig lawyer from Georgia, was curious. "I should like, with all respect and deference to the learned and venerable gentleman from Massachusetts, to ask him a question," he said. By what authority did Polk proclaim that the nation's right to Oregon was "clear and unquestionable"?

"I say that our title is *'clear and unquestionable,'* " Adams answered tartly.

"Then why did not the gentleman from Massachusetts give that definition when he was Secretary of State?"

Adams got up slowly again and stepped into the aisle beside his desk.

"The state of my health has been so poor lately," he said, "that I had rather despaired of taking part in this debate." He stood for a moment looking silently at Speaker Davis. "The little book you have upon your table, which you employ to administer a solemn oath—be so good as to pass it to the clerk, and I will ask him to read what I conceive to be the foundation of our title."

To the clerk he said, "The twenty-sixth, twenty-seventh and twenty-eighth verses of the first chapter of Genesis."

The clerk read:

" 'And God said, Let us make man in our image, after our likeness: and let them have dominion over the fish of the sea, and over the fowl of the air, and over the cattle, and over all the earth, and over every creeping thing that creepeth upon the earth.

" 'So God created man in his *own* image, in the image of God created He him; male and female created He them.' "

"Go on! Go on!" Adams commanded as the clerk's puzzled voice hesitated. "The twenty-eighth verse."

" 'And God blessed them, and God said unto them, Be fruitful, and multiply, and replenish the earth, and subdue it: and have dominion over the fish of the sea, and over the fowl of the air, and over every living thing that moveth upon the earth.' "

"There, sir, in my judgment," said Adams, his voice vibrant, "is the foundation not only of our title to Oregon but the foundation of all human title to all human possessions."

If the controversy were with a non-Christian nation—with China, for example—he went on, "I could not cite that book." But Britain and the United States were both ruled by the laws of God as spoken by Him in the Bible. "It is between Christian nations that the foundation of title to land is laid in the first chapter of Genesis, and it is in this book that title to jurisdiction, to eminent domain, has its foundation. I ask the clerk to read another passage, . . . the eighth verse of the Second Psalm."

" 'Ask of me, and I shall give *thee* the heathen *for* thine inheritance, and the uttermost parts of the earth *for* thy possession.' "

No one knew his Bible better than Adams. "Turn back a verse or two," he told the clerk, "so it will be seen to whom it is said He will give them. To 'Yet have I set my King.' "

" 'Yet have I set my King upon my holy hill of Zion.

" 'I will declare the decree: the Lord hath said unto me, Thou *art* my Son; this day have I begotten thee.'

" 'Ask of me—' "

Adams raised his arm. "There! That is how Great Britain holds Ireland; Pope Adrian gave, by that same power, to Henry I of England, the island of Ireland, and England has held it from that day under that title, and no other."

Back in 1818, when the original division of authority over

Oregon Territory had been established, and later, during his own Presidency, he said, he had agreed to it because the region was then unsettled, a wilderness left to the Indians and nomadic trappers. Since then hundreds of pioneers from the United States had moved into it, had cleared land for themselves, established settlements, provisional government; they were obeying God's injunction to "be fruitful and multiply." Missionaries were among them, teaching Christianity to the heathen Indians.

"We claim that country to make the wilderness blossom," he concluded, "to establish laws, to increase . . . and subdue the earth, which we are commanded to do by the first behest of God Almighty. She [Great Britain] claims it . . . for navigation, for her hunters to hunt the wild beast. There is the difference between our claims."

The resolution to terminate the treaty passed the House by a lopsided 163 to 54. The Senate concurred, and the northwestern boundary, from Lake of the Woods to the Pacific, was on the way to settlement—by compromise at the forty-ninth parallel, as Adams had expected.

The Twenty-ninth Congress was now deep into its first session. Evenings when the sky was clear Adams frequently stopped off on his way home at the little frame building of the United States Naval Observatory, below the Capitol. On an April night the year before, Lieutenant Matthew Maury, the naval hydrographer under whom the Depot of Charts and Instruments had established the observatory, had called at Adams' house. Adams was "one of the most active and zealous friends" the observatory had, the scholarly, middle-aged naval officer said. "Your efforts to advance in America the cause of practical astronomy are known to the world." He took Adams in his carriage to the building on Capitol Hill, and he and the astonomer, Lieutenant James Gillis, opened the hatches over the skylights and cranked the telescope into position. Adams sat enthralled, staring into the eyepiece "at the nebula of Orion, at the blazing light of Sirius, and at the double stars, orange and blue, in Andromeda." Since then he had been a familiar visitor.

For ten years now he had been trying to get Congress to act

on the Smithsonian bequest. A peripheral result of his campaign had been this observatory and, in good part, those at Cincinnati and Harvard and scattered others. But the special committees of the House and Senate had been unable to agree on how the institution should be set up. Adams himself had been responsible for some of the delay because of the restrictions he demanded: not another educational establishment for the young, no sinecure for aging scholars or for politicians, only the interest on the fund to be used. Now he had finally managed to get the joint committee to draft a bill, still vague and unsatisfactory, but at least a bill. On April 28, 1846, three months before Adams' seventy-ninth birthday, it came up for debate in the House, and he was quickly embroiled with the agrarian opponents of "this gift horse."

Alexander Sims of South Carolina argued that the bequest should be peremptorily returned to the British chancery; it was beneath the dignity of the United States to indulge the "vanity" of an illegitimate Englishman, "build up his name for posterity." Furthermore, he said, "I inquire of the gentleman from Massachusetts by what power Congress is authorized to accept and administer this fund."

If Sims would "point me to the power in the Constitution *to annex Texas,*" Adams retorted, "I will answer his question." He went on, "I am delighted that an observatory—not perhaps so great as it should have been—has been smuggled into the number of institutions of the country, under the mask of a small depot for charts, etc. I would like to ask the gentleman where was the power under the Constitution to make this appropriation?"

Sims said he did not know, "but since the doctrine promulgated by a distinguished President of the United States, of erecting lighthouses in the skies, has grown into popular favor, I presume the gentleman will find no difficulty as to the question of power."

"I am glad to hear it has grown into popular favor," Adams answered. "I claim no merit for the erection of the observatory, but in the course of my life no honor, of interest, of office, has given me more delight than the belief that I have contributed, in some small degree, to producing these astronomical observatories, both here and elsewhere. I no longer wish any portion of this fund applied to an observatory."

Young Andrew Johnson from rural Tennessee, who would be elevated to the Presidency by Lincoln's assassination, was serving his second term in the House. His homespun anti-British, anti-aristocracy, anti-scholastic oration ended, "I would send the money back to the source from which it came."

Adams ignored him. Standing beside his desk, leaning on it occasionally for brief support, his voice now hoarse and strident, now barely a tired whisper, he repeated in painstaking detail what he had been saying for years, in committee, to Presidents and Cabinet members, to his scholar friends. When he finished, Robert Dale Owen, a Democrat from Indiana, who had taken over the chairmanship of the Smithsonian House committee from his weary colleague, said, "The gentleman from Massachusetts has labored more zealously in this good cause than any other individual." He added, "If anyone who has ever debated with him has come off the better, it was while I was out of the House."

The bill was on its way. Revised, it established the Smithsonian Institution as a corporation to be controlled by a board of regents made up of the President of the United States, the Chief Justice of the Supreme Court and the members of the Cabinet, and administered purely for "the increase of knowledge among men." It passed both houses without further contention. But Adams' victory created little public interest at the time. By then the nation was at war. President Polk had sent General Zachary Taylor to defend the border of Texas, which Mexico contended was at the Nueces River and the United States placed 100 miles to the southwest, at the Rio Grande. When Taylor's force moved across the disputed terrain to the east bank of the Rio Grande, under Polk's orders, Mexico warned it was an act of war; a small reconnoitering party was attacked by a Mexican patrol and several Americans were killed. Polk, solidly supported by his Cabinet, told the Congress: "Mexico has passed the boundary of the United States, has invaded our territory, and shed American blood on American soil. She has proclaimed that hostilities have commenced, and the two nations are now at war. . . . Notwithstanding all our efforts to avoid it [war] exists by the act of Mexico herself."

Adams was certain that Polk had plotted to provoke Mexico so that he could force her to give up California as well as Texas. Once he had supported his enemy, Jackson, because he believed Jackson was in the right in his dispute with France. Now he was as inflexibly on the side of Mexico for the same reason. But only 13 members of the House were willing to vote with him against supporting the war declaration, while 174 voted for it. In the Senate the vote was 40 to 2, although both Calhoun and Benton argued that Polk had violated the constitutional provision that only "Congress shall have the power to declare war."

Occupied with measures supporting the war effort, the session was the second longest up to that time, extending into the first week of August. On July 11 Adams wrote in his diary, which now filled nineteen bulky volumes of crowded script, "This day I enter upon my eightieth year." He noted that it was exactly a half century since he had begun his custom of rising at four o'clock. Before then he had been a late sleeper. A book he picked up in 1796, while serving his first diplomatic assignment as Washington's minister to The Hague, had changed that. It was a life of John Wesley, the founder of Methodism. Wesley, he read, rose methodically at four, and so put in several hours of writing and reading before his contemporaries were out of bed. "I said to myself," Adams recalled, " 'what John Wesley accomplishes, cannot I undertake?' "

Two mornings later, responding to "an irresistible impulse," he once more crossed the footbridge over Tiber Creek behind the White House to his old spot on the Potomac. Dawn was just breaking, and the shore below the bluff was still deserted. He swam for a half hour, dried himself leisurely with his shirt, and started home. Near another rock three boys were now in the water. He heard one of them say, "There is John Quincy Adams." The next day he returned, and the next, but the third morning the temperature was down to seventy-four and a stiff breeze rippled the river. He shivered getting dressed, and had to walk fast to warm himself. That was his last swim in the Potomac.

Back in Quincy for the tag end of the summer, he seldom left his study and garden. When the evenings became chilly, the family closed the frame mansion and joined Charles Francis in his Boston house at 57 Mount Vernon Street. Louisa and Mary and the two servants left for Washington in mid-November, Adams expecting to follow in a few days. The morning of November 20 he was up at four as usual, bathed and massaged himself with his horsehair strap and mitten, and had finished breakfast when his old friend, Dr. George Parkman, came to take him on an inspection of the new medical college at Harvard. The day was crisp under a gray overcast. They started away together, their canes tapping in unison down the brick sidewalk. Suddenly Adams' knees buckled; he staggered, started to fall. Dr. Parkman threw his arms around him and looked up and down the street for help, but there was no one in sight. Slowly the two old men struggled back to the house, Adams' face the color of cold ash, his legs limp.

A servant ran for the family doctor, John Bigelow, who put Adams to bed and told the family he believed he had had a slight stroke. They sent word to Louisa. A nephew traveled as far as Baltimore with her, from where she came on alone, by the railroads and the sound steamer *Atlantic,* making the trip from Washington in only thirty-six hours. In a few weeks Adams' legs began to regain their strength, but Dr. Bigelow's cheerful prognostications that he was on the way to full recovery did not convince him. "From that day [November 20, 1846]," he said, "I date my decease, and consider myself for every useful purpose to myself or to my fellow creatures, dead."

On New Year's Day he left the house for a short carriage ride, and by February 8 he was well enough to start back to Washington with Louisa. The House was in session when he walked in five days later. As he came down the aisle Speaker Davis stood up, and the entire membership stood up with him. Two members escorted him ceremoniously to his old desk below the rostrum. His friends and old enemies crowded around him, the men from the plantation South holding out their hands together with those from the West and the North in sudden reverence and good will. Adams was plainly uncomfortable. He waited till the last of them had spoken, and when they still did not move away answered hesitantly. He was "happy to be among them again," he said. "Had I a more powerful voice, I might respond to the congratulations of my friends and"—even now he could not temporize—"the members of this House. But enfeebled as I am, I beg that you will excuse me."

For the three remaining weeks of the session, he was at his desk punctually at noon every day. Polk's war was going well. General Taylor, "Old Rough and Ready," was marching deep into Mexico and meeting only sporadic resistance. But the North and West were becoming increasingly critical and rebelling against the mounting expense. When Polk sent an angry message to the Congress charging that all those who opposed the war were giving "aid and comfort to the enemy," Adams listened silently and let his friend Giddings answer for him. Nevertheless, when only four members of the House dared to vote for a resolution, by Charles Hudson of Massachusetts, proposing that the administration order the Army back to the border and offer peace to Mexico, Adams was one of the four.

He took the floor only once, the day before adjournment. Secretary of State James Buchanan had asked for an appropriation of $50,000 to dispose of the long-standing indemnity claim of the owners of the *Amistad* for the loss of their ship and Negro cargo. When Adams raised himself out of his chair and lifted his hand for the Speaker's attention, the members up the aisles left their desks and moved down near him. The reporter for the *Congressional Globe* sensed that the occasion was exceptional and pressed in as close as he could "to the venerable speaker." Adams' voice, he remarked, "though feeble, was firmer than it had been when he spoke a few words [three weeks before] on resuming his seat."

"Mr. Speaker, the Secretary of State cannot be acquainted with the facts," Adams protested, "or he never would have sanctioned the demand for indemnity as a fair claim on this government. . . . The Spanish minister demanded the *Amistad* captives not as slaves but as assassins. He wanted them tried and executed for liberating themselves. . . . The Supreme Court pronounced them free men and as such entitled to the value of the vessel which they had taken possession of, and this after two years' imprisonment. Now the Spanish minister comes and asks the people of the United States to pay $50,000 to the pretended proprietors of those men." He lifted his arms in supplication. *"God forbid that any claim should ever be allowed!"* The House supported him, 94 to 28.

But the Mendis would not know of this last appeal by their benefactor. Most of them had disappeared joyfully into their Sierra Leone jungle. Their return, however, had not been as soon as Adams had expected when he wrote the New York philanthropist, Lewis Tappan, that—"Thanks! Thanks, in the name of humanity and justice!"—they were free at last. Of necessity their departure had been delayed to raise the money for their passage. But the public exhibitions and the sale of the *Amistad* had taken care of that. Still the little people had not been sent home.

The reason was religious zealotry. Tappan had decided they needed further indoctrination in the Scriptures. "We must grapple their hearts to God," he told his devout followers. "I am in favor of keeping them in America at least another year, that they may be more thoroughly instructed in the Christian faith and way of life. Such assurance against return to native customs and beliefs is necessary. . . . The name of Christ must be writ large to shine in the darkness of Africa."

The New Haven abolitionist-preacher, Simeon Jocelyn, fervently agreed. The Mendis were moved to a new barracks in nearby Farmington and two catechists from Jocelyn's Negro congregation were assigned to complete their indoctrination. The Mendis brooded over the delay. "We want to go home," said Cinqué. He had not spoken much about himself to the white people. Now they learned that back in his village he had left a father, the chieftain, and a wife, whom he called Tafe, and chil-

302

dren. Cinqué was unhappy, too, about the Negro catechists. So long as the teachers had been white men, the Mendis had accepted his leadership without question. Now more and more that role was being taken by the Negro catechists.

For another long New England winter and summer and into the next winter the black people were confined in their barracks before a schooner, the *Gentleman,* was chartered to take them back to Africa. Three New England missionaries went with them to set up stations, their first on the Sierra Leone coast far from the Mendi homeland. As soon as the Negroes got their bearings, they started to desert, the impatient Cinqué among the first. Traveling swiftly, unerringly northward along the jungle trails, he cautiously skirted the hostile territory of Birmaja, the chief who had captured and sold him into slavery, and came to the village site of his family. He found fire-blackened ruins and the jungle foliage closing over them.

Back at the station, he told the story as he had gotten it from neighboring tribesmen. Birmaja and his warriors had raided the village some moons back and sold the inhabitants to a slave trader. Cinqué's father and wife and children, if they were still alive, were by now in bondage somewhere in the land he had come back from. Naïvely, he believed the white people could rescue them. When the missionaries said they were helpless, he became bitter and sullen. He drifted among the neighboring natives, getting drunk on palm wine and roistering. From one long absence he returned with a Negress wearing only a breechclout and said she was his wife, Tafe. William Raymond, leader of the missionaries, made him send her away and denounced him as a bad influence on the other Mendis still at the station. But Cinqué's dissipation was only the first flush of grief. In time his inherent pride and natural intelligence reclaimed him. But he was an angry man, deeply, savagely angry. He went away again.

The rest of his story is told in fragments sent back to America by missionaries. Cinqué took up with a white trader and prospered as a dealer in ivory and the red camwood used for dyeing; and, said the horrified missionaries, sometimes dealing in slaves. But the Africans delivered from him to the traders all had one thing in common: every one bore the tattoo marks of his enemy Birmaja's tribe.

By the time the Civil War in America closed the last outlet for the slave traders, Cinqué, his vengeance satisfied, was an honored and powerful leader among his people; he had obeyed God's word to the children of Israel: "Eye for eye, tooth for tooth." Long afterward he came back to the Mendi mission, tribesmen bearing his old body on a litter. "I have come to die," he said. A few days later they buried him there.

During the summer of 1847 back in Quincy, Adams appeared to recover some of his old stamina. On clear mornings his neighbors, driving into the village or out to their woodlots, frequently met him, his gait slow but his back erect, waving his cane in answer to their salutes. He still spent most of his afternoons in his nursery, where the seedlings he had started from cherry and peach and plum pits in his study were now mature trees heavy with fruit and the oaks and hickories he had watched sprout in glasses of water reached over his head. Old friends who came to visit found his study table as cluttered as ever with open books and newspapers, among them a brown apple core or two. Charles Francis came regularly in the evening, and Adams brought out the Madeira bottle and they sipped a glass together, sometimes two, and talked of Polk's "unrighteous war," of the prospects of Whig victories in the midterm elections, of the slow but persistent growth of the antislavery impulse in the North. Charles was now deeply committed to abolition, but he was by nature the more judicious and reserved, and he let his father do most of the talking.

Toward the evening's end Adams occasionally fell into long silences; a veiled look came into his face; his eyes seemed to be on something far beyond the dim lamplight of the study. The new volume of his diary had a strange heading: *Posthumous Memoirs,* and only a few entries were in his shaky handwriting. The others, and his letters, he dictated to his twenty-year-old granddaughter, Louisa Catherine. On July 27 he and Louisa celebrated their fiftieth wedding anniversary with a quiet fam-

ily dinner in the old house where his father and mother had observed theirs thirty-six years before. All in all, his had been a
good marriage, Adams thought, and Louisa's, too. Living with
him, he knew, had not always been easy, considering his puri-
tanical—yes, and cantankerous—nature, and his devotion to
public service. They had had their heartbreaks, first George's
suicide, then John's death and the two little granddaughters;
shared tragedies that had slowly brought them closer together.

Louisa still hoped he would retire. Surely, it was time. Why
go on until he could no longer stand on his feet? Couldn't he,
Charles asked, enjoy a little of the quiet life? He had won the
reverence of half the country, had given the antislavery crusade solid direction and vitality. Adams answered, "Because I
will die the moment I give up public life."

On December 6, 1847, now going on eighty-one, he was back
in his seat in the House. The fall elections, reflecting the increasing disenchantment with Polk and his war with Mexico,
had given the Whigs a working majority, 117 to 108, and he
helped elect one of his son's colleagues from Boston, Robert
Winthrop, the new Speaker. Giddings and his fellow boarders at
Abolition House took over the burden of presenting the petitions that had piled up in Adams' mail while he was away. But
a few that particularly concerned him he insisted on presenting
himself. Two of them prayed for peace with Mexico, and he
saw them respectfully referred to the Committee on Foreign
Affairs. A packet from New York brought him an embossed
resolution from Lewis Tappan and his executive committee of
the growing new American and Foreign Anti-Slavery Society.
They thanked him for the work he had done for the cause and
extended their "respectful wishes for his health and usefulness
during the approaching session of Congress and while his valuable life shall be preserved."

The first order of business on Monday, February 21, was a
resolution to extend the thanks of Congress and approve gold
medals for eight generals who had performed meritoriously in
the Mexican campaign. Speaker Winthrop asked if the main
question should be put. Adams answered to his name with an
angry "No!" but the motion carried. The Speaker called on the

clerk to read the resolution preparatory to the vote. As be began, H. B. Stanton of the Boston *Emancipator and Republican,* at the press table, saw Adams grasp the edge of his desk as though about to rise in protest. His lips moved, but no sound came from them. His head fell forward. Washington Hunt, a Congressman from New York, yelled, "Mr. Adams!" David Fisher of Ohio, at the desk next to Adams', jumped up and grabbed him as he started to slump out of his chair. Joseph Grinnell of Massachusetts, who had been Adams' companion on his Western trips, called to a page to bring water, and bathed his forehead.

The word spread across the desks: "Mr. Adams is dying!" Speaker Winthrop called for a motion to adjourn. It came quickly, and the House responded in a somber viva voce. A sofa was brought in; Adams was lifted onto it, unconscious, and carried to the rotunda. Senator Benton had just stepped out of the Senate chamber. He turned back and shouted the news, and the Senate adjourned. Five physicians were members of the House. They bent over Adams. He was breathing stentoriously. His eyes were closed. The rotunda was cold and drafty, and crowded now. They carried him into the Speaker's room and laid him on a big mahogany-framed sofa. It was half past one. The doctors bled him, applied mustard plasters to his chest. At two o'clock he stirred. Hopefully, they bled him again. At two-thirty Louisa and Mary arrived. At three o'clock the physicians agreed that his right side was completely paralyzed, and there were "only involuntary motions" in the muscles of his left side. But a few minutes later he opened his eyes and looked up at the circle of doctors. His lips moved. They heard him whisper, "This is the last of earth." A silence, then, "I am content."

He lived on for two more days, but never regained consciousness again. Each day the House and Senate met at noon and immediately adjourned. At seven o'clock the evening of February 23 he died, by destiny's design under the old copper-roofed dome of the Capitol where for seventeen years he had done his finest work—the champion of the muted slave and the Bill of Rights.

BIBLIOGRAPHY

BOOKS

Adams, Charles Francis, Jr., *Three Episodes of Massachusetts History*. New York, 1903.

Adams, Henry, *The Education of Henry Adams*. Boston, 1918.

Adams, James Truslow, *The Adams Family*. New York, 1930.

Adams, John Quincy, *Dermot MacMorrough, or the Conquest of Ireland, an Historical Tale of the Twelfth Century*. Boston, 1832.

———, *Memoirs of John Quincy Adams, Comprising Part of His Diary from 1795 to 1848*, 12 vols., edited by Charles Francis Adams. Philadelphia, 1875-77.

———, *Poems of Religion and Society*. New York, 1847.

Barber, John W., *A History of the* Amistad *Captives*. New Haven, 1840.

Barnes, Gilbert Hobbs, *The Anti-Slavery Impulse, 1830-1944*. New York, 1933.

Barnes, Gilbert, and Dwight L. Dumond, *Letters of Theodore Dwight Weld, Angelina Grimké Weld and Sarah Grimké, 1822-44*, 2 vols. New York, 1934.

Bates, Ernest Sutherland, *The Story of Congress*. New York, 1936.

Beard, Charles A., *The American Party Battle*. New York, 1928.

Bemis, Samuel Flagg, *John Quincy Adams and the Foundations of American Foreign Policy*. New York, 1949.

———, *John Quincy Adams and the Union*. New York, 1956.

Benedict, S. W., *Argument of John Quincy Adams Before the Supreme Court of the United States, Appellants vs. Cinqué and Others*. New York, 1841.

Bennett, Whitman, *Whittier, Bard of Freedom*. Chapel Hill, 1941.

307

Binkley, W. E., *American Political Parties, Their Natural History*. New York, 1943.

Binkley, William C., *The Texas Revolution*. Louisiana State U., 1952.

Blakeslee, George H., *The History of the Antimasonic Party*. Cambridge, 1903.

Bobbé, Dorothie, *Mr. and Mrs. John Quincy Adams*. New York, 1930.

Buell, Walter, *J. R. Giddings, a Sketch*. Cleveland, 1882.

Burgess, J. W., *The Middle Period*. New York, 1897.

Clark, Bennett Champ, *John Quincy Adams, "Old Man Eloquent."* Boston, 1933.

Channing, William E., *Works*. Boston, 1875.

Cross, Whitney R., *The Burned-Over District*. Ithaca, N.Y., 1950.

Darling, Arthur B., *Political Changes in Massachusetts, 1828-1848*. New Haven, 1925.

Goodrich, Samuel G., *Recollections of a Lifetime*, 2 vols. New York, 1856.

Grund, Francis J., *Aristocracy in America*. London, 1839.

Hone, Philip, *Diary of Philip Hone, 1828-1851*, edited by Bayard Tuckerman. New York, 1889.

Jay, William, *A Review of the Causes and Consequences of the Mexican War*. Boston, 1849.

Julian, George W., *The Life of Joshua Giddings*. Chicago, 1892.

Lawrence, George A., *Benjamin Lundy, Pioneer of Freedom*. Illinois, 1913.

Lipsy, George A., *John Quincy Adams, His Theory & Ideas*. New York, 1950.

Lloyd, Arthur Y., *The Slavery Controversy, 1831-1860*, Chapel Hill, 1939.

Lundy, Benjamin, *Life, Travels and Opinions, Compiled Under the Direction and on Behalf of His Children*. Philadelphia, 1847.

Martineau, Harriet, *Society in America*. London, 1837.

McLemore, Richard Aubrey, *Franco-American Diplomatic Relations, 1816-1836*. Louisiana State U., 1941.

Mock, Stanley Upton, *The Morgan Episode in Free-masonry*. East Aurora, N.Y., 1930.

Morgan, William, *Illustrations of Masonry, by One of the Fraternity Who Has Devoted Thirty Years to the Subject*. New York, 1827.

Morris, John T., Jr., *John Quincy Adams*. American Statesmen Series. Cambridge, 1895.

Nevins, Allan, *The Diary of John Quincy Adams, 1794-1845*, 1 vol. New York, 1928.

Nye, Russell B., *Fettered Freedom, Civil Liberties and the Slavery Controversy*. Michigan, 1949.

Owens, William A., *Slave Mutiny: the Revolt on the Schooner* Amistad. New York, 1953.

Peters, Richard, Jr., *Reports of Cases Argued and Adjudged in the Supreme Court*, Vol. 15. Philadelphia, 1828-43.

Pierson, George Wilson, *Tocqueville and Beaumont in America*. New York, 1938.

Quincy, Josiah, *Memoirs of the Life of John Quincy Adams*. Boston, 1860.

Rhees, William J., ed., *Documents Relating to the Origin and History of the Smithsonian Institution*. Washington, 1880.

Rives, George Lockhart, *The United States and Mexico, 1821-1848*, 2 vols. New York, 1913.

Schlesinger, Arthur M., Jr., *The Age of Jackson*. Boston, 1945.

Seitz, Don, *Famous American Duels*. New York, 1929.

Seward, William H., *Autobiography, from 1801 to 1834*, 3 vols., edited by F. W. Seward. New York, 1877-91.

——, *Life and Public Services of John Quincy Adams*. New York, 1849.

Smith, Justin H., *The Annexation of Texas*. New York, 1911.

Smith, Walter Buckingham, *Economic Aspects of the Second Bank of the United States*. Cambridge, 1953.

Snyder, Charles S., *The Development of Southern Sectionalism, 1819-1846*. Louisiana State U., 1948.

Spaulding, Myra L., *Dueling in the District of Columbia*. Records of the Columbia Historical Society, Washington, 1928.

Stanwood, Edward, *American Tariff Controversies in the Nineteenth Century*. Boston and New York, 1903.

Thomas, Benjamin P., *Theodore Weld*. New Brunswick, N.J., 1950.

Trollope, Frances, *Domestic Manners of the Americans*. London, 1832.

Turner, Frederick Jackson, *The United States, 1830-1850*. New York, 1935.

Tyler, Alice Felt, *Freedom's Ferment*. Minneapolis, 1944.

Warren, Charles, *The Supreme Court in United States History*, 3 vols. Boston, 1923.

Weed, Thurlow, *Autobiography*. Boston, 1883.

Weld, Theodore Dwight, *American Slavery As It Is, Testimony of a Thousand Witnesses*. New York, 1839.

Whitney, George, *Some Accounts of the Early History and Present State of the Town of Quincy, in the Commonwealth of Massachusetts*. Boston, 1827.

Wilson, Henry, *History of the Rise and Fall of the Slave Power in America*, 3 vols. Boston, 1872-3.

Wise, Barton H., *The Life of Henry A. Wise*. New York, 1899.

Wise, Henry A., *Seven Decades of the Union*. Philadelphia, 1881.

NEWSPAPERS AND PERIODICALS CONSULTED

Albany *Argus*.
Auburn *Journal*

Niles Weekly Register, 1811-49 (Baltimore)
Boston *Argus*
Boston *Daily Advertiser*
Boston *Daily Advocate*
Boston *Daily Evening Transcript*
Boston *Whig*
Cincinnati *Gazette*
Cincinnati *Journal*
Cleveland *Herald*
Cleveland *Whig*
Weekly Ohio State Journal (Columbus)
New Haven *Palladium*
New London *Gazette*
New York *American*
New York *Evening Post*
New York *Express*
New York *Times,* predecessor of the present *Times*
New York *Whig*
Quincy *Patriot*
Utica *Democrat*
Washington *National Intelligencer*
Washington *Globe*
United States Telegraph (Washington)

ANTISLAVERY JOURNALS

The leading publications of the day were:

The Genius of Universal Emancipation, edited by Benjamin Lundy from
1821 to 1835, first in Mt. Pleasant, Ohio, then in Greenville, Tenn.,
Baltimore and Washington.
The National Enquirer, edited by Lundy from 1836 to 1838 in Phila-
delphia.
The Pennsylvania Freeman, successor to the *Enquirer,* edited by John
Greenleaf Whittier in Philadelphia.
The Emancipator, journal of the American Anti-Slavery Society in New
York, of which Joshua Leavitt was for some years editor.
The Liberator, Boston, published and edited by William Lloyd Garrison.
Others were: *The National Anti-Slavery Standard,* the New York *Evan-
gelist, The Philanthropist, The Friend of Man, The Anti-Slavery
Reporter, The Herald of Freedom,* the Massachusetts *Abolitionist.*

Index

INDEX

313

Bouldin, James, 161
Bowie, Jim, 128
Briggs, George, 121, 193
Bronson, David, 245
Brooks, Peter Chardon, 21, 94, 269, 272
Brown, Moses, 52, 103
Buchanan, James, 301
Buckingham, Joseph Tucker, 20, 21
Bynum, Jesse, 140, 142, 215, 283, 285

Calhoun, John, 13, 33, 36, 45, 59, 60, 72-3, 90, 98, 107, 125-7, 141, 179, 187-8, 266, 288, 293, 299
Calhoun, William B., 245
Camberleng, Churchill, 91, 93, 95-8, 106, 115-6, 161, 179
Carson, Samuel, 63
Cass, Lewis, 56, 167
Catron, John, 231
Causten, John, 234
Chambers, John, 152
Channing, William Ellery, 269
Charles X of France, 89
Chittenden, Thomas, 245
Cincinnati Astronomical Society, 271, 277
Choate, Rufus, 164, 223
Cicero, 12, 18, 19, 26
Cilley, Jonathan, 191-2, 258
Cinqué, 203-6, 211, 219-20, 228, 302-4
Clayton, Augustus S., 53, 74-6, 93
Clay, Clement, 64
Clay, Henry, 13, 21, 41, 45, 47, 49, 53, 54, 56, 58, 79, 89, 90, 97-8, 105-6, 107-8, 141, 150, 181, 279, 290
Cleveland *Herald*, 275
Cleveland *Whig*, 275
Coke, Richard, 105
Colt, Roswell, 229
Colt, Samuel, 234

Condict, Lewis, 49, 50
Congressional Globe, 249, 254, 257, 301
Cooper, James Fenimore, 229
Crawford, William H., 13, 33
Creek Indian Uprising, 131-5
Creole, 245-6, 255, 282
Crockett, Davy, 128
Cushing, Caleb, 194

Davis, Gideon, 184
Davis, John, 21, 23, 24, 56, 83, 90, 94
Davis, John W., 153, 294, 300
Dawson, John, 251
Day, George, 228
Day, Jeremiah, 228
Dickens, Charles, 259
Doddridge, Philip, 51
Drayton, William, 54-5, 67, 69, 78
Dromgoole, George, 140, 189, 193, 195
Dyer, Edward, 181

Eaton, John H., 59, 60
Ellicott, Andrew, 35
Ellsworth, H. L., 288
Emancipator, The, 141, 156, 205-6, 209, 228, 242
Emerson, Ralph Waldo, 153, 269
Essex Junto, 16, 22, 23
Everett, Alexander, 41
Everett, Edward, 14-21, 23, 44, 48, 49, 69, 93-4, 96, 269
Ewing, Thomas, 114

Fairfield, John, 122
Fieschi, Giuseppe, 101
"Fifty-four Forty or Fight," 292
Fillmore, Millard, 45, 255, 270-1
Finney, Charles, 36, 83, 145, 273
Fisher, David, 306
Force, Peter, 183

DATE DUE	BORROWER'S NAME	ROOM NUMBER